The amulet

A novel

Charles Egbert Craddock

Alpha Editions

This edition published in 2024

ISBN : 9789366387833

Design and Setting By
Alpha Editions
www.alphaedis.com
Email - info@alphaedis.com

As per information held with us this book is in Public Domain.
This book is a reproduction of an important historical work. Alpha Editions uses the best technology to reproduce historical work in the same manner it was first published to preserve its original nature. Any marks or number seen are left intentionally to preserve its true form.

Contents

CHAPTER I ....- 1 -
CHAPTER II ....- 14 -
CHAPTER III ....- 21 -
CHAPTER IV ....- 31 -
CHAPTER V ....- 40 -
CHAPTER VI ....- 55 -
CHAPTER VII ....- 63 -
CHAPTER VIII ....- 74 -
CHAPTER IX ....- 82 -
CHAPTER X ....- 96 -
CHAPTER XI ....- 106 -
CHAPTER XII ....- 118 -
CHAPTER XIII ....- 129 -
CHAPTER XIV ....- 139 -
CHAPTER XV ....- 150 -
CHAPTER XVI ....- 160 -
CHAPTER XVII ....- 170 -
CHAPTER XVIII ....- 177 -
CHAPTER XIX ....- 188 -

CHAPTER I

THE aspect of the lonely moon in this bleak night sky exerted a strange fascination upon the English girl. She often paused to draw the improvised red curtain at the tiny window of the log house that served as the commandant's quarters and gaze upon the translucent sphere as it swung westering above the spurs of the Great Smoky Mountains, which towered in the icy air on the horizon. Beneath it the forests gleamed fitfully with frost; the long snowy vistas of the shadowy valleys showed variant tones of white in its pearly lustre. So dominant was the sense of isolation, of the infinite loneliness of the wilderness, that to her the moon was like this nowhere else. A suspended consciousness seemed to characterize it, almost an abeyance of animation, yet this still serene splendor did not suggest death. She had long ago been taught, indeed, that it was an extinct and burnt-out world. But in this strange new existence old theories were blunted and she was ready for fresh impressions. This majestic tranquillity seemed as of deep and dreamless slumber, and the picturesque fancy of the Indians that the moon is but the sun asleep took strong hold on her imagination. She first heard the superstition one evening at dusk, as she stood at the window with one end of the curtain in her hand, and asked her father what was the word for "moon" in the Cherokee language.

"Don't know! The moon in English is bright enough for me!" exclaimed Captain Howard, as he sat in his easy-chair before the fire with his glass of wine. A decanter was on the table beside him, and with venison and wild-fowl for the solid business of dinner, earlier in the afternoon, and chocolate-and-cocoanut custard, concocted by his daughter, for the "trifle," he had fared well enough.

Very joyous he was in these days. The Seven Years' War was fairly over, the treaty of peace concluded, and the surrender of the French forts on the American frontier already imminent, even thus early in the spring of 1763. His own difficult tour of service, here at Fort Prince George, the British stronghold on the eastern edge of the Cherokee country, was nearing its close. He, himself, was to be transferred to a post of ease and comfort at Charlestown, where he would enjoy the benignities of social courtesies and metropolitan association, and where his family, who had come out from England for the purpose, could join him for a time. Indeed, on his recent return from South Carolina, where he had spent a short leave of absence, he had brought thence with him his eldest daughter, an intelligent girl of eighteen years, who was opening great eyes at the wonders of this new world, and who had specially besought the privilege of a peep into the wilderness, now that the frontier was quiet and safe.

George Mervyn, a captain-lieutenant of the garrison, a youth whom her father greatly approved,—the grandson of his nearest neighbor at home in Kent, Sir George Mervyn,—was inclined to pose as a picturesque incident himself of the frontier, the soldier who had fought its battles and at last pacified it. Now he suddenly developed unsuspected linguistic accomplishments. He was tall, blond, and bland, conventional of address, the model of decorous youth. He seemed quiet, steady, trustworthy. His was evidently the material of a valuable future. He rose and joined her at the window.

"There is no more moon," he said with a somewhat affected but gentlemanly drawl. "You must realize that, Miss Howard. This is 'the sleeping sun,' You must not expect to see the moon on the frontier."

"Only a stray moonling, now and then," another subaltern struck in with a laugh.

There was something distinctly sub-acid in the quick clear-clipped tones, and Captain Howard lifted his head with a slightly corrugated brow. He looked fixedly into his glass as if he discerned dregs of bitterness lurking therein. He was experiencing a sentiment of surprise and annoyance that had earlier harassed him, to be dismissed as absurd; but now, recurring, it seemed to have gathered force. These two young men were friends of the Damon-and-Pythias type. Their one-ness of heart and unanimity of thought had been of infinite service to him in the many difficult details of his command at Fort Prince George,—a flimsy earth-work with a block-house or two, garrisoned by a mere handful of troops, in a remote wilderness surrounded by a strong and savage foe. These officers had been zealous to smooth each other's way; they had vied to undertake onerous duties, to encounter danger, to palliate short-comings. They were always companions when off duty; they hunted and fished together; they were on terms of intimate confidence, even privileged to read each other's letters. They were sworn comrades, and yet to-day (Captain Howard did not know how to account for it—he was growing old, surely) neither had addressed a kindly word to the other; nay, Ensign Raymond was sharply and apparently intentionally sarcastic.

Captain Howard wondered that Arabella did not notice it, but there she stood by the window, the curtain in her hand, the light of the great flaring fire on the hair, a little paler than gold, which she had inherited from her Scotch mother, and the large, sincere, hazel English eyes which were like Captain Howard's own. The delicate rose tint of her cheek did not even fluctuate; she looked calmly at the young men as they glared furiously at each other. But for her presence Captain Howard would have ordered them to their respective quarters to avoid a collision. Fort Prince George was not usually the scene of internecine strife. He resented the suggestion as an indignity to himself. It impaired the flavor of the dinner he had enjoyed, and jeopardized digestion. It was a disrespect to the formality with which he had complimented the occasion of his daughter's arrival, inviting his old neighbor's grandson, with his especial friend, and wearing his powdered wig, his punctilious dress uniform, pumps, and silk hose. It had been long since his table was graced by a woman arrayed ceremoniously for dinner, and the sight of his daughter in her rose-hued tabby gown, with shining arms and shoulders and a string of pearls around her throat, was a pleasant reminder to him, in this bleak exile, of the customs of old times, soon to be renewed, the more appreciated for compulsory disuse. Captain Howard, watching the group as the young men glowered at each other, was amazed to think that she looked as if she enjoyed it, the image of demure placidity.

"The Cherokees call the moon *Neusse anantoge*, 'the sleeping sun,'" said the captain-lieutenant, making no rejoinder to Raymond.

"La! How well you speak their language, Mr. Mervyn, to be sure. Oh-h, how musical! As lovely as Italian! Oh-h-h—how I wish I could learn it before I go back to England! Sure, 'twould be monstrous genteel to know Cherokee in London. *Neusse anantoge*. I'll remember that. 'The sleeping sun.' I'll say that again. *Neusse anantoge. Neusse anantoge.*"

"*Neusse anantoge!*" cried Raymond, with a fleering laugh. "Gad, Mervyn, you *are* moon-struck."

His bright dark eyes were angry, although laughing. They seemed to hold a light like coals of fire, sometimes all a-smoulder, and again vivid with caloric or choler. With his florid complexion and dark hair and eyes the powder had a decorative emphasis which the appearance of neither of the other men attained. The lace cravat about his throat was of fine texture and delicately adjusted, but it was frayed along the edge in more than one place and the lapels of his red coat hardly concealed this. Woman-like she was quick to discern the insignia of genteel poverty, and she pitied him with a sympathy which she would not have felt for a rent of the skin or a broken bone. These were but the natural incidents of a soldier's life; blows and bruises must needs be cogeners. She divined that his education and his commission were all of value at his command,—the younger son of a good family, but poor and proud,—and it was hard to live in a world of lace and powder on so slender an endowment. She began to hate the precise and priggish George Mervyn who roused him so, although the provocation came from Raymond, and she was already wondering at her father that this dashing man, who had a thousand appeals to a poetic imagination, stood no higher in favor. She did not realize that a long command at Fort Prince George was no promoter of a poetic imagination.

As Raymond spoke Miss Howard turned eagerly toward him, the dark red curtain still in her hand, showing a section of the bleak, moonlit, wintry scene in the distance, and in the foreground the stockaded ramparts, the guard-house, its open door emitting an orange-tinted flare of fire, the blue-and-black shadows lurking about the block-house and the hard-trodden snow of the deserted parade.

"What do *you* say it should be, then?" she demanded peremptorily, as if she were determined not to be brought to confusion by venturing incorrect Cherokee in London,—as if there a slip of the tongue would be easily detected!

"How much Cherokee does *he* know?" interposed Mervyn, satirically. "We keep an interpreter in constant employ,—expressly for him."

Raymond was spurred on to assert himself.

"*Neusse anantoge!*" he jeered. "Then what do you make of *Nu-da-su-na-ye-hi?* That is 'the sun sleeping in the night.' And see here, *Nu-da-ige-hi*. That is 'the sun living in the day.'"

"*That?*—why, that is the Lower town dialect."

"Oh, the Lower town dialect!" Raymond, in derision, whirled about on the heels of his pumps, for he too was displaying all the glory of silk hose. "The Lower town dialect,—save the mark! It is Overhill Cherokee."

"Oh,—oh,—are there *two* dialects of the Cherokee language?" cried Arabella. "How wonderful! And of the different towns! Oh-h—which *are* the lower towns? and oh,—Mr. Raymond, how prodigiously clever to know both the dialects!"

Captain Howard lifted his head with a brusque challenge in his eye. He tolerated none but national quarrels. He did not understand the interests in conflict. But he thought to end them summarily. The words "moonling," "moon-struck," and the tone of the whole conversation were not conducive to the conservation of the peace. Raymond had conducted himself in a very surly and nettling manner all through the day toward his quondam friend, who, so far as Captain Howard could see, had given him no cause of offence.

He was obviously about to strike into the conversation, and all three faces turned toward him, alert, expectant. The suave inscrutable countenance of the young lady merely intimated attention, but it was difficult for the two young men to doff readily their half scoffing expressions of anger and defiance and assume the facial indicia of respect and deference and bland subservience due to their host, their senior, and their superior officer.

His sister, however, quickly forestalled his acrid comments. Mrs. Annandale ostensibly played the part of duenna to her niece and of acquiescent chorus to her brother's dictatorial opinions. But in her secret heart she controverted his every prelection, and she countermarched his intentions with an unsuspected skill that was the very climax of strategy, for she brought him to the conviction that they were his own plans she had furthered and his own orders she had executed. Her outer aspect aided her designs—it was marvellously incongruous with the character of tactician. She had a scanty little visage, pale and wrinkled, with small pursed-up lips, closely drawn in meek assent, and small bright eyes that twinkled timorously out from gray lashes. A modish head-dress surmounted and concealed her thin gray locks, and an elaborately embroidered kerchief, crossed over the bosom of her puce-colored satin gown, conforming in the décolleté cut to the universal fashion of the day, hid the bones of her wasted little figure. She was very prim, and mild, and upright, as she sat in the primitive arm-chair, wrought by the post-carpenter and covered with a buffalo-skin. In a word she turned the trend of the discourse.

"M—m—m," she hesitated. "Sure, 'twould seem one dialect might express all the ideas of the Indians—they have a monstrous talent for silence."

She looked directly at Raymond from out her weak, blinking little eyes.

"They talk more among themselves, madam, and when at home," responded Raymond, turning away from the young people at the window, and leaning against the high mantel-piece, one hand on the shelf as he stood on the opposite side of the fire from Mrs. Annandale. "They are ill at ease here at the fort,—the presence of the soldiers abashes and depresses them; they are much embittered by their late defeat."

Mrs. Annandale shuddered. She was afraid of wind and lightning; of waters and ghosts; of signs and omens; of savages and mice; of the dark and of the woods; of gun-powder and a sword-blade.

"And are you not frightened of them, Mr. Raymond?" she quavered.

He stared in amazement, and Captain Howard, restored to good temper, cocked up his eyes humorously at the young soldier. The vivid red and white of Raymond's complexion, his powdered side-curls, and his bold, bright hazel eyes, were heightened by the delicacy of his lace cravat, and his red uniform was brought out in fine effect by the flaring light of the deep chimney-place, but Mrs. Annandale's heart was obdurate to all such appeals, even vicariously. A side glance had shown her that the young people at the window had drawn closer together and a low-toned and earnest conversation was in progress there,—the captain-lieutenant was talking fast and eagerly, while the girl, holding the curtain, looked out at the dreary wintry aspect of the sheeted wilderness, the frontier fort, and the "sleeping sun" resting softly in the pale azure sky, high, high above the Great Smoky Mountains. The duenna pressed her lips together in serene satisfaction.

"M—m—m. I should imagine you would be so frightened of the Indians, Mr. Raymond," she said.

"Ha—ha—ha—!" laughed Captain Howard, outright.

Mrs. Annandale claimed no sense of humor, but she was a very efficient mirth-maker, nevertheless.

"I am beholden to you, madam," said the young soldier, out of countenance. He could not vaunt his courage in the presence of his commander, nor would he admit fear even in fun. He was at a loss for a moment.

"It is contrary to the rules of the service to be afraid of the Indians," he said after a pause; "Captain Howard does not permit it."

"Oh,—but how can anyone help it!—and they are so monstrous ugly!"

"They are considered very fine men, physically," said Raymond.

"But they will never make soldiers," interpolated Captain Howard. The English government had done its utmost with the American Indians, as with other subdued peoples of its dependencies, both earlier and later, to incorporate their martial strength into the British armies, but the aborigines seemed incapable of being moulded by the discipline of the drill and the regulations of the camp, and deserted as readily as they were enlisted, rewards and penalties alike of no effect.

"Oh, Mr. Raymond, no one could think them handsome!—they are—greasy!"

"The grease is to afford a surface for their paint, you must understand. But it is a horribly unclean and savage custom."

He never could account for a shade of offence on the lady's expressionless, limited face and a flush other than that of the rouge on her delicate, little flabby cheek. How should he know that that embellishment was laid on a gentle coating of pomade after the decrees of fashion. He was not versed in the methods of cosmetics. He had been on the frontier for the last three years—since his boyhood, in fact, and that grace and gentlemanliness which so commended his address were rather the results of early training and tradition than the influence of association with cultured circles of society. He knew that he had said something much amiss and he chafed at the realization.

"I am fitter for an atmosphere of gun-powder than attar of roses," he said to himself with a half glance over his shoulder at the window, the pale moonlight making the face of the girl poetic, ethereal, and shimmering on her golden hair.

The next moment, however, Mrs. Annandale claimed his attention, annulling the idea that there had been aught displeasing in his remark.

"But sure, Mr. Raymond, there were never towns, called towns, such as theirs—la!—what a disappointment, to be sure!"

"Ha! ha! ha!" exclaimed Captain Howard, mightily amused. "So you are looking for the like of Bond Street and Charing Cross and the Strand—eh!—in Estatoe, and Kulsage, and Seneca,—ha! ha! ha!"

Raymond winced a trifle lest the fragile little lady should find this soldier-like pleasantry too bluff for a sensitive nature, but she laughed with a subdued, deprecating suggestion of merriment. He could not imagine, as she lent herself to this ridicule, that she construed it as humoring the folly of the commandant, of whom indeed she always spoke behind his back in a commiserating way as "poor dear Brother." She had so often outwitted the tough old soldier that she looked upon his prowess as a vain thing, his fierce encounters with the national foe mere figments of war compared with those subtle campaigns in which she so invariably worsted him. She laughed at herself. She could afford it.

"Dear Brother," she said, "Charlestown is not London, to be sure, but we found it vastly genteel for its size. There is everything a person of taste requires for life—on a scale, to be sure—on a minute scale. But there is a theatre, and a library of books, so learning is not neglected, and a race-course, and a society of tone. Lord, sir, strangers, well introduced, have nothing to complain of. I'm sure Arabella and I were taken about till we could have dropped with fatigue, Mr. Raymond—what with Whisk and Piquet for me and a minuet for her, night after night, everywhere we went, we might well have thought ourselves in London. And Lord, sir, the British officers there are so content they seem to think they have achieved Paradise."

"I'll warrant 'em," and Captain Howard wagged his head scoffingly, meditating on the contrast with his past hardships in the frontier service.

"And being mightily charmed with what I had seen of the province I was struck with a cold chill by the time I'd crossed Ashley Ferry—the woods half dark by day and a cavern by night; and such howlings of owls, and lions, and tigers, I presume—"

"Oh, ho—ho—ho!" exclaimed Captain Howard. "I'll detail you, Ensign Raymond, to drill the awkward squad in natural history."

Raymond, responsive to the spirit of the jest, stood at attention and saluted, as if receiving a serious assignment to duty.

He was not of a wily nature, nor especially suspicious. He had keen perceptions, however, and his own straightforward candor aided them in detecting a circuitous divergence from the facts; when Mrs. Annandale declared herself so terrified that she had begged and prayed her niece and her brother to turn back, he realized dimly that this was not the case, that it was by her own free will the party had kept on, and that Arabella would never have had the cruelty to persist in the undertaking against her aunt's desire, nor had she the authority to compass this decision. But why had the little woman mustered the determination, he marvelled, for this long and arduous journey. He looked at her with the sort of doubtful and pitying yet fearful repulsion with which a scientist might study a new and very eccentric species of insect. He could realize that she had suffered all the fright and fatigue she described. Her puny little physique was indeed inadequate to sustain so severe a strain, bodily and mentally. Her fastidious distaste to the sight and customs of the Indians was itself a species of pain. Why had she come?

"Before we reached Ninety-Six I saw the first of the savages. Oh,—Mr. Raymond,—it seems a sort of indecency in the government to make war on people who wear so few clothes. They ought to be allowed to peacefully retire to the woods."

"Oh—ho—ho—ho!—that's the first time I ever heard the propriety of the government called in question," said Captain Howard. He glanced over his shoulder to make sure that Arabella had not overheard this jest of doubtful grace.

"She's busy," Mrs. Annandale reassured him with a sort of smirk of satisfaction, which impressed Raymond singularly unpleasantly. He too glanced over his shoulder. The tall, fair, graceful young officer could hardly appear to greater advantage than Mervyn did at this moment, in the blended light of the fire and the moon, for the candles on the table scarcely sent their beams so far. The rich dress of the girl was accented and embellished by the simplicity of the surroundings. Her head was turned aside—only the straight and perfect lines of her profile showed against the lustrous square of the window. She still held the curtain and, while he talked, she silently listened and gazed dreamily at the moon. There was a moment of embarrassment in the group at the fireside, as they relinquished their covert scrutiny, and Raymond's ready tact sought the rescue of the situation.

"It has been urged that we armed the Indians against ourselves through the trade in peace," he suggested.

"And now Mrs. Annandale thinks they ought to be put in the pink of the fashion before being shot at—ha—ha—ha!" returned Captain Howard.

"Then their towns,—a-lack-a-day,—to call them towns! A cluster of huts and wigwams, and a mound, and a rotunda, and a play-yard. They frightened me into fits with their proffers of hospitality. The women—dressed in some vastly fine furs and with their hair plaited with feathers—came up to our horses and offered us bread and fruit; oh, and a kind of boiled meal and water; and Arabella partook and said it was nice and clean but I pressed my hands to my stomach and rolled up my eyes to intimate that I was ill; and indeed I was at the very sight of them," Mrs. Annandale protested.

Once more she glanced over her shoulder, thinking her niece might hear her name; again that smirk of satisfaction to note the mutual absorption of the two, then, lest the pause seem an interruption, she went on:

"And have these wretches two sets of such towns? lower and upper—filthy abominations!"

"No, no, Claudia," said the captain, shaking his head, "they are clean, they are clean—clean as floods of pure water can make them. Every town is on a rock-bound water-course, finest, freshest, freest streams in the world, and every Indian, big and little, goes under as a religious duty every day. No, they are clean."

"Dear heart!" exclaimed the lady, without either contention or acquiescence.

"And they wear ample clothes, too. The buck-skin hunting-shirt and leggings of our frontiersmen are copied from the attire of the Indians. If you saw savages who were scantily clothed they must have been very poor, or on the war-path against other Indians—for they wear clothes, as they construe them, on ordinary occasions."

"How nice of them," commented Mrs. Annandale. "Shows their goodness of heart."

Once more Raymond bent the gaze of an inquiring scrutiny upon the lady— simple as she was, he had not yet classified her. She had begun to exert a sort of morbid fascination upon him. He did not understand her, and the enigma held him relentlessly.

He had not observed a motion which Arabella had made once or twice to quit the *tête-à-tête* beside the window, and he was taken by surprise when she suddenly approached the fire. Standing, tall and slender and smiling, between him and her father, with her hand on the commandant's chair, she addressed the coterie at large:—

"What a jovial time you seem to be having!"

Raymond's heart plunged, and Mervyn reddened slightly with an annoyance otherwise sedulously repressed. She spoke with a naïve suggestion as of an enforced exclusion from the fun. "What is all this talk about?"

"Mr. Raymond has been admiring the Indians' taste in dress," said Mrs. Annandale, titteringly,—"he says they wear the hides of beasts,—their own hides."

Captain Howard frowned. It did not enter into his scheme of things to question the discretion of a professed duenna. He was confused for a moment, and it seemed to him that the fault lay in Raymond's bad taste in the remark rather than in its repetition. It did not occur to him that it was made for the first time.

Raymond, realizing that for some reason Mrs. Annandale sought to place him at a disadvantage, was on the point of gasping out a denial, but the gaucherie of contradicting a lady, and she the sister of his host, deterred him.

Though the young girl was convent-bred with great seclusion and care, she had emerged into an atmosphere of such sophistication that she was able to seem to have apprehended naught amiss. She bent her eyes with quiet attention on her aunt's face when Mrs. Annandale said abruptly:—

"Tell George Mervyn how oddly those gypsies were dressed—gypsies, or Hindoos, or whatever they were—that camped down on the edge of the copse close to his grandfather's park gates last fall, and told your fortune!"

"Was it on our side of the ha-ha, or your side?" asked Mervyn, eagerly. For as Raymond understood the property of the two families adjoined, large and manorial possessions on the part of the Mervyns, and with their neighbors a very modest holding—a good old house but with little land.

"Oh, to think of the copse!" cried Mervyn with a gush of homesick feeling,—"to think of the beck! I could almost die to be a boy again for one hour, bird-nesting there once more!"

"Even if I made you put the eggs back?" Arabella smiled.

"Though they would never hatch after being touched," he corroborated.

"But tell the story, Arabella. Tell what the gypsy said," urged Mrs. Annandale, significantly.

The young lady still stood, her hand resting on her father's chair. She looked down into the fire with inscrutable hazel eyes. Her face seemed to glow and pale, as the flames flared and fell and sent pulsations of shoaling light along the glistening waves of her pink tabby gown.

"I don't care what the gypsy said," she returned.

"But you cared then—enough to cross her hand with silver!" cried Mrs. Annandale. "And, George, your grandfather, Sir George, came riding by—I think that gray cob is a rather free goer for the old gentleman—and he reined up by the hedge and looked over. And he said, 'Make it gold, young lady, if you want it rich and true. Buy your luck—that's the way to get it!'"

Captain Howard stirred uneasily. "Sir George is right—the gypsy hussy is bought; she gives a shilling fortune for a shilling and a crown of luck for a crown. I have no faith in the practice."

"You will when you hear this, dear Brother. Tell what the gypsy said, Arabella!" Mrs. Annandale leaned forward with her small mouth tightly closed and her small eyes twinkling with expectation.

"Oh, I have clean forgot," declared Arabella, her eyes still on the coals and standing in the rich illumination of the flare.

"I have not forgot. I heard every word!" exclaimed the wily tactician.

Now Arabella lifted her long dark lashes, and it seemed to Raymond that she sent a glance of pleading expostulation, of sensitive appeal to meet the microscopic glitter in the pinched and wizened pale face. Mervyn waited in a quiver of expectation, of suspense; and Raymond, wounded, excluded, set at naught, as he had felt, was sensible of a quickening of his pulses. But why did the old woman persist?

"There is nothing in such prophecies," said Captain Howard, uneasily.

"She said you had a lover over seas,—didn't she, my own?"

The girl, looking again at the red fire, nodded her golden head casually, as if in renewing memory.

"One who loved you, and whom you loved!"

Mervyn caught his breath. The blood had flared into his face. He held himself tense and erect by a sheer effort of will, but any moment he might collapse into a nervous tremor.

"She said—oh, she said—" exclaimed Mrs. Annandale, prolonging the suspense of the moment and clasping her mittened hands about her knees, leaning forward and looking into the fire, "she said he was handsome, and tall, and blond. And you—you didn't know in the least who he was; though you gave her another crown from pure good will!" And Mrs. Annandale tittered teasingly and archly, as she glanced at Mervyn.

"Oh, yes, I did know who he was,"—the girl electrified the circle by declaring. "That is why I gave her more money."

Her eyes were wide and bright. She tossed her head with a knowing air. Her cheeks were scarlet, and the breath came fast over her parted red lips.

Mrs. Annandale sat in motionless consternation. She had lost the helm of the conversation and it seemed driving at random through a turmoil of chopping chances. Mervyn looked hardly less frightened,—as if he might faint,—for he felt that his name was trembling on Arabella's lips. It was like the chaos of some wild unexplained dream when she suddenly resumed:—

"The gypsy meant Monsieur Delorme, my drawing-master at Dijon—all the pupils were in love with him—I, more than all—handsome and adorable!"

Raymond's eyes suddenly met Mervyn's stony stare of amazement. He did not laugh, but that gay, bantering, comprehending look of joyful relish had as nettling a sting as a roar of bravos.

Captain Howard was but just rescued from a dilemma that had bidden fair to whelm all his faculties, but his disgust recovered him.

"Oh, fie!"—he said rancorously. "The drawing-master! Fudge!"

Mrs. Annandale had the rare merit of knowing when she was defeated. She had caused her brother to invite Raymond merely that the invitation to Mervyn might not seem too particular. But having this point secure she had given him not one thought and not a word save to engage his attention and permit Mervyn's *tête-à-tête* with her niece. Since her little scheme of bantering the two lovers, as she desired to consider them, or rather to have them consider each other, had gone so much awry, she addressed herself to obliterate the impression it had made. She now sought to ply Raymond with her fascinations, and with such effect that Mervyn, who had been occupied with plans to get himself away so that he might consider in quiet the meaning of her demonstration and the girl's unexpected rejoinder, was amazed and dismayed. Mrs. Annandale was of stancher stuff than he thought, and though afterward she much condemned the result of her inquiries touching family relations and mutual acquaintance in England, this seemed to be the only live topic between a young man and an elderly woman such as she, specially shaken as she had been by the downfall of all her plans in the manipulation of the treacherous Arabella. She had not, indeed, intended to elicit the fact that Raymond was nearly connected with some of the best people in the kingdom, that his family was so old and of so high a repute that a modern baronetcy was really a thing of tinsel and mean pretence in comparison. Among them there was no wealth of note, but deeds of distinction decorated almost every branch of the family tree. When at last she could bear no more and rose, admonishing her niece to accompany her, terminating the entertainment, as being themselves guests, Arabella, sitting listening by the side of the fire, thrown back in the depths of the arm-chair among the furs that covered it, exclaimed naively: "What! So early!"

CHAPTER II

WHEN Mrs. Annandale and her niece repaired to the quarters assigned them, the young lady passed through the room of the elder to the inner apartment, as if she feared that her contumacy might be upbraided. But if Mrs. Annandale felt her armor a burden and was a-wearied with the untoward result of the evening's campaign she made no sign, but gallantly persevered, realizing the truism that more skill is requisite in conducting a retreat than in leading the most spirited assault. She followed her niece and seated herself by the fire while Arabella at the dressing-table let down her mass of golden hair and began to ply the brush, looking meanwhile at a very disaffected face in the mirror. The youthful maid who officiated for both ladies, monopolized chiefly by Mrs. Annandale, was busied with some duties touching a warming-pan in the outer room, and thus the opportunity for confidential conversation was ample.

"These soldiers talk so much about their hard case," said the elder lady, looking about her with an appraising eye. "Many folks at home might call this luxury."

For Captain Howard had exerted his capacity and knowledge to the utmost to compass comfort for his sister and daughter, with the result that he was held to complain without a grievance. A great fire roared in a deep chimney-place—there were no andirons, it is true, but two large dornicks served as well. The log walls were white-washed and glittered with a vaunt of cleanliness. The bed-curtains were pink, and fluttered in a draught from the fire. Rose-tinted curtains veiled the meagre sashes of the glazed windows. The chairs, of the clumsy post manufacture, were big and covered with dressed furs. Buffalo rugs lay before the wide hearth and on the floor. A candle flickered unneeded on the white-draped dressing-table, and there was the glitter of silver and glass and of such *bijouterie* as dressing-case and jewel-box could send forth. The young girl, now in a pink *robe de chambre*, seemed in accord with the rude harmony of the place.

"They line their nests right well, these tough soldiers," said the elder woman. "If it were not for the Indians, and the marching, and the guns, and the noisy powder, and the wild-cats, and the wilderness, one might marry a soldier with a fair prospect. George Mervyn is a handsome young man, Bella."

"He looks like a sheep," said Arabella, petulantly. "That long, thin, mild face of his, pale as the powder on his hair, without a spark of spirit, and those stiff side-curls on each side of his head, exactly like a ram's horns! He looks like a sheep, and he *is* a sheep."

With all her unrevealed and secret purposes it was difficult to hold both temper and patience after the strain of the mishaps of the evening. But Mrs. Annandale merely yawned and replied, "I think he is a handsome young man, and much like Sir George."

"Ba-a-a!—Ba-a-a!"—said the dutiful niece.

The weary little woman still held stanchly on. "I believe you'd rather marry the grandfather."

"I would—but I don't choose to marry either."

Mrs. Annandale had a sudden inspiration. "No, my poor love," she said with a downward inflection, "a girl like you, with beauty, and brains, and good birth, and fine breeding,—but no money, too often doesn't *choose* to marry anybody, for anybody that *is* anybody doesn't want her."

There was dead silence in front of the mirror. A troublous shade settled on the fair face reflected therein. The brush was motionless. An obvious dismay was expressed in the pause. Self-pity is a poignant pain.

"Lord! Lord!—how unevenly the good things of this world are divided," sighed the philosopher. "The daughter of a poor soldier, and it makes no difference how lovely, how accomplished!—while if you were the bride of Sir George Mervyn's grandson—bless me, girl, your charms would be on every tongue. You'd be the toast of all England!"

There was a momentary silence while the light flashed from the lengths of golden hair as the brush went back and forth with strong, quick strokes. The head, intently poised, betokened a sedulous attention.

"Out upon the injustice of it!" cried Mrs. Annandale, with unaffected fervor. "To be beautiful, and well-bred, and well-born, and well-taught, and faultless, and capable of gracing the very highest station in the land, and to be driven by poverty to take a poor, meagre, contemned portion in life, simply and solely because those whom you are fit for, and who are fit for you, will not condescend to think of you."

"I am not so sure of that!" cried Arabella, suddenly, with a tense note of elation. The mirror showed the vivid flush rising in her cheeks, the spirit in her eyes, the pride in the pose of her head. "And, Aunt, mark you now,—no man can *condescend* to me!"

"Lord! you poor child, how little you know of the ways of the world. But they were not in the convent course, I warrant you. Wealth marries wealth. Station climbs to higher station. Gallantry, admiration, all that is very well in a way, to pass the time. But men's wounded hearts are easily patched with title-deeds and long rent-rolls. Don't let your pride make you think that your bright eyes can shine like the Golightly diamonds. Bless my soul, Miss Eva had them all on at the county ball last year. Ha! ha! ha! I remember Sir George Mervyn said she looked a walking pawn-shop,—they were so prodigiously various. You know the Mervyns always showed very chaste taste in the matter of jewellery—the family jewels are few, but monstrous fine; every stone is a small fortune. But he was vastly polite to her at supper. I thought I would warn you, sweet, don't bother to be civil to young George, for old Sir George is determined on that match. Though the money was made in trade 'twas a long time ago, and there's a mort of it. The girl has a dashing way with her, too, and sets up for a beauty when *you* are out of the county."

"Lord, ma'am, Eva Golightly?" questioned Arabella, in scornful amaze.

"Sure, she has fine dark eyes, and she can make them flash and play equal to the diamonds in her hair. Maybe I'm as dazzled as the men, but she fairly looked like a princess to me. Heigho! has that besom ever finished fixing my bed? Good night—good night—my poor precious—and—say your prayers, child, say your prayers!"

The face in the mirror—the brush was still again—showed a depression of spirit, but the set teeth and an intimation of determination squared its delicate chin till Arabella looked like Captain Howard in the moment of ordering a desperate assault on the enemy's position. There was, nevertheless, a sort of flinching, as of a wound received, sensitive in a thousand keen appreciations of pain. The word "condescend" had opened her eyes to new interpretations of life. Her father might realize that a captain, however valorous, did not outrank a major-general, but in the splendor of her young beauty, and cultured intelligence, and indomitable spirit, she had felt a regal preëminence, and the world accorded her homage. That it was a mere *façon de parler* had never before occurred to her—a sort of cheap indulgence to a pretension without solid foundation. Her pride was cut to the quick. She was considered, forsooth, very pretty, and vastly accomplished, and almost learned with her linguistic acquirements and the mastery of heavy tomes of dull convent lore, yet of no sort of account because her people were not rich and she had no dowry, and unless she should be smitten by some stroke of good fortune, as uncontrollable as a bolt of lightning, she was destined to mate with some starveling curate or led captain, when as so humbly placed a dame she would lack the welcome in the circles that had once flattered her beauty and her transient belleship. The candle on the dressing-table was guttering in its socket when its fitful flaring roused her to contemplate the pallid reflection, all out of countenance, the fire dwindling to embers, and the shadows that had crept into the retired spaces of the bed, between the rose-tinted curtains, with a simulacrum of dull thoughts for the pillow and dreary dreams.

The interval had not passed so quietly within the precincts of Mrs. Annandale's chamber. The connecting door was closed, and Arabella did not notice the clamor, as the maid was constrained to try the latches of the outer door and adjust and readjust the bars, and finally to push by main force and a tremendous clatter one of the great chairs against it, lest some discerning and fastidious marauder should select out of all Fort Prince George, Mrs. Annandale's precious personality to capture, or "captivate," to use the incongruous and archaic phrase of the day. Now that the outer door was barricaded beyond all possibility of being carried by storm or of surreptitious entrance, Mrs. Annandale was beset with anxiety as to egress on an emergency.

"But look, you hussy," she exclaimed, as she stood holding the candle aloft to light the tusslings and tuggings of the maid with the furniture and the bar, "suppose the place should take fire. How am I to get out! You have shut me in here to perish like a rat in a trap, you heartless jade!"

"Oh, sure, mem, the fort will never take fire—the captain is that careful—the foine man he is!" said the girl, turning up her fresh, rosy, Irish face.

"I know the 'foine man' better than you do," snapped her mistress. The victory of the evening had been so long deferred, so hardly won at last, that the conqueror was in little better case than the defeated; she was fit to fall with fatigue, and her patience was in tatters. The War Office intrusted Captain Howard with the lives of its stanch soldiers and the value of many pounds sterling in munitions of war. But his sister belittled the enemy she had so often worsted, and who never even knew that he was beaten. "And those zanies of soldiers—smoking their vile tobacco like Indians!"

"Lord, mem," said the girl, still on her knees, vigorously chunking and jobbing at the door, "the sojers are in barracks, in bed and asleep these three hours agone."

"Look at that guard-house, flaring like the gates of hell! What do you mean by lying, girl!" Mrs. Annandale glanced out of the white curtained window, showing a spark of light in the darkness.

"Sure, ma'am, it's the watch they be kapin' so kindly all night, like the stars, or the blissed saints in heaven!"

"Mightily like the 'blissed saints in heaven,' I'll wager," said the old lady, sourly.

"I was fair afeard o' Injuns and wild-cats till I seen the gyard turn out, mem," said the maid, relishing a bit of gossip.

Mrs. Annandale gave a sudden little yowl, not unlike a feline utterance.

"You Jezebel," she cried in wrath, "what did you remind me of them for—look behind the curtains—under the valance of the bed—yow!—there is no telling who is hid there—robbers, murderers!"

Norah, young, plump, neat, and docile to the last degree, sprang up from her knees and rushed at these white dimity fabrics, tossing their fringed edges, with a speed and spirit that might have implied a courage equal to the encounter with concealed braves or beasts. But too often had she had this experience, finding nothing to warrant a fear. It was a mere form of search in her estimation, and her ardor was assumed to give her mistress assurance of her efficiency and protection. Therefore, when on her knees by the bedside she sprang back with a sudden cry of genuine alarm, her unexpected terror out-mastered her, and she fled whimpering to the other side of the room behind the little lady, who, dropping the candle in amazement and a convulsive tremor, might have achieved the conflagration she had prefigured without the aid of the zanies of the barracks, but that the flame failed in falling.

"Boots!—Boots!—" cried the girl, her teeth chattering.

Mrs. Annandale's courage seemed destined to unnumbered strains. It was not her will to exert it. She preferred panic as her prerogative. She glanced at the door, barred by her own precautions against all possibility of a speedy summons for help. Even to hail the guard-house through the window was futile at the distance; to escape by way of the casement was impossible, the rooms being situated in the second story of the large square building; a moment of listening told her that her niece was all unaware of the crisis, asleep, perhaps, silent, still. There was nothing for it but her own prowess.

"I have a blunderbuss here, man," she said, seizing the curling-iron from her dressing-table and marking with satisfaction the long and formidable shadow it cast in the firelight on the white wall. "Bring those boots out or I'll shoot them off you!"

There was dead silence. She heard the fire crackle, the ash stir, even, she fancied, the tread of a sentry in the tower above the gate.

"It's a Injun—a Injun—he don't understand the spache, mem!" said Norah, wondering that the unknown had the temerity to disregard this august summons.

"Norah," said Mrs. Annandale, autocratically, and as she flourished the curling-tongs Norah cowered and winced as from a veritable blunderbuss, so did the little lady dominate by her asseverations the mind of her dependent—and indeed stancher mental endowments than poor little Norah's—"fetch me out those boots."

"Oh, mem—what am I to do with the man that's in 'em?" quavered the Abigail, dolorously.

"Fetch him, too, if he's there. Give him a tug, I say, girl."

The doubt that this mandate expressed, nerved the timorous maid to approach the silent white-draped bed. That she had nevertheless expected both resistance and weight was manifest in the degree of strength she exerted. She fell back, overthrown by the sheer force of the recoil, with a large empty boot in her hand, nor would she believe that the miscreant had not craftily slipped off the footgear till the other came as empty, and a timorous peep ascertained that there were no feet to match within view.

"Some officer's boots!" soliloquized Mrs. Annandale. "He must have left them here when he was turned out of these snug quarters to make room for us. I wonder when that floor was swept."

"Sure, mem, they're not dusty," said Norah, all blithe and rosy once more. "I'm rej'iced that he wasn't in 'em."

"Who—the officer?" with a withering stare.

"No'm, the Injun I was looking for"—with a quaver.

"Or the wild-cat you was talking about! Nasty things! Never mention them again."

Mrs. Annandale was a good deal shaken by the experience and tottered slightly as she paused at the dressing-table and laid down the curling-tongs that had masqueraded as a blunderbuss. The maid, all smiling alacrity to make amends, bustled cheerily about in the preparations for the retirement of her employer. "Sure, mem, yez would love to see 'em dead."

"You've got a tongue now, but some day it will be cut out," the old woman remarked, acridly.

"I'm maning to say, mem, they have the beautifulest fur—them wild-cats, not the Injuns. There's a robe or blanket av 'em in the orderly room—beautiful, mem, sure, like the cats may have in heaven."

As Mrs. Annandale sat in her great chair she seemed to be falling to pieces, so much of her identity came off as her hand-maiden removed her effects. She was severally divested of her embroidered cape, the full folds of her puce-colored satin gown, her slippers and clocked stockings; and when at last in her night-rail and white night-cap, she looked like a curious antique infant, with a malignant and coercive stare. Norah handled her with a fearful tenderness, as if she might break in two, such a wisp of a woman she was! Little like a conquering hero she seemed as she sat there before the fire, now girding at the offices of her attendant, now whimpering weakly, like a spoiled child, her white-capped head nodding and her white-clad figure fairly lost in the great chair, but she was the most puissant force that had ever invested Fort Prince George, though it had sustained both French military strategy and Indian savage wiles. And the days to come were to bear testimony to her courage, her address, and her dominant rage for power. When her little fateful presence was eclipsed at last by the ample white bed-curtains and Norah was free to draw forth her pallet and lay herself down on the floor before the fire, the girl could not refrain a long-drawn sigh, half of fatigue and half self-commiseration. It seemed a hard lot with her exacting and freakish employer. But the cold bitter wind came surging around the corner of the house, and she remembered the bleak morasses across the wild Atlantic, the little smoky hovel she called home, the many to fend from frost and famine, the close and crowded quarters, the straw bed where she had lain, neighboring the pig. She thought of her august room-mate in comparison.

"But faix!—how much perliter was the crayther to be sure!"

CHAPTER III

IT was one of the peculiarities of the officers of the Fort Prince George garrison that they were subject to fits of invisibility, Mrs. Annandale declared. She had been taciturn, even inattentive, over her dish of chocolate at early breakfast. More than once she turned, with a frostily fascinating smile, beamingly expectant, as the door opened. But when the dishes were removed, and the breakfast-room resumed its aspect as parlor, and her niece sat down to her embroidery-frame as if she had been at home in a country house in Kent, and the captain rose and began to get into his outdoor gear, Mrs. Annandale's sugared and expectant pose gave way to blunt disappointment.

"Where are those villains we wasted our good cheer upon overnight?" she brusquely demanded. "I vow I expected to find them bowing their morning compliments on the door-step!"

"You must make allowances for our rude frontier soldiers,"—the commandant began.

"Were they caught up into the sky or swallowed up by the earth?"

The commandant explained that the tours of service recurred with unwelcome frequency in a garrison so scantily officered as Fort Prince George, and that Mervyn and Raymond were both on duty.

"You should have excused them, dear Brother, since they are our acquaintances, and let some of those rowdy fellows in the mess-hall march, or goose-step, or deploy, or what not, in their stead."

"Shoot me—no—no!" said the commandant, wagging his head, for this touched his official conscience, and the citadel in which it was ensconced not even this wily strategist could reach. "No, no, each man performs his own duty as it falls to him. I would not exchange or permit an exchange to—to, no, not to be quit forever of Fort Prince George."

"Poor Arabella—she looks pale."

"For neither of them," the niece spoke up, tartly.

"Now that's hearty," said her father, approvingly.

"I shall be glad to be quiet a bit, and rest from the journey," Arabella declared. "I don't need to be amused to-day."

"Lord—Lord! I pray I may survive it," her aunt plained.

Mrs. Annandale was so definitely disconsolate and indignant that the captain held a parley. Lieutenant Bolt, the fort-adjutant, was a man of good station, he said, and also a younger lieutenant and two ensigns; should he not bespeak their company for a game of Quadrille in his quarters this evening?

Truly "dear Brother" was too tediously dense. "A murrain on them all!" she exclaimed angrily. "What are they in comparison with young Mervyn?"

"As good men every way. Trained, tried, valuable officers—worth their weight in gold," he retorted, aglow with *esprit de corps*.

She caught herself up sharply, fearing that she was too outspoken; and, realizing that "dear Brother" was an uncontrollable roadster when once he took the bit between his teeth, she qualified hastily. "An old woman loves gossip, Brother. What are these strangers to me? George Mervyn and I will put our heads together and canvass every scandal in the county for the last five years. Lord, he knows every stock and stone of the whole country-side, and all the folks, gentle and simple, from castle to cottage. I looked for some clavers such as old neighbors love."

"Plenty of time—plenty of time,"—said the commandant. "George Mervyn will last till to-morrow morning."

"To-morrow—is he in your clutches till to-morrow morning?" the schemer shrieked in dismay.

"He is officer of the day, Claudia, and his tour of duty began at guard-mounting this morning, and will not be concluded till guard-mounting to-morrow morning," the captain said severely. Then in self-justification, for he was a lenient man, except in his official capacity, he added gravely: "You must reflect, Sister, that though we are a small force in a little mud fort on the far frontier, we cannot afford to be triflers at soldiering. A better fort than ours was compelled to surrender and a better garrison was massacred not one hundred and fifty miles from here. Our duties are insistent and our mutual responsibility is great. We are intrusted with the lives of each other."

He desired these words to be of a permanent and serious impression. He said no more and went out, leaving Mrs. Annandale fallen back in her chair, holding up her hands to heaven as a testimony against him.

"Oh, the ruffian!" she gasped. "Oh—to remind me of the Indians—the greasy, gawky red-sticks! Oh, the blood-thirsty, truculent brother!"

Arabella was of a pensive pose, with her head bent to her embroidery-frame, her trailing garment, called a sacque, of dark murrey-colored wool, catching higher wine-tinted lights from the fire as the folds opened over a bodice and petticoat of flowered stuff of acanthus leaves on a faint blue ground. She seemed ill at ease under this rodomontade against her father, and roused herself to protest.

"Why, you can't have *forgotten* the Indians! You were talking about them every step of the way from Charlestown. And if you have seen one you have seen one hundred."

"Out of sight out of mind—and *me*—so timid! Oh—and that hideous Fort Loudon massacre! Oh, scorch the tongue that says the word! Oh—the Indians! And me—so timid!"

"Lord, Aunt—" Arabella laid the embroidery-frame on her knees and gazed at her relative with stern, upbraiding eyes, "you know you lamented to discover that we were not to pass Fort Loudon on our journey, for you said it would be 'a sight to remember, frightful but improving, like a man hung in chains.'"

Mrs. Annandale softly beat her hands together.

"To talk of guarding life with his monkey soldiers against those red painted demons who drink blood and eat people—oh!—and me, *so timid!*"

She desisted suddenly as a light tap fell on the door and the mess-sergeant entered the room. She set her cap to rights with both her white, delicate, wrinkled, trembling hands, and stared with wild half-comprehending eyes as the man presented the compliments of Lieutenants Bolt and Jerrold, and Ensigns Lawrence and Innis, who felt themselves vastly honored by her invitation to a game of Quadrille, and would have the pleasure of waiting upon her this evening at the hour Captain Howard had named.

She made an appropriate rejoinder, and she waited until the door had closed upon the messenger, for she rarely "capered," as her maid called her angry antics, in the presence of outsiders. Then she said with low-toned virulence to her niece:—

"The scheming meddler! That father of yours! *That* father of yours! Talk of treachery! Wilier than any Indian! Quadrille! Invite them! Smite them! Quadrille! Why, Mervyn is not complimented at all. The same grace extended to each and every!"

"And why should *he* be complimented, Aunt Claudia?"

"No reason in the world, Miss, as far as you are concerned," retorted her aunt. "Our compliments won't move such as George Mervyn!" Then recovering her temper,—"I thought a little special distinction as a dear old friend and a lifelong neighbor might be fitting. Poor dear Brother must equalize the whole garrison!"

It seemed to Captain Howard as if with the advent of his feminine guests had entered elements of doubt and difficulty of which he had lately experienced a pleasant surcease. The joy which he had felt as a fond parent in embracing a good and lovely child, after a long absence, was too keen to continue in the intensity of its first moments and was softened to a gentle and tender content, a habitude of the heart, even more pleasurable. He was fond, too, in a way, of his queer sister, and grateful for her fostering care of his motherless children; he had great consideration for her whims and not the most remote appreciation of her peculiar abilities. The abatement of the joy of reunion was manifest in the fact that her whims now seemed to dominate her whole personality and tempered the fervor of his gratitude. He was already ashamed that he had not invited to the dinner of welcome the four other gentlemen who seemed altogether fit for that festivity and made the occasion one of general rejoicing among his brother officers and fellow-exiles, rather than a nettlesome point of exclusion. He was realizing, too, the disproportionate importance such trifles as the opportunity for transient pleasures possess in the estimation of the young, although they have all the years before them, with the continual recurrence of conventional incidents. Perhaps the long interval, debarred from all society of their sphere, rendered the exclusion a positive deprivation. He regretted that he had submitted to Mrs. Annandale's arrogation of the privilege of choosing the company invited to celebrate the arrival of the commandant's daughter at the frontier fort. He seized upon the first moment when the rousing of his official conscience freed him, for the time, to repair the omission. The projected card-party would seem a device for introducing the officers in detail, as if this were deemed less awkward than entertaining them in a body, especially as there were only two ladies to represent the fair sex in the company.

To his satisfaction this implied theory of the appropriate seemed readily adopted. Lieutenant Jerrold was a man of a conventional, assured address, his conversation always strictly in good form and strictly limited. He was little disposed to take offence where the ground of quarrel seemed untenable or, on the other hand, to thrust himself forward where his presence was not warmly encouraged. He welcomed the invitation as enabling him to pay his respects to the ladies, which, indeed, seemed incumbent in the situation, but he had been a trifle nettled by the postponement of the opportunity. He had dark hair and eyes; he was tall, pale, and slender, with a narrow face and a flash of white teeth when he smiled. He was in many respects a contrast to the two ensigns—Innis, blue-eyed, blond, and square visaged, his complexion burned a uniform red by his frontier campaigns, and Lawrence, who had suffered much freckling as the penalty of the extreme fairness of his skin, and who always wore his hair heavily powdered, to disguise in part the red hue, which was greatly out of favor in his day. Bolt, the fort-adjutant, was not likely to add much to the mirth of nations, or even of the garrison—a heavily-built, sedate, taciturn man, who would eat his supper with appreciation and discrimination, and play his cards most judiciously.

Captain Howard left the mess-hall where the recipients of his courtesy discussed its intendment over the remainder of breakfast, and took his way, his square head wagging now and then with an appreciation of its own obstinacy, across the snowy parade.

The gigantic purple slopes of the encompassing mountains showed here and there where the heavy masses of the drifts had slipped down by their own weight, and again the dark foliage of pine and holly and laurel gloomed amongst the snow-laden boughs of the bare deciduous trees. The contour, however, of the great dome-like "balds" was distinct, of an unbroken whiteness against the dark slate-tinted sky, uniform of tone from pole to pole.

Many feet had trampled the snow hard on the parade, and there was as yet no sign of thaw. Feathery tufts hung between the points of the high stockade surmounting the ramparts and choked the wheels of the four small cannon that were mounted on each of the four bastions. The cheeks of the deep embrasures out of which their black muzzles pointed were blockaded with drifts, and the scarp and counterscarp were smooth, and white, and untrodden. The roofs of the block-houses were covered, and all along the northern side of the structures was a thin coating of snow clinging to the logs, save where the protuberant upper story overhung and sheltered the walls beneath. Close about the chimney of the building wherein was situated the mess-hall, the heat of the great fire below had melted the drifts, and a cordon of icicles clung from the stone cap, whence the dark column of smoke rushed up and, with a vigorous swirl through the air, made off into invisibility without casting a shadow in this gray day. He could see the great conical "state-house" on a high mound of the Indian settlement of Old Keowee Town, across the river; it was as smooth and white as a marble rotunda. The huddled dwellings were on a lower level and invisible from his position on the parade. As he glanced toward the main gate he paused suddenly. Before the guard-house the guard had been turned out, a glittering line of scarlet across the snow. The little tower above the gate was built in somewhat the style of a belfry, and through the open window the warder, like the clapper of a bell, stood drooping forward, gazing down at a group of blanketed and feather-crested figures, evidently Indians, desiring admission and now in conference with the officer of the guard. Captain Howard quickened his steps toward the party, and Raymond, perceiving his approach, advanced to meet him. There was a hasty, low-toned colloquy. Then "Damn *all* the Indians!" cried Captain Howard, angrily. "Damn them *all*!"

"The parson says 'No'!" Raymond submitted, with a glance of raillery.

"This is no occasion for your malapert wit, sir," the captain retorted acridly.

Ordinarily Captain Howard was accessible to a pleasantry and himself encouraged a jovial insouciance as far as it might promote the general cheerfulness, but this incident threatened a renewal of a long strain of perplexity and dubious diplomacy and doubtful menace. It was impossible to weigh events. A trifle of causeless discontent among the Indians might herald downright murder. A real and aggravated grievance often dragged itself out and died of inanition in long correspondence with the colonial authorities, or the despatch of large and expensive delegations to Charlestown for those diplomatic conferences with the governor of South Carolina which the Indians loved and which flattered the importance of the head-men.

He strove visibly for his wonted self-balanced poise, and noticing that the young officer flushed, albeit silent, as needs must, he felt that he had taken unchivalrous advantage of the military etiquette which prevented a retort. He went on with a grim smile:—

"Where is this missionary now, who won't give the devil his due."

"The emissaries don't tell, sir. Somewhere on the Tugaloo River, they give me to understand."

"And what the fiend does he there?"

"Converts the Indians to Christianity, sir, if he can."

"And they resist conversion?"

"They say he plagues them with many words."

Captain Howard nodded feelingly.

"They say he unsettles the minds of the people, who grow slack in the observance of their 'old beloved' worship. He reviles their religion, and offends 'the Ancient White Fire.'"

"There is no rancor like religious rancor, no deviltry like pious strife," said Captain Howard, in genuine dismay. "Nothing could so easily rouse the Indians anew."

He paused in frowning anxiety. "Stop me, sir, this man is monstrous short of a Christian, himself, to jeopardize the peace and put the whole frontier into danger for his zeal—just now when the tribe is fairly pacified. This threatens Fort Prince George first of all."

He set his square jaw as he thought of his daughter and his sister.

Raymond instinctively knew what was passing in his mind, and forgetful of his sharp criticism volunteered reassurance.

"The delegation speak, sir, as if only the missionary were in danger."

"Why don't they burn him, then, sir—kindle the fire with his own prayer-book!" cried Captain Howard, furiously. Danger from the Indians—now! with Arabella and Claudia at Fort Prince George! He could not tolerate the idea. Even in their defeated and disconsolate estate the Cherokees could bring two thousand warriors to the field—and the garrison of Fort Prince George numbered scant one hundred, rank and file.

"It might be the beginning of trouble," suggested Raymond, generously disregarding the acerbity with which his unsought remarks had been received. "You know how one burning kindles the fires of others—how one murder begins a massacre."

"Lord—Lord—yes!" exclaimed Captain Howard. "What ails the wretch?—are there no sinners at Fort Prince George that he must go hammering at the gates of heaven for the vile red fiends? And what a murrain would they do there! I can see Moy Toy having a 'straight talk' with Saint Peter, and that one-eyed murderer, Rolloweh, quiring to a gilded harp! Is there no way of getting at the man? Will they not let him come back now?"

"They have asked him to leave the country."

"And what said he?" demanded Captain Howard.

"The delegation declare that he said, 'Woe!'"

"Whoa!" echoed Captain Howard, in blank amaze.

"Yes, sir,—that was his answer to them in conclave in their beloved square. 'Woe!'"

"Whoa!" repeated Captain Howard, stuck fast in misapprehension. "I think he means, Get-up-and-go-'long!"

Raymond had a half-hysteric impulse to laugh, and yet it was independent of any real amusement.

"I fancy he meant, 'Woe is unto him if he preach not the gospel,'" he said. "The Indians remember one word only—'Woe!'"

"He shall preach the gospel hereafter at Fort Prince George! Is there no way to quiet the man?"

"You know the Indians' methods, sir. I think they have some demand to make of you, but they will not enter on it for twenty-four hours. They want accommodations and a conference to-morrow."

"Zounds!" exclaimed Captain Howard, in the extremity of impatience. In this irregular frontier warfare he had known many a long-drawn, lingering agony of suspense—but he felt as if he could not endure the ordeal with all he now had at stake, his daughter, his sister, as hostages to the fortunes of war. He had an impulse to take the crisis as it were in the grasp of his hand and crush it in the moment. He could not wait—yet wait he must.

"They only vouchsafed as much as I have told you in order to secure the conference," said Raymond. "I gave them to understand that the time of our 'beloved man' was precious and not to be expended on trifles. But they held back the nature of the demand on you and the whereabouts of the parson."

"I pray God, they have not harmed the poor old man!" exclaimed Captain Howard fervently, with a sudden revulsion of sentiment.

They both glanced toward the gate where the deputation stood under the archway. The sun was shining faintly and the wan light streamed through the portal. The shadows duplicated the number and the attitudes of the blanketed and feather-crested figures, all erect, and stark, and motionless, looking in blank silence at the conference of the two officers. The shadows had a meditative pose, a sort of pondering attention, and when suddenly the sun darkened and the shadows vanished, the effect was as if some dimly visible councillors had whispered to the Indians and were mysteriously resolved into the medium of the air.

They received Raymond on his return with their characteristic expressionless stolidity, and when the quarter-master appeared, hard on Captain Howard's withdrawal, with the order for their lodgement in a cluster of huts just without the works, reserved for such occasions and such guests, they repaired thither without a word, and Raymond, looking after them from the gate, soon beheld the smoke ascending from their fires and the purveying out of the good cheer of the hospitality of Fort Prince George. He noticed a trail of blood on the snow, where the quarter-master's men had laid down for a moment a quarter of beef, and in this he recognized a special compliment, for beef was a rarity with the Indians—venison and wild-fowl being their daily fare.

As the day waxed and waned he often cast his eye thither noting their movements. They came out in a body in the afternoon and repaired together to the trading-house, situated near the bank of the river, and occupied as a home as well as a store by the Scotch trader and his corps of assistants. That fire-water would be in circulation Raymond did not doubt, for to refuse it would work more disturbance than to set it forth in moderation. There were many regulations in hindrance of its sale, but rarely enforced, and he doubted if the trader would forego his profit even at the risk of the displeasure of the commandant. Some difficulty they evidently encountered, however, in procuring it. They all came back immediately and disappeared in their huts, and there was no sign of life in all the bleak landscape, save the vague smoke from the Indian town across the river and the dark wreaths from the fires of the delegation. The woods stood sheeted and white at the extremity of the space beyond the glacis, cleared to prevent too close an approach of an enemy and the firing into the fort from the branches of trees within range. The river was like rippled steel, its motion undiscerned on its surface, and its flow was silent. The sky was still gray and sombre; at one side of the fort the prongs and boughs of the abattis thrust darkly up through the snow that lodged among them.

Somewhat after the noon hour he noticed a party of Indians, vagrant-like, kindling a fire in a sheltered space in the lee of a rock and feeding on the carcass of a deer lately killed. The feast was long, but when it was ended they sat motionless, fully gorged, all in a row, squatting, huddled in their blankets and eying the fort, seemingly aimless as the time passed and the fire dwindled and died, neither sleeping nor making any sign. When the Indians of the delegation accommodated in the huts issued again and once more hopefully took their way to the trading-house, they must have seen, coming or going, this row of singular objects, like roosting birds, dark against the snow, silently contemplating with unknown, unknowable, savage thoughts the little fort. There was no suggestion of recognition or communication. Each band was for the other as if it did not exist. The delegation wended its way to the trading-house, and presently returned, and once more sought the emporium, and again repaired to the temporary quarters. The snow between the two points began to show a heavily trampled path.

That these migrations were not altogether without result became evident when one of the Indians, zig-zagging unsteadily in the rear, wandered from the beaten track, stumbled over the stump of a tree concealed by a drift, floundered unnoticed for a time, unable to rise, and at last lay there so still and so long that Raymond began to think he might freeze should he remain after the chill of the nightfall. But as the skies darkened two of the Indians came forth and dragged him into one of their huts, which were beginning to show as dull red sparks of light in the gathering dusk. And still beyond the abattis that semblance of birds of ill-omen was discernible against the expanse of white snow, as with their curious, racial, unimagined whim the vagrant savages sat in the cold and watched the fort. They did not stir when the sunset gun sounded and the flag fluttered gently down from the staff. The beat of drums shook the thick air, and the yearning sweetness of the bugle's tone, as it sounded for retreat, found a responsive vibration even in the snow-muffled rocks. Again and again it was lovingly reiterated, and a tender resonance thrilled vaguely a long time down the dim cold reaches of the river.

Lights had sprung up in the windows. A great yellow flare gushed out from the open door of the mess-hall, and the leaping flames of the gigantic fireplace could be seen across the parade. The barracks were loud with jovial voices. Servants bearing trays of dishes were passing back and forth from the kitchen to the commandant's quarters. The vigorous tramp of the march of soldiers made itself heard even in the snow as the corporal of the guard went out with the relief. A star showed in the dull gray sky that betokened in the higher atmosphere motion and shifting of clouds. A faint, irresolute, roseate tint lay above the purple slope to the west with a hesitant promise of a fair morrow. The light faded, the night slipped down, and the sentries began to challenge.

CHAPTER IV

IT was the fashion of the time and place to be zealous in flattering the Indian's sense of importance, and the hospitality of the fort was constantly asserted in plying the delegation with small presents. Shortly after nightfall the quarter-master-sergeant went out to the Indian huts with some tobacco and pipes, and tafia, and the compliments of the commandant. He returned with the somewhat significant information that they needed no tafia. A few, he stated, were sober, but saturnine and grave. Others were blind drunk. The most troublesome had reached the jovial stage. From where they lay recumbent they had caught the soldier by one leg and then by the other, tumbled him on the floor, and tripped him again and again as he sought to rise; finally, he made his way by scrambling on all fours out into the snow, and running for the gate with two or three of the staggering braves at his heels.

"Faix, if the commandant has any more complimints to waste on thim Injun gossoons," he remarked, as he stood, panting and puffing, under the archway while the guard clustered at gaze in the big door of the guard-house, "by the howly poker, he may pursint them in person! For the divil be in ivery fut I've got if I go a-nigh them cu'rus bogies agin! They ain't human. Wait, me b'ye, till I git me breath, an' I'll give ye the countersign, if I haven't forgot ut. I'm constructively on the outside yit, seein' ye cannot let me in till I gives ye the countersign."

There was a low-toned murmur.

"Pass, friend," said the sentinel.

"Thankin' ye fur nothin'," the quarter-master-sergeant rejoined as he paused under the archway to gaze back over the snow.

"If Robin Dorn ain't a frog or a tadpole to grow a new laig if one is pulled off," he remarked, "he'll hardly make the fort to-night."

The sentinel, left alone at the gate, peered out into the bleak dark waste. All suggestion of light had faded from the sky, and that the ground was white showed only where the yellow gleams from the doors and windows of the fort fell upon the limited space of the snowy parade. Soon these dwindled to a lantern in front of the silent barracks and a vague glimmer from the officers' mess-hall, where the great fire was left all solitary to burn itself out. A light still shone through the windows of the commandant's quarters, where he was entertaining company at cards. But otherwise the fort was lapsing to quiescence and slumber.

A wind began to stir in the woods. More than once the sentinel heard the dull thud of falling masses of snow and the clashing together of bare boughs.

Then the direction of the current of the air changed; it wavered and gradually its force failed, a deep stillness ensued and absolute darkness prevailed. The sound of crunching, as wolves or dogs gnawed, snarling, the bones of the deer that the vagrant savages had killed beyond the abattis, was distinct to his ear. It was a cold night and a dreary. The vigilance of watching with naught in expectation is a strain upon the attention which a definite menace does not exert. There was now no thought of danger from the Indians, who were fast declining from the character of warriors and marauders to that of mendicants and aimless intruders and harmless pests. The soldier knew his duty and was prepared to do it, but to maintain a close guard in these circumstances was a vexatious necessity. He paced briskly up and down to keep his blood astir.

A break in the dull monotony can never be so welcome as to a dreary night-watch. He experienced a sense of absolute pleasure in the regulation appearance of the officer of the day, crossing the parade and challenged by the sentinel before the guard-house door. The brisk turning out of the guard was like a reassurance of the continued value and cheer of life. The flare from the guard-house door showed the lines of red uniforms, the glitter of the bayonets, the muskets carried at "shoulder arms!" the officer of the guard, Raymond, at his post, and the sergeant advancing to the stationary figure, waiting in the snow. He watched the familiar scene, on which in the day-time he would not have bestowed a glance, as if it had some new and eager significance—so do trifles of scant interest fill the void of mental inactivity.

The crisp young voices were musical to his ear as they rang out in the night with the stereotyped phrases. "Advance, officer of the day, and give the countersign!" cried the sergeant. Then as Mervyn advanced and a whispered colloquy ensued, the dapper sergeant whirled briskly, smartly saluting the officer of the guard with the cry—as of discovery—"The countersign is right!"

"Advance officer of the day," said Raymond.

The two officers approached each other and the sentinel, losing interest in their unheard, whispered conference as Mervyn gave the parole, turned his eyes to the wild waste without. He was startled to see vaguely, dubiously, in some vagrant, far glimmer of the flare from the guard-house door or the swinging flicker of the lantern carried by one of the two men who, with a non-commissioned officer, was preparing to accompany the officer of the day on his rounds, a strange illusion, as close as the parapet of the covered way. There were dark figures against the snow, crouching dog-like or wolf-like—and yet he knew them to be Indians. They were gazing at the illuminated military manœuvre set in the flare of yellow light in the midst of the dark night. The sentinel could not be sure of their number, their distance. He cried out harshly—"Who goes there! The guard! The guard!"

In one moment the guard, put to double-quick, was under the archway of the gate. A detail was sent out in swift reconnaissance with the corporal's lantern and returned without result. There was naught to be found. The barren wintry expanse of the glacis was vacant. Nothing stirred save a wind blowing in infrequent, freakish gusts that struck the snow with sudden flaws and sent a shower of stinging icy particles upward into the chill red faces as the men rushed hither and thither. The huts of the Indians were silent, dark, the inmates apparently locked in slumber. Bethinking himself of the untoward possibilities of a sudden tumult among the Indians in the confusion and darkness,—whether they might interpret the demonstration from the fort as aggression or consternation,—Raymond on this account ordered the party to return silently to Fort Prince George through the sally-port. The same idea had occurred to Mervyn, for when the ensign rejoined him at the main gate he was administering a sharp rebuke to the sentry for raising a false alarm. It seemed, however, to Raymond that it left much to the discretion of an ordinary soldier to permit him to discriminate between inaction and the reference to his officer's judgment of such a demonstration as he had described.

"You saw nothing," Mervyn said, severely. "You are either demented, or drunk, or dreaming."

He turned away, then suddenly stepped back to admonish the sentry to raise no such disturbance when Robin Dorn should return from the trader's.

"Don't mistake the drummer-boy for an army with banners!" he said, scornfully. And having concluded his visit to the guard he once more flung off and disappeared in the darkness of the parade. Raymond lingered after ordering the guard within. Perhaps it was a bit of meddlesome jealousy, perhaps a resentment of Mervyn's manner, which seemed unwontedly high-handed to-night, although there had been naught but the official business between them, perhaps he thought it dangerous to curb so severely the zeal of a sentry under these peculiar circumstances, but he plied the soldier with questions and considerately weighed his contradictory statements and seemed sympathetically aware that these inconsistencies were not intentional perversions of fact, but the impossibility of being sure of aught when all was invested with mystery. Raymond's mind bent to the conviction that there was no admixture of fancy in the sentry's story. Whatever was the intent of the demonstration on the part of the Indians,—whether to rush the gate and overpower the guard, or merely the malicious joy in creating an alarm and a fierce relish of being an object of terror, or even, simpler still, a childish curiosity in the military routine of going the rounds—it was certainly a genuine fact and no vision, drowsy or drunken.

It had latterly been the habit to leave the gates open for the sheer sake of convenience, after the foolhardy fashion of the frontier. Strange as it may seem in view of the universal distrust of the good faith of the Indians, the universal conviction of their inherent racial treachery, the repeated demonstration of their repudiation of the sanctities of all pledges, many a massacre found its opportunity in the heedless disregard of the commonest precautions. Raymond now ordered the gates to be closed and barred, and instructed the sentinel to send Robin Dorn for admittance to the sally-port beneath the rampart. He repaired to the guard-house, and, still doubtful, he ordered the corporal with two men to attend him, stating to the sergeant, as next in rank, his intention to reconnoitre from the northern ramparts and the slope of the abattis, to discover if the curious birds of ill-omen still crouched at gaze or whither they had betaken themselves and with what intent. It was understood that he would return in a quarter of an hour, and quiet settled down on the precincts of the guard-room.

Robin Dorn was of that unclassified species, too tall, too long of limb, too stalwart of build for a boy, and yet too young, too raw, too inconsequent and unreasoning for a man. The simple phrase, "hobble-de-hoy," might adequately describe his estate in life. His errand had been to secure from the trading-house the drum-sticks of a new drum to replace one with a burst cylinder, which the commandant had ordered in Charlestown, through the trader. The instrument had been duly delivered, but the drum-sticks had been overlooked. Upon this discovery the drummer had requested leave to repair to the trader's in the hope that the sticks were among the smaller commodities of the cargo, just arrived by pack-train, the convoy, indeed, under whose protection the ladies of the captain's household and he himself had travelled. The confusion incident upon opening a variety of goods which had been packed with the sole effort to compress as much as possible in the smallest compass was not a concomitant of speed. Robin's efforts to tousle and tumble through the whole stock in his search were sternly repressed by the trader's assistants, and even the merchant now and then admonished him with—"Wow, pig, take your foot out the trough!" He was fain at last to sit on a keg of gun-powder, and watch the unrolling of every bit of merchandise, solemnly disposed in its place on the shelf before the next article was handled. Now and again a cheerful,—"Heigh, sirs! Here they are!" called out in the unrolling of a piece of stroud cloth, wherein was folded wooden spoons, or a dozen table-knives, or a long pistol, heralded a disappointment which Robin manifested so dolorously that the trader was fain to mutter— "Bide a wee, Robbie, bide a wee—" and offer a sup of liquid consolation. So long the search continued that the new goods were all sorted and fairly ranged upon the shelves before the drum-sticks revealed themselves, stuffed separately in a pair of leggings which they inadequately filled out, and the night had long ago descended upon the snowy environs of the little fort.

"If the sentry winna pass me ye'll hae to gie me a bit sup o' parritch an' my bed the nicht," he stipulated, modestly, in reply to the profuse apologies and commiseration of his host. "I kenna the countersign, an' ye wad na hae me shake down wi' them Injuns in the huts yon. I mis-doubt they hae fleas, though 'tis winter."

"Dinna ye gae nigh 'em, bairn," the kindly trader seriously admonished him. "Fleas is not the way thae dour savages will let your blood. Gif the sentry winna let ye come ben e'en turn back, callant;—but if ye are thinkin' they winna sort ye for it, ye are welcome to stay the nicht here, without seeking to win the fort."

"Na—na—I'm fair fain to hear how these birkies will march to the tune of 'Dumbarton's Drums'!"

Robin caught up the sticks between his practised fingers, and in dumb show beat a spirited measure on the empty air. His red uniform, his cocked hat, showing his flaxen curls, his frank sun-burned face, and his laughing blue eyes, all combined to make up an appealing picture to the elder men, and despite a qualm of reluctance the trader could not refrain from saying, "Take a horn, callant, before you gae out in the air—you've a sair hoast now."

With this reinforcement to his earlier potations,—still he was not what a Scotchman would call drunk,—Robin set out with swift strides in the black night, a drum-stick in either hand, in the direction of the fort. He might only know where it lay by a vague suffusion in a certain quarter of unappeasable bleak darkness—a sort of halo, as it were, the joint effect, he was aware, of the occasional opening of the guard-room door, the feeble glimmer of the lanterns hanging in the barrack galleries and outside the officers' quarters, and the light that dully burned all night in the hospital, gleaming from the windows.

After a time a dim red spot toward the left showed him where lay the Indian camp. Now it became invisible as some undulation of the ground interposed, or some drift heavily submerged one of the myriad stumps of the cleared-away forest. Sometimes he ran into these in the blinding night, and once he stumbled, floundering so deep that he thought he had fallen into some pit sunk there in the days of the war to entrap an enemy—the remnants of an exploded mine, perhaps, or *trous-de-loup*. But he came upon hard ground with no mishap, save the loss of one of his drum-sticks, found after much groping. As he regained the perpendicular he noted that the red glow, indicating the Indian camp, seemed, now that he was nearer, but the light from embers. It was odd that their fires should die down. Ordinarily the flames were kept flaring high throughout the night, to scare away wolves and panthers. When this thought struck him he drew a long knife from his belt and passed his fingers gingerly along its keen edge, then thrust it anew into its sheath. But if the Indians were not there, whither had they vanished? The unfriendly, veiled night, with a suggestion as of an implacable enmity in its unresponsive silence, its bitter chill, its sinister, impenetrable obscurity, was appalling in the possibility that its vast invisibilities harbored these strange, savage beings, wandering, who knew where and with what ferocious intent. Robin Dorn suddenly began to run impetuously, stumbling where he could not heed, falling if he needs must, with his right arm advanced, as if the night were a palpable thing and he shouldered through obstacles in the obscurity. He met naught. He crossed the glacis, ran along the covered way, reached the brink of the counterscarp, and wavered at the little bridge above the ditch as the warder from the lookout tower challenged him with a stern—"Halt! Who goes there?"

"Robin Dorn. An' I hinna the countersign. There's a wheen Injuns flittering around yon. Let me come ben. What for have ye got the great yett steekit?"

"Come around to the little gate, Sawney!" said the sentinel below, after a word to his comrade aloft. "The sally-port is big enough for the likes of you."

"I'm fair froze," Robin whimpered, as the smaller postern at last opened to admit him. "Ohone! You've kep' me jiggling an' dauncing till my ears are fair frosted!"—he touched them smartly with his drum-sticks—"an' me out on the business of the post! I did na think ye'd have served me sic a ill turn, Benjie! Steek the yett agin me!"

"Oh, stow your tongue!" retorted the sentinel. "I had nothing to *do* with closing the gate—the guard closed it. Get along with you."

Robin shuffled along through the snow, bent half double and feeling pierced with the chill which he had sustained while waiting at the gate, over-heated as he was from running. He paused as he passed in front of the guard-house.

"What for did the guard steek the yett agin me?" he demanded of the sentinel on the step. "I'll complain to the officer of the guard!"

"Go to bed, you zany!" returned the sentinel, "the officer of the guard is not here."

"Heigh, sirs," cried the harum-scarum boy. "Say ye sae! I'll e'en tak a keek at the guard-room fire!" He sprang past the sentinel and was in the room in a moment.

The great fire flared tumultuously in the deep chimney-place; the white-washed room, despite its ample proportions, was warm, and snug, and clean.

The light glittered on the arms stacked in the centre of the floor in readiness at a moment's warning. On the broad hearth of stone flagging, the soldiers, all fully accoutred and arrayed, despite the hour, in their scarlet uniforms, were ranged; several sat on each of the high-backed settles on either side of the chimney. All looked up as the door opened and the drummer shot in, the sentinel protesting behind him. The door of the prison beyond was half ajar, the sergeant having stepped in to examine an inmate, confined for some military misdemeanor, who was complaining of sudden illness.

"Why, Robin," one of the guard called out, jocosely. "Avaunt! Depart! This is no place for you!"

He was a big, clumsy, red-faced young Briton, and he rose and came with a lurching gait toward the drummer, who stood, smiling, a mischievous glint in his blue eyes, his cocked hat set back on his flaxen curls, his face flushed with the nipping chill without, and his red coat and leggings covered with a frosting of snow, evidently relishing the freak of his intrusion here in the absence of the officers, and full of animal spirits and fun.

"Wha's gaun to mak me gae, the noo?" he demanded, capering on his long legs.

"Faix, thin, I will, me b'ye!" cried an Irishman, springing up from the hearth, eager for even the semblance of a shindy. As he ran at the drummer, head down, Robin lifted the drum-sticks and beat a brisk rub-a-dub on his crown; then as his English comrade came to the rescue, the boy whisked about and, being the taller by a head, despite his youth, he made the drum-sticks rattle about the older man's ears and his skull ring like the drawn membrane of the new snare drum. The others sprang up in a body and rushed gayly at the light and agile drummer, still plying his sticks on every cranium that came within his reach, whisking among them, darting from one to another, slipping under their out-stretched arms and setting many a head to ringing with a tune all its own, till finally he was surrounded, collared, caught up bodily and fairly flung outside in the deepest drift near at hand. There he wallowed futilely struggling, for a moment overcome with laughter and frantic exertion; finally, he found his feet and made off, tingling with warmth and jollity, toward the barracks. He was fairly housed there when the guard-house door opened to admit the officer of the guard, the corporal, and the two men with the lantern, and the opposite door closed by the re-entrance of the sergeant from the sick patient. Both officers stood at gaze; the men were shambling and shuffling, a trifle shame-facedly, about the room, deeply flushed, some still mechanically laughing, and breathing hard and fast, though all assumed the stiff regulation attitude of the soldier.

"What is all this, Sergeant?" demanded Raymond.

"I don't know, sir," answered the second in command. "I've been looking after Peters—he seems better now."

"What is the matter, men?" Raymond turned to the soldiers.

"Just a bit of fun, sir," one of them responded, puffingly, his breath still short.

"This is no time or place for wrestling and horse-play," Raymond admonished them.

"Oh, no, sir," another replied, "that little fool drummer stopped here as he came in the fort, and we put him out."

"Half frozen, I dare say. I see no fun in that," responded Raymond. Then because the night was long and monotonous, and the reconnaissance unfruitful, and the fire genial, as he stood before it, and subversive of unbending—"What was the joke?" he demanded, feeling that a flavor of joviality might season the arid and tasteless interval of time.

The men hesitated, looking doubtfully from one to the other. But Raymond was a favorite among them, and his query could not be disregarded. In view of their sentiment toward him they did not seek a subterfuge or to baffle his curiosity.

"'Twon't be like reporting on the gossoon, Ensign?" demanded the Irishman, anxiously, and with the negative reply he burst into a spirited detail of the drum-beating episode and the freakish drum-sticks.

"We were not goin' to put up with the loikes av that, Ensign, av course," he concluded. "As soon as we cud lay hands on the slippery little baste, we doubled up the long legs av him an' flung him out into a snow-drift."

Raymond smiled indulgently as he stood before the fire, looking down thoughtfully into the bed of coals, glistening to a white heat under the flaming logs. Then he turned away.

"I think I'll see Peters, Sergeant. If he is as bad as he was, he must be sent to the hospital." Thus he disappeared into the inner room.

The group of soldiers resumed their places on the settle and on the hearth before the flaming fire. By slow degrees the long night wore away. Now and again the fire was replenished, but as the hours passed it was suffered to burn low, for the weather had moderated. The clouds thinned and fell apart, and when the relief went out there were stars in a chill glitter in a clear dark sky. The wind was astir; it was blowing from the south. Again and again a commotion within the forest verges told of dislodged drifts from the branches of the trees. The thaw set in before dawn, and when the sun appeared in a gorgeous emblazonment of deep red, and purplish pink, and roseate saffron on the opaline sky, its light suffused a world all adrip with moisture, and the slopes of the neighboring mountains, darkly purple, were half veiled in shimmering mists, that reached from creek and valley to the zenith and hung in the air in motionless suspension. The Keowee River was of a dull, rippled slate-color, till a sudden shaft of light struck out a steely gleam as if a blade had been suddenly unsheathed. The bugle's stirring acclaim of the reveille rang out to far distant coverts of the mountain, where the deer, coming down to drink, paused to listen, and the marauding wolf, and catamount, and panther, cogeners of the night, slunk to their caverns and dens, as if warned by the voice of the morn to vex no more for a season the peace of harmless wildlings. The sun-rise gun smote the air with all its dull echoes booming after. The flag rose buoyantly to the tip of the staff. The Indian town of Old Keowee, on the opposite bank of the river, was all astir, and now and again the sonorous note of the conch-shell, a detail of the matutinal savage worship, blended oddly with the martial resonance of the British drums beating for roll-call as the garrison of Fort Prince George lined up in front of the barracks.

CHAPTER V

THE influence of the masterful Mrs. Annandale at Fort Prince George was felt on the parade that morning ere guard-mounting was fairly concluded. The old guard had been paraded, presenting arms, as the new guard, with arms shouldered, marched past, the band playing, the officers punctiliously saluting, the whole conducted with as much ceremony as if the garrison numbered ten thousand men. These strict observances were held to foster the self-respect of the soldier as well as conserve discipline. Even off duty the rigors of military etiquette, as between the rank and file and the officers, were never permitted to be relaxed. Among the officers, themselves, however, formality, save as strictly official, was altogether ignored. So few they were, in exclusive constant association by reason of the loneliness, that they were like a band of brothers, and the equality always pervading a mess, in which the distinctions of rank are by common consent annulled in the interests of good fellowship, was peculiarly pronounced. Therefore Raymond, walking across the parade to the mess-hall, now off duty,—his sentinels had been relieved and his report duly sent by a non-commissioned officer to the officer of the day,—was somewhat surprised by a very commanding gesture from Mervyn signing him to pause.

Captain-Lieutenant Mervyn certainly had no aspect resembling a sheep as he crossed the parade. He was erect, alert; he stepped swiftly; his eyes were bright and intent, his cheek was flushed, and he had an imperious manner. So uncharacteristic was his look that Raymond was conscious of staring in surprise as they met. Mervyn cast so significant a glance at the subaltern's hand that it was borne in upon the junior that he considered the occasion official, and expected the formal salute. Raymond, half offended, had yet a mind to laugh, Mervyn's manner being so pervaded by a sense of his superiority in rank as well as all else. The ensign saluted with a half-mocking grace, and the captain-lieutenant gravely responded.

"Ensign Raymond," said Mervyn, "you were officer of the guard yesterday and relieved to-day."

"Even so," assented Raymond.

Mervyn lifted his eye-brows, and Raymond knew that he desired the formal "Yes, sir." He was suddenly angered by this unusual proceeding. He saw that something was much amiss with his senior, but he could not imagine that still rankling in Mervyn's consciousness was the recollection of the laughing delight and ridicule in his eyes the evening of the dinner upon the dénouement of the gypsy story. He knew of naught that should render their relations other than they had hitherto been. He protested to himself that he would not be a fool, and stand here saluting, and frowning, and majoring with importance, as if they had some military matter of moment pending between them.

"What the devil, Mervyn, do you want?" he demanded.

Mervyn gave him a stony stare. Then, still formally, he went on. "As officer of the day I received your report as officer of the guard. No mention was made—" he unfolded a paper in his hand and referred to it—"of a very unusual proceeding which took place during your tour of service."

"Was not the arrival of the delegation mentioned?"

"Certainly," Mervyn said, his eyes still on the paper. Raymond reached forth his hand, as if to take it, but his superior held it fast; Raymond felt as if he were suspected of a design upon it, to suppress it. Therefore he desisted, merely asking, "Was there not a statement of their intoxication?"

"Of course."

"Their sudden appearance at the gates,—watching the guard turn out for the officer of the day, and the closing of the gates?"

"Assuredly."

"Then, what else?" Raymond demanded, bewildered.

"You omitted a circumstance known to no officer but yourself," said Mervyn, severely.

"I mentioned Peters and his illness—isn't it there?" he could hardly forbear snatching the paper to see for himself.

"You did not mention the intrusion of the drummer," said Mervyn, sternly. "I overheard the men laughing about it to-day."

"Oh, the little drummer's frolic—that was a trifle," said Raymond, trying to smile.

"You suppressed this matter in your report. It was your duty to report any unusual circumstances. You will see on this paper under the head of 'Remarks' no mention of this circumstance."

"Lord, man, it was altogether immaterial!" cried Raymond, excessively nettled by this reflection on his conduct as an officer.

"Disorderly behavior, interference with guard-duty, intoxication, and buffoonery out of place are serious breaches of conduct, of evil example, and subversive of discipline. These seem to me very material subjects for report."

"Stop me—Mervyn—but you are playing the fool!" cried Raymond, quite beside himself with rage.

"I find it my duty as officer of the day in adding my report to the guard report to mention this failure of duty on your part. And unless you change your tone, sir, I shall also report you for insolence and insubordination to your superior officer."

His steady, steely look forced a mechanical salute from Raymond as Mervyn turned away with the same energy of step, burning cheek, and flashing eye. He resolved within himself that he would be nobody's fool, and he certainly looked "nobody's sheep."

Raymond, hurt, amazed, and angry, dashed off across the parade over the trampled snow, which was melting in the sun and honey-combed with myriads of dark cells that cancelled all its remaining whiteness. Where tufts still clung between the points of the stockade that surmounted the heavy red clay ramparts, it still had its pristine glister and purity. Now and again great masses slipped down from some roof where it had clung on the northern exposure, and it was obvious that all would vanish before the noonday. He hardly paused until he reached the mess-hall, and when he entered it was with so hasty a step, so absorbed a mien, that the officers dully loitering there looked up surprised, expectant of some disclosure or sensation.

The apartment was spacious and commodious, but ill-lighted, save for the largess of the great fireplace, where huge logs blazed or smouldered red and deeply glowing in a bed of ashes. It was of utility as a block-house, and the loop-holes for musketry served better for ventilation than illumination. The walls illustrated the prowess of the mess as sportsmen. They were hung with trophies of the chase,—great branching horns of elk and deer, a succession of scarlet flamingo feathers and white swan's wings, all a-spread in a gorgeous fiction of flight, and the wide, suggestive pinions of the golden eagle. Among these were many curios,—quivers, tomahawks, aboriginal pictures painted on the interior of buffalo hides, quaint baskets, decorated jugs, and calabashes a kaleidoscopic medley. The red coats of the officers gave a note of intense color in the flare of the flames. On a side table were silver candle-sticks and snuffers—where the tapers of the previous night had not been renewed, and had burned to the socket—a token of luxury in these rude surroundings, intimating the soldier alien to the wilds, not the pioneer. A punch-bowl and goblets of silver gilt, suggestive of post-prandial zest, were on a shelf of sideboard-like usage. A service of silver and china, with the remnants of the breakfast, evidently a substantial meal,—trout, and venison, and honey in the comb, and scones of Indian meal,—was yet on the table in the lower end of the room, and a belated partaker still plied knife and fork.

Raymond might have joined him, for he had not broken his fast, but he had forgotten physical needs in the tumult of his feelings. He had great pride in his efficiency as an officer. He had, too, great hopes of his military career. All that was best and noblest in him vibrated to the idea of honor, responsibility, fitness for high trusts. He could not brook a disparagement in these essentials. He felt maligned, his honor impugned, his fair intentions traduced, that he should be held to have failed in a point of duty—that he should be made the subject of a report for negligence or wilful concealment of a breach of discipline.

He had intended to say nothing of the contention. It seemed a subject which he could not canvass with the mess. He felt that he could not lend his tongue to frame the words that he was accused of a failure of duty. But the languid conversation which had been in progress was not resumed. Raymond's tumultuous entrance had proved an obliteration rather than an interruption of the subject.

"Anything the matter, Raymond?" asked Lieutenant Jerrold, who had had a glimpse of the two officers in conversation on the parade.

"Nothing," said Raymond. He had flung himself down in one of the huge, cumbrous, comfortable chairs of the post-carpenter's construction, covered by buffalo skins. "That is—well—"

The eyes of all were upon him, inquisitive but kindly. The yearning for sympathy, for reassurance, for justification, broke down his reserve.

"Mervyn, as officer of the day, is going to report me for suppressing a breach of discipline, as officer of the guard."

Only one of the men, the quarter-master, an old campaigner, was smoking; this habit he had acquired from the Indians, for pipes were temporarily out of fashion, save the cutty of the lower classes. He was of a ruder type than the others,—a burly, red-faced, jovial blade, inclined to be gray, and much disposed to lament what he called the shrinking of his waistcoat, as he grew portly on fine fare. He took the long pipe-stem from his lips, lowered the curiously carved bowl, and looked inquisitively at the young man's face.

"Gad-zooks!" incredulously exclaimed the blond young ensign of the name of Innis.

The fort-adjutant was an older man, and had seen much service. He was grave, concerned. He sought a polite palliative.

"The first time since you have been in the service, I take it."

Raymond noticed that none of them was swift to speech. Mervyn's disapproval of him carried weight with them all. The thought sent him wild,—Mervyn, always so dispassionate, so calm, so self-contained, with good, slow judgment and an impeccant record! In his own defence, for his own repute, they must know the truth. He leaned forward, eagerly.

"Now I put the case to you,—not that I expect you to express any opinion as between us—" he added, hastily, marking a general expression of embarrassed negation. "I was officer of the guard, and about eleven of the clock, the night being very dark and a party of Indians having been lying down among the stakes of the abattis after eating a deer they had killed, I took the corporal and two men and visited the sentry posted on that side of the fort. Then I went out to where we had seen the bucks, but they had gone. This required some little time. When I got back to the guard-house I found the men in great glee. They were laughing and chuckling. They had a secret that mightily amused them. And, the night being long and the time dull, to pass it a bit I asked them—like a fool—what the fun was. They didn't wish to tell, yet as I have always been fair to them, and considered their comfort and favored them as far as I could, they didn't wish to refuse. So out it came. That little Scotch scamp, Robin Dorn, had leave to go down to the Scotch trader's, and it seems the two Sawneys didn't drink water. He came back while I was gone, very handsomely fuddled, I suppose, with two new drumsticks for which he had been sent. The sentry at the gate passed him, and the guard-house door was open. In he flew like a whirlwind, with his new drumsticks, and beat a rally on as many heads as he could before they could catch him and pitch him out into the snow. When I came in a moment later their heads were all roaring. It was a rough soldier's joke of a fine relish to them. They were laughing, and grinning, and plotting to get even with Robin Dorn."

There was a languid smile around the circle.

"Now, if this had happened in my presence, or if I had gained cognizance of it in any way except as a jest told at my request, for my amusement, or if it had been material to any interest of the garrison, I should have mentioned it in my report."

"Is this what Mervyn calls your failure of duty?" demanded Bolt, the fort-adjutant.

Raymond nodded a silent assent. The others exchanged glances of surprised comment, and made no rejoinder.

"In his report as officer of the day," said Raymond at length, "he includes this detail among his remarks on my report as officer of the guard."

"Zounds! The commandant can't take a serious view of a bit of horse-play behind an officer's back," said Lieutenant Jerrold. He fell to meditating on Mervyn's priggish arrogations of gentlemanly perfection, and he rather wondered that he should place himself in the position of a persecutive martinet. The incident was not without its peculiar relish to Lieutenant Jerrold. Not that he wished aught of ill to Ensign Raymond, but he secretly resented, naturally enough, that he had not been selected instead, as a guest for the dinner of welcome to the captain's daughter. Mervyn's invitation was, of course, a foregone conclusion—in the double capacity of old friend and close neighbor. But it seemed to Jerrold that since a make-weight was needed, he, himself, was heavier metal than Raymond. He felt, in a measure, passed over, excluded, and the subsequent invitation with the other officers to play a game of Quadrille hardly made amends, for he claimed some superior distinction in point of age, in service, in rank, in personality. He might have been flattered and his wounded self-love assuaged if he had known that it was for these identical reasons he had been passed over. Mrs. Annandale had schemed to avoid any interference with Mervyn's opportunity to impress the young lady and to be impressed in turn. She had waived away Jerrold's name when she had declared that it would be too personal and particular to invite Mervyn alone, although as old friend and neighbor she cared only for him,— but since he was a man of wealth and gilded expectations, she would not like the officers of the garrison to think she was throwing precious Arabella at his head. "Doited dear Brother" took instant alarm at this, and proposed the next in rank—Lieutenant Jerrold. But she objected to so considerable a man. She had by no means the intention of furnishing Captain-Lieutenant Mervyn with a rival, after she had come all the way from England to ensnare him for her niece.

"Save us!" she had exclaimed. "We don't want two lieutenants! Send for some simple little ensign, man; just to balance the table."

Her heart had sunk into her shoes when she beheld the face and figure of the make-weight that Captain Howard, all unconscious of her deep and subtle schemes, had provided. This Raymond—to balance the table! But for her own careful exploitation of the evening the dashing ensign would have unwittingly destroyed every prospect that had lured her on so long and grievous a journey. She had enough rancor against the unconscious and dangerous marplot to enable her to receive with great relish the tidings that he was in disfavor with the commandant, for the cause, always most reprehensible in a soldier, wilful neglect of duty.

"Don't talk to me! There is no excuse for that sort of thing," she said, virulently, for Captain Howard was showing great concern for the incident, and was of the opinion, evidently, that Mervyn might well have let the matter rest. "I am not a soldier, dear Brother, and know nothing of tactical details. But reason argues that guard-duty is one of the dearest trusts of a soldier, and will bear no trifling."

"True, true, indeed," assented Captain Howard.

"While that rapscallion was playing Killie-crankie on the heads of those numskulls, the sentry at the gate might have shouted for the guard in vain. The gate might have been rushed by an enemy—"

"There was a sentry at the guard-room door who would have heard; it is his business to notify the guard," Captain Howard interpolated, but without effect. Mrs. Annandale went on as if he had not spoken.

"—and though the officer in charge was within his duty in visiting distant and exposed sentinels, he should have reported the disturbance occurring during his absence. No!—no—! Don't talk to me!"

"He has the promise of becoming a fine officer, and it irks me to check and bait him. He means for the best."

"Dear Brother, we might be massacred every one, if the service proceeded on such indulgence to negligence. The rules and regulations must be observed. The Articles of War ought to be as sacred as the Thirty-nine Articles of Religion."

"True—true—very true—" assented "dear Brother," for who could gainsay her.

She was in earnest hope that for a time no more would be said of the handsome marplot. So serious, indeed, did she deem his interference that now that it was removed her spirits mounted high, her wit sparkled, her flabby, pallid cheek flushed, and her microscopic eyes glimmered and twinkled among her wrinkles. So distinct was her sense of carrying all things before her that she did not notice at first the change in Mervyn's manner when he called in formal fashion to pay his respects to his recent host and the ladies of the household. The transformation was complete—no longer mild, pale, docile of aspect. He held himself tensely erect; his face was flushed; his eyes glittered with a light not altogether friendly, even when he turned them upon the beautiful Arabella. He had not forgotten—he promised himself he would never forget—the lure by which the artful duenna had made him believe that he himself was the beloved one of the gypsy's prophecy, for which the delighted girl had added a gratuity for pure good will. His cheek burned when he remembered that Raymond—nay, all the fireside group—had perceived his agitation, his joyful tremor, yet a degree of vacillation, and alack, his coxcombical prudery lest one or the other should openly speak his name. He recognized the whole of the wily aunt's scheme to put it into his mind that if he were not in love with Arabella he might well be, and was thought to be. The treacherous anti-climax, by which Arabella had interfered to spare his blushes,—her protestation of adoration of the drawing-master who, he was persuaded, was fictitious,—had a peculiar bitterness in being deemed a necessity. Yet in thus thwarting his obvious expectations and self-consciousness he had been rendered ridiculous in the eyes of Raymond,—who seemed actually to have the temerity to contemplate a competition with him for Miss Howard's favor,—and openly and signally punished for his self-conceit. They thought too slightingly of him—to play with him thus. He was neither to be managed by the adroit old tactician nor flouted by the imperious young beauty. He was remembering his worldly consequence, which he generally had the magnanimity to forget,—his expectations, as heir of his grandfather's title and estates, for he was the only son of his father, years ago deceased. He had summoned all his instinct for the social conventions, since he was too young to have learned worldly wisdom from experience, and was very definitely asserting himself in a restrained and incidental fashion. Under no coercion would bluster be practicable for his temperament.

He was talking of himself—of himself, continually, and Mrs. Annandale beamed upon him with the most intent solicitude, and Miss Arabella's charming hazel eyes expressed a flattering interest. Her pride, too, had been cut down—was it indeed true that nobody who was *anybody* would care for her?

His grandfather was much on his lips to-day—recent letters had brought the home news; naught of great moment, he said, eying not the lovely girl but a clouded cane which he poised with a deft hand, be-ringed with some costly gauds that he was not wont to wear. There had been a storm. Some timber was down in the park. His grandfather grudged every stick.

"Of course. Trees are such beautiful objects," said Arabella, consciously inane, struggling against an embarrassment induced by his manner and all unaware of a cause for a change.

"Fairly good-looking, I suppose; but I have seen several here—in the wilderness. Not a rarity, you know."

"Oh, you sarcastic boy!" cried Mrs. Annandale, visibly out of countenance, and sending her niece a side glance of exhortation and upbraiding.

"Even the mere outline is fascinating to me," said Arabella. "I often spend hours in delineating merely the tree form in sepia. It is such an apt expression of the idea of symmetry."

This was an unhappy reminder of the incident of the drawing-master. The two ladies were altogether unperceptive of any subtler significance in the remark, but with Mervyn it set the recollection rankling anew.

"For myself, I always thought the park too dense, except, perhaps, toward the north, but my grandfather reports to me each tree fallen, as rancorously as if it were a deserter from the main body."

"To be sure—to be sure—it will all be yours one day," said Mrs. Annandale, clear adrift from her wonted moorings.

The young man haughtily changed color. "A far day, I earnestly hope," he said, gravely. "I never look to it. I am more than content with my mother's little property."

"Oh, to be sure—to be sure—a handsome provision," said Mrs. Annandale, wildly. What was the matter with the conversation—a murrain on it!—She could have taken Arabella by her handsome shoulders and shaken her with a will. Every word that the girl spoke was a word awry. It did not occur to her that the interpretation was inimical. As for herself she incontinently wished that her tongue were blistered. For Mrs. Annandale had no leniency for herself unless she were triumphantly demonstrating her right to consideration. She glanced about the room nervously for an inspiration. The circle of great clumsy chairs ranged round the fire, covered with buffalo robes, were several of them empty—she might have fared better, perhaps, if "dear Brother," with his military bluntness, and the direct glance of his eye, and his candid habit of mind were ensconced in one of them—even in her extremity she did not wish for Raymond as a reinforcement. Her adversity, she felt, would be that young villain's opportunity. But what lacked she herself? What perversity had metamorphosed this propitious occasion! It seemed of phenomenal advantage. What more could she ask! Arabella was lovely in a simple gown of lilac sarcenet, all sprigged with white violets. Though the bodice was cut low according to the universal fashion, her neck was covered by a tucker, as behooved the day-time, but her shoulders gleamed through the sheer muslin and the tambour embroidery with a fascinating fairness and softness, enhanced by the modesty of the veiling. Her golden hair was surmounted by a tiny cap of plaited gauze, also a diurnal adjunct, and her slender slippered feet rested with dainty incongruousness upon a great wolf-skin. Her lute, lying in the ample window-seat, for the logs of the walls were thick, offered no suggestion.

"The poor lamb would sing off the key in all this commotion," thought Mrs. Annandale, venturesome no more. A rustic table, wrought of twisted grape-vines, thick as a man's arm, held the young lady's open work-box, full of skeins of silks, and beside it her embroidery-frame. On a large and clumsy table in the centre of the floor was a silver tankard, emblazoned with the family arms, and a pair of goblets, showing handsomely on a scarlet blanket utilized as a table cover, wrought with beads and porcupine quills, a foot and a half in depth. The usual frontier decorations on the walls were buffalo hides, painted in aboriginal art, quivers, blankets, baskets, Indian head-dresses, and collars of swan's feathers, and on the mantel-piece, decorated jugs and bowls, with Captain Howard's swords crossed above them. Still above was a small oval portrait of Arabella when she was a smiling, rosy infant. Mrs. Annandale's hard little eyes softened as they rested upon it.

This affection for her elder niece was the only proof that Mrs. Annandale had or had ever had a heart. Her husband, an ill-advised country squire, who wanted a clever wife and got her, gave up the enigma of life and died within the year. The jointure was the only certain reason why she had married him, for obviously she had not wanted a clever husband. But to this motherless niece, her whole nature paid tribute. She could not be said to soften—for she grew hard, and keen, and tough in endurance in Arabella's interest. The trust which her brother had confided to her was not misplaced. Her acumen, her vigilance, her training, all exerted to one end, had resulted in a charming and finished product of feminine education. And now the schemer was looking to the future. The war was over; leave of absence was granted in profusion to the officers whose duty had been so nobly done. George Mervyn at home would be surrounded with all the match-making wiles which lure an unexceptionable young man, already well endowed with this world's goods and the heir to a title and a fortune. The gay world would be a pleasant place for him. He was docile, tractable, and the delight of his grandsire's heart, and if the youth had no special ambitions to gratify in marriage, which his quiet, priggish, restrained manner seemed to promise, be sure Sir George Mervyn would not be without mercenary designs on his account. The old man would say the boy was good enough, well-born enough, handsome enough, wealthy enough, to deserve well of matrimonial fate. He should have a beautiful and richly dowered bride, and become, with these accessories of fortune and importance, preëminent among the magnates of the country-side. Thus Mrs. Annandale had beheld with prophetic dismay the septuagenarian's gallant attentions to Miss Eva Golightly at the supper-table of the county ball, and thus it was that she had determined to intercept George Mervyn's unpledged heart, still in his own keeping, in the frontier fastnesses of America. Moreover, Sir George Mervyn, as tough as one of the English oaks whose downfall he deplored, was as old in his type of creation—his downfall as certain. His grandson would one day be summoned home to assume the title and inherit the estates, and in the nature of things that day could not be far distant.

How well the primordium of her schemes had fared—the successful journey, the eager welcome, the ample leisure, all the possibilities that propinquity might betoken! But suddenly a distortion like the dislocations of a dream had befallen her symmetrical plan. The young officer had seemed yesterday the ingenuous, pliable, confiding youth she remembered of yore. He had showed her an almost affectionate respect; for Captain Howard he evidently entertained a deep regard and appreciation; the beautiful young lady whom he had last seen as a mere schoolgirl had roused in him a delighted admiration and an earnest solicitude to monopolize her society. While to-day he was haughty, stiff, only conventionally deferential, disposed to consider himself, and with no inclination to converse on any other topic.

The pause frightened Mrs. Annandale. It was a provocation to terminate a formal call. She bolted at the nearest subject in hand.

"Who is your friend, Mr. Raymond?" she asked. Then the recollection of the difficulty that had arisen between the two young men smote her with the aim of a bolt of lightning.

Mervyn cast a keen glance at her, but she held her pinched little features well together and gave no sign. A very small face she had, with but little expression, and but little was required of it.

"I thought I heard him giving you his autobiography the other evening," he said with a formal, frosty smile.

"Oh, but we need the estimate of a friend to come at the truest truth," she opined, sagely.

"I could add nothing to what he has already said," Mervyn replied succinctly. And Mrs. Annandale felt as if reproved as a gossip, baffled in the hope of slander, and disregarded as a cynic.

She hardly knew where to turn. In desperation she gave up the personal conduct of the action.

"Why do you two young people sit moping in the house this fine day?" she cried. "Arabella, why don't you ask Captain Mervyn to take you to walk on the ramparts? He will not let the cannon bite you, and the snow is almost gone!"

She glanced at the young officer with her coercive smile, and certainly he could not refuse. He rose instantly—"At your service," he said, turning with a polite bow to the young lady.

The demonstration certainly had not the eager enthusiastic urgency with which he had offered to show her the fort when she first arrived;—it hardly suggested an appreciation of the prospect of a delightful walk with a charming young lady, nor expressed gratitude for an unexpected pleasure and honor conferred upon him. Mrs. Annandale restrained her sentiments till the two young people were fairly out of the house; then her first sensation was one of rejoicing that the window was so small and the glass so thick that she might unobserved shake her fist at him as he walked away.

"I'd like to gnaw your bones," she said, unaware how savage she looked. Then she narrowed her eyes intently to mark if Arabella's pelisse did not hang short in the back, much relieved to perceive a moment later that the suggested calamity was merely the result of her leaning a trifle forward as she ascended the ramp of the barbette to reach the level of the terre-pleine. Mervyn had courteously offered his hand to assist her.

"Throttle him!" muttered the fierce little duenna. But the folds of the pelisse swung back in place as Arabella stood erect on the rampart and looked about her with interest. A violet-hued cloth was the fabric of this garment, and it was trimmed about the edges with a narrow band of swan's-down. A hood of like material was on her head, and the glitter of her golden hair, rolled high, was framed by white down like some lingering wreath of the snow. It had indeed disappeared; the ramparts were clear; the foot-path hard-trodden; the banquettes beside the parapet, where the soldiers were wont to stand to fire through loop-holes in the stockade, still dripped, having been shaded by the high pointed stakes when the sun shone.

"You can have little view here, except the ulterior of the fort," Mervyn said, as they strolled along. So disillusioned, so disaffected was he that he was quite open to the fact that a walk with Arabella along the ramparts was but a device of Mrs. Annandale's, and of no interest in itself.

"I have a glimpse of the mountains above the stockade, and I am breathing the sun, not the fire."

"Very true," assented Mervyn. "The sun is a welcome visitor—a rare honor."

Arabella had a fair share of pride, of enterprise in a way. Too inexperienced to understand her aunt's schemes, too affectionate to divine them, she only realized that this young man was holding his head higher than became him in her company, and that her aunt seemed to regard him as somehow rated superior to her station, and incidentally to her. She had an aptitude for ascendency—she could not look up. Her neck, too, was stiff. And she did not find Mervyn amusing on his pedestal. Moreover, if he valued his peace he must come down.

"How little did I ever think in England I should some day walk along the rampart of a fort in America with you,"—she turned her suave and smiling eyes upon him, and he almost melted for the nonce.

"None of us can read the future," he rejoined at random. And straight the unlucky recollection of the gypsy's prophecy smote him anew.

The men in the galleries of the barracks, and others pitching horse-shoes in lieu of quoits near the stable precincts, all marked the lady with interest and admiration, a rare apparition indeed in these far wilds, and noted without wonder the prideful port of the captain-lieutenant, in such charming company.

"A-pea-cockin' along loike a major-general, be-dad!" the warder in the tower vouchsafed in a whisper to the sentry below.

She could not account for Mervyn's lofty and distant air—he, who used to be, who seemed indeed but yesterday, an unassertive and modest youth.

"Are there any fish in this river?" she asked as passing one of the embrasures she saw above the cannon the steely gleam of the Keowee, stretching out to the defiles of the mountains, which were splendidly purple and crowned with opalescent mists that shimmered with an intense white glister when they caught the sheen of the westering sun.

"The fish are hardly worth the taking," he returned, disparagingly.

"Do you remember the flies I made for you when you came home that Easter with Cousin Alfred?" she suggested, glancing up a trifle coyly. He hesitated to seem ungrateful.

"Oh, yes. Fine flies—beautiful flies," he replied at random, for indeed he had forgotten them,—he was almost a young man at the time, and had taken scant note of the little girl yet in the schoolroom.

She was laughing quietly to herself, as she stood gazing out for a moment on the scene—for she had made them no flies; they had sought her assistance, and she had denied them.

"What amusements have they in this country?" she demanded, as she began to walk on slowly, and he kept step at her side.

"Well—scalpings, and burnings, and the torture are the most striking recreations of the country," he said, perversely.

"You can't make me afraid of the Indians," she returned, lifting her head proudly, "while my father is in command."

He had a sudden appalled realization of the limitations of the commandant's power in which she trusted so implicitly; he was recollecting that her father's predecessor in command, Captain Coytmore, had been treacherously slaughtered by the Cherokees in a conference at the gate of this fort, within twenty paces of the spot where she now stood.

"I did not mean to alarm you," he said hastily.

"I *know* you didn't." She cast on him a look seeming full of sweet generosity. "You only meant to be witty."

"An unappreciated jest. Apparently I did not succeed."

"You are not of that caliber," she suggested.

He was not pleased that she should express her judgment of his mental endowments. His nerves were all tense and vibrated with keen dissonance at every unconsidered touch. Nevertheless it was impossible not to reply in kindred vein.

"Do you allude to a large or a small caliber?" he revolted at the question.

"It depends on the charge—too large for some—too small for others."

"I feel as if I were guessing riddles," he said, floutingly.

"Life is a riddle—a dark riddle, and there is no answer this side of eternity," she returned, seriously.

"Now I am hearing a sermon. Do you often preach?" he asked, mockingly.

"What are they going to do about the dear old missionary?" she queried, suddenly. "The poor old man who is risking his life among the Indians to bring their souls to salvation!"

"The commandant will request him to come down here to Fort Prince George, and leave their souls to their deserts. He is sending a boat up to-morrow. I think he goes with it to use his influence in person."

"Papa—is going—" She paused in dismay.

"It is not far; there is no danger for him; he takes an escort."

"And he will leave *me* here?" She spoke tremulously, half to herself. She could hardly rest without the sense of the puissant paternal protection.

"His influence at Little Tamotlee is necessary," explained Mervyn. "The Indians have great regard for him. His presence there will avert danger from the post,—Fort Prince George,—and may actually be necessary to save the old missionary's life."

"Then—who is to be left in command at Fort Prince George?" she asked.

"I shall be in command here, being next in rank."

She still paused, facing him as they stood together on the rampart. She had turned a little pale. The breeze blowing gently from the shining river ruffled the tendrils of the hair on her forehead beneath the white fur of her violet hood and lifted the one long, soft golden curl that hung between its strings on her left shoulder. The simple attire, the wistful look, the doubtful, tremulous pause, made her seem very young, and appealing, and tender.

"You will be in command?" she repeated, interrogatively. Then—"Take care of Aunt Claudia," she said, urgently. "Take care of—me."

"I will, indeed," he cried, heartily, wholly won. "Trust me, I will indeed!"

CHAPTER VI

WHEN the rescuing party set forth the following day, Arabella and her aunt, with much perplexity and disapproval of frontier methods, watched through an embrasure on the southern bastion the boats pulling down the river. The men of the escort were evidently in the highest spirits; great hilarity prevailed amongst those warned for duty as they ran to and fro on the parade and in and out of the barracks, making their preparations for the expedition. They were loud of voice, calling directions, suggestions, admonitions, hither and thither, in clear, resonant tones; swift of movement, hardly a step taken that was not at a double-quick. They were notably clean and dapper of aspect, in their cocked hats, red coats, long leggings, drawn high over the trousers, and white cross-belts, glittering from the effects of pipe-clay, their hair in stiff plaited queues, decorously powdered.

"And not one of them knows whether he will have so much as his own scalp to bring home with him, by the time this fashionable, aboriginal Drum is over," remarked Mrs. Annandale. "I always thought that men are constitutionally knaves, my dear, but I begin to fear, I greatly fear, they are instead constitutionally fools."

They were obviously regarded with envy by their stay-at-home comrades, and there was a sort of sullen plaint in the very glance of the eye of the silent sentinels at their various posts as the details of the preparations passed within the range of their vision. The quarter-master-sergeant and the cooks were enjoying great prominence, and were the centre of much of the fluster and bustle. The chief of this department, however, the quarter-master, himself, who conferred from time to time with Captain Howard, seemed to harbor the only despondent sentiments entertained pending the packing. It was necessary to jog his memory more than once touching supplies that were more luxuries than necessities, which had been required by the commandant, and especially was this the case in regard to the contents of the great budgets made up for the presents to Tamotlee Town, which Captain Howard intended to convey with the party. The quarter-master gave an irritated shake of his big round head and his big red face, as if this demonstration were officially necessary to the pained and reluctant relinquishment of his charge, as he stood in the precincts of his store-room, a great log building illumined from a skylight that the walls might be utilized by shelves from top to bottom, and with many barrels and boxes and sacks of various commodities ranged along the floor, narrow aisles permitting a passage. More than once, the sergeant and his assistant, both handsomely be-floured and be-sugared in their haste, fostering awkward handling, were fain to say—"An' the terbaccy, sor?"

"Oh, Gad!—as if they didn't have tobacco of their own and to spare—" he cried out. Then in a weakened voice—"How many pounds does the list call for, Peters?"

"Then the brandied sweetmeats, sor?" The sergeant made toward a series of jars, brought expressly for the delectation of the officers and by no means intended for the rank and file.

"Hell!" The quarter-master squeaked out the exclamation as if it had laid hold on him and half choked out his voice. "*They* ain't on the list? Lord! the commandant is clean crazed! The Injuns have got no palates. They can't taste."

The sergeant cocked up a beguiling eye at his chief and smacked his lips.

"Them brandied cher's, sor, is sthrong enough, an' swate enough to make 'em grow a palate a-purpose," he said.

"And how do *you* know?" demanded the quarter-master, suddenly intent.

"Faix, sor, yez remember that one of the jars was bruken in onpackin', an' only half full. An' though Peters said glass wuz pizin, an' wouldn't tech 'em—sure, sor, I thought a man cudn't die in a sweeter way!" And once more he smacked his lips.

"There's a case-bottle of brandy for Rolloweh,"—the quarter-master's face fell as he gazed at the list on the head of a barrel. "Why, 'tis known that the Injuns will drink pepper vinegar as soon as sherry wine! And a jug of raspberry shrub—the finest ever made, I'll swear. Get 'em out. Get 'em out!"—and once more he stood over the commodities, and eyed them funereally, and shook his head in melancholy farewell.

"And the cheeses, sor. Would ut be convanient fur yer honor to furgit the cheeses?" suggested the sergeant with a roguish eye.

"What?—not at all—not at all," said the quarter-master, out of countenance, nevertheless.

"Thin, sor, if yez be aimin' to presarve yer memory, there's a box o' snuff—fine Rappee—at the top of the list, passed by."

"Get it out! Get it out!" said the quarter-master, pacing back and forth, as if preoccupied, in the narrow aisle between the baled goods, his red face grave and bent, his portly figure erect, his hands clasped behind him, with the list held carelessly in his fingers.

"I'll engage the commandant niver thinks how low the sthore is running," suggested the sergeant.

"And if we get out—out we will be; for the government will send no more goods here, and we just awaiting orders to evacuate and march for Charlestown. Have you finished—the order filled? Then call the boat's crew and get it aboard."

They were embarked at last, the oars striking the water with a masterful impact, the boats then skimming off like a covey of birds with wings spread. There went first the commandant and his escort, followed by the pettiaugre laden with the necessaries for the expedition, and lastly by the Indian delegation, who had come afoot of their own motion, and were now going back at the expense of Fort Prince George with transportation furnished. Very drunk several of them were, all a trifle unsteadied by the signal success of their mission, and the fervor of the hospitality of Fort Prince George. To their own place in his estimation they ascribed Captain Howard's instant concession to their demand, the compliment of his official presence on this mission, their return to their confrères in this triumphant state, and they pridefully interpreted the desire of the government to preserve the peace as fear still entertained of the prowess of the Indian. They took no heed of the commandant's solicitude for the life of the old missionary.

Captain Howard felt justified in bestirring himself smartly for the rescue of the old man.

"It is for the obvious good of the frontier and in the interest of the government, for one murder now would be the precursor of an outbreak," he had said in a council of the officers summoned the previous morning; "and I am glad that it is thus, for I cannot in conscience, in humanity, leave the old missionary to his horrible fate. The thought would not let me sleep a wink last night."

He was cheerful and hilarious now as he sat in the stern, listening to the orders to the crews. The voices carried far on the water, echoed by the crags on either bank, then striking back from the foothills of the mountains, which were marshalled in close defiles on each side further and further along the reaches of the river. He took scant notice of other echoes—the mouthings and mockings of young braves of the Indian town of Keowee on the opposite bank, as they ran glibly along in a line with the craft, yelling in their broken English,—"Let fall!—Give way!—Back oars!—Keep stroke!" as the orders successively rang over the water.

On shore to the two watching women on the bastion, gazing through the embrasure, this demonstration seemed queerly rancorous, and as inimical as uncouth. They noted that the delegation in the boat, who had been so honored, so generously entreated, took up the fantastic flout and continued it even after the mockings from along shore had flagged and failed. When the crew of soldiers began to sing, after the time-honored custom of the pettiaugre afloat, and the crude young voices rang out not inharmoniously in a strong and hearty chorus, the Indian guests interpolated derisive comments as they followed—now a short howl, now a cry of *Hala! Hala!* now a bleat, as of sheep, now the crowing of cocks—a raillery little suggestive of mirth or rollicking good-humor. The soldiers seemed as disregardful as if they did not hear, and bent to the oars with a will. The commandant never turned his head. But his sister and daughter looked at each other with an aghast questioning stare, to which neither could suggest a consolatory response.

Arabella seemed all the more slender and willowy in her long violet pelisse, with its edge of soft white down, as she stood beside the little lady, who was bundled in a thick coat of gray, lined and bordered with squirrel fur. She had a great calash to match, and as she peered out with her preternaturally sharp eyes with their furtive glance, she looked not unlike some keen little animal of no great strength, perhaps, but capable of some sharp exploit of mischief.

The craft of the expedition became visible once more far across the wooded spur of a hill which the steely river rounded. The sun on the stream was so bright that the three boats, skimming the dazzling surface, seemed as if they were airily afloat on floods of light instead of the denser medium of water. Still the singing sounded, richly, still the echoes answered clear, and once and again the harsh note of derision marred the harmony. Then they were gone, and the woods were silent. The fragment of a stave—a hesitant echo—the vague impact of an oar on water—! No more.

"They are gone!" said Arabella, turning to her aunt, a sort of desolation in her fair young face.

"Yes—I don't see them now." Mrs. Annandale had already turned to descend the ramp, and the captain-lieutenant remembered with a start to offer her his hand. He himself filled now the field of vision of the little schemer, though he had only eyes for Arabella. She came lightly down the steep incline without assistance, and once more he noted the pallid suspense in her face, the dilation of anxiety in her beautiful eyes. He had long ago been inured to the fierce suspense of frontier life, but he appreciated that to her untried heart it had all the poignancy of a realized grief. He sought to divert her attention.

"I have a favor to ask of you, ladies."

Mrs. Annandale paused as she trudged stoutly along on the miry ground and glanced up keenly from out her fur.

"An invitation to dine and spend the evening with you," he continued.

The old lady, a benign glow stirring in her stanch heart, had yet the tact to plod silently for a few minutes.

"You want to see how dull an evening can be—for we are in no case to be merry," she said.

"I want to show you how we spend the intervals of suspense on the frontier—how we pass the time as best we may—and hold up our hearts."

"But we did not bargain for this—for suspense—on the frontier," plained Arabella. "Did we, Aunt Claudia?"

The fur head of the little animal in advance wagged in earnest corroboration. "They told me the war was over," she said, without turning, "—and *me*—so timid!"

"You have nothing but your unfounded fears to frighten you," he urged. "There is no danger—nothing to frighten you—nothing threatening. You are not used to the manners of the Indians, that is all!"

"Manners! they have no manners, drat 'm!" exclaimed Mrs. Annandale, remembering the marred melody of the boat-song.

"You have not been here to agonize over Captain Howard even when there was real war," he persisted.

"Ah, but we couldn't realize how strange—how uncertain—how dangerous, till we see something of it!" Arabella declared.

"You see nothing of it—this is absolutely nothing."

"Why, I tremble to think even of the others," said Arabella, and Mrs. Annandale had a sudden recollection of the distant figure of Raymond in a gallant pose as he stood in the bow of the foremost boat, taking off his cocked hat and bowing low to Arabella as he glimpsed her standing by the cannon at the embrasure, while the boat passed slowly beyond the range of the bastion.

"Yes—yes—and that dear good man, the missionary. When the Reverend Mr. Morton comes to Fort Prince George, precious love, you must embroider for him a sermon-case or a silk poor-bag."

"I fancy a man who wants to save Indians' souls doesn't care for gauds of embroidery, and the poor don't get much comfort from a fine silk bag," said Arabella, with sudden contumacy.

Mrs. Annandale swiftly put her in the wrong.

"Oh, my own, don't reflect on the minister for trying to save the souls of Indians. God made them, child, God made them. Humanly speaking, He might have done better. But everything has a purpose. Perhaps Providence created them with souls, and no manners, to give the Mr. Mortons of this life something to do, to keep them going up and down in the waste places where the Indians are safely out of sight of civilized people—except fools who journey from London to see how near they can come to being scalped without losing hair or hide. Oh, no, my dear; realize human limitations and never, *never* reflect on the purposes of creation."

Mervyn, noticing the frowning cogitation on Arabella's fair brow as she listened, interposed in his own interest—"All this is aside from the question. May I come in to dinner?"

Once again Mrs. Annandale vacillated, and Arabella, marking her hesitation, was a little ashamed of a suspicion she had entertained. She had fancied that, although her aunt had said that Mervyn was far too highly placed and too richly endowed with worldly goods to make a possible parti for her, there had been some scheme in Mrs. Annandale's mind, nevertheless, to try for his capture. Now as he fairly begged for an hour of her society the old lady doubted, and hesitated, and was hardly hospitable to her old friend's grandson and her neighbor. She even began to make terms with him.

"You won't want to fetch over with you any of the villains at the mess-hall? For I don't know what is the state of the larder—or if we have *anything* to eat."

"No—no, only myself, madam. And I'll bring my own dinner, if you like."

"What have you got for dinner?" Mrs. Annandale asked as she stood on the step of the commandant's quarters, and looked over her shoulder with a benign jocosity.

"The finest trout you ever tasted, madam," he protested. "Do let me send them in to you."

"I thought you said yesterday that the fish in this river are hardly worth the taking," the young lady interrupted, surprised.

Mervyn colored a trifle, remembering his perversity during the morning walk of the day before.

"Oh, I was sad—and rather bad," he remarked.

Her aunt had disappeared within, and she put her foot on the step where her relative had just stood. It brought her face almost on a level with his, and the gaze of her beautiful eyes at these close quarters was rather bewildering.

"It is very bad for you to be sad," she said softly, and his heart beat so fast and so loud that he feared she might hear it. "And it is very sad for you to be bad," she stipulated, and went smiling into the house with a languid relish of her jest.

He followed into the parlor, begging Mrs. Annandale for the coveted invitation, protesting that what he wanted was a bit of talk to keep them all from being lonely, and—with a glance at the lute on the window-seat—to hear the new songs they were singing at Vauxhall Gardens and Ranelagh, and to hear the old songs that Arabella used to sing down in Kent. Might he come? And might he send the fish?

"No supper—no song," Mrs. Annandale at last assented, and Mervyn went off in a glow of happiness to confer cautiously with the officer of the day, to order the great gate closed, to himself inspect the guard and visit each sentinel, to climb to the warder's tower and thence gaze over the great spaces of the picturesque country—the stretches of mountains looming purple and dark, save where the residuum of snow still glimmered in a deep ravine, the river between the silent hills, the fluctuating lights of Keowee Town on the opposite side of the stream, and the stars whitely a-gleam in the great concave of the sky, all clear, save to the west, where a dark cloud, voluminous, of variant degrees of density and with flocculent white verges, was slowly rising above the horizon. It held rain—mayhap wind. It would strike the rescue expedition before it would reach Fort Prince George. But Mervyn's interests were within the work. He personally looked to every precaution for its safety before, arrayed anew with great particularity, he repaired to the commandant's quarters, whither his dish of fish had preceded him.

Arabella, sick at heart, nervous and anxious, sitting in her own room with her aunt before the wood fire, with every detail of its scant and simple furnishings reminding her of the love and care of her father and his thought and devices with such meagre materials for her comfort,—the rose-tinted hangings, the large mirror, so difficult to transport through the wilderness, the chairs and tables, each constructed by his orders,—felt that she could hardly support the ordeal of an evening with a stranger—at least a comparative stranger. She wished the occasion to be one of scant ceremony. She said to her aunt that she intended to appear in the dress she had worn throughout the day.

"I have no mind for bedizenment and festivity," she complained. "My head aches. I can hear those savage yells every time I listen."

"Then—don't listen," interpolated her aunt.

"And I can see—" she pressed her hands to her eyes—"can see those boats pushing out from the shore—taking the soldiers off into the shining water—who knows where!"

"They tell me the town's fiendish name is Little Tamotlee," put in Mrs. Annandale.

"I can see the first pettiaugre with my father in the stern and Ensign Raymond standing in the prow, and waving his hat to me and—"

"Captain Howard is able to take care of himself," Mrs. Annandale interrupted hastily, "and if Ensign Raymond is not—so much the worse for him! Has that besom laid out my frock yet?" She lifted her voice for the edification of Norah in the outer room.

"And you will excuse me, Aunt, if I don't change my dress?" Arabella said, plaintively.

"I don't suppose it would hurt the young man's feelings," Mrs. Annandale affected to consider. "He is too sodden in pride—those Mervyns all are. I suppose he *might* think, as we are so poor, that you have but a frock or two. Well, it is none of *his* business how little money Captain Howard can spare for your maintenance."

"Oh, Aunt Claudia!" cried Arabella, genuinely offended—"if you think *that*!—And what are you wearing? Your murrey-colored satin?"

Thus it was that the young lady was resplendent in silver-shot gray paduasoy, shoaling and shimmering with white lights, made with short puffed sleeves slashed with cerise velvet, and she wore a fillet of cerise velvet in her golden hair. A delicate fichu of filmy Mechlin lace was draped over her shining neck and was caught with shoulder-knots of cerise velvet. She cast a very imperious glance upon Mervyn as she entered the parlor, which challenged his homage, but she had no need to assert her pride, for he was again in his old docile character, assuming naught of pre-eminence because of his worldly advantages, satisfied to bask in her smiles, yet a trifle conscious of his personal endowments, and carrying himself with a species of gallant self-confidence not displeasing in a handsome youth.

CHAPTER VII

It was Captain Howard's faithful belief that a good cook was as important to the commander of a garrison as an efficient fort-adjutant. The soup was redolent of sherry; the trout had been prepared with an earnest solicitude that might be accounted prayer, and made a fine show arranged on a bed of water-cress that had sprouted before the late snows; the lamb, a rarity on the frontier, sent up an aromatic incense of mint sauce. All the brandied cherries had not gone as gifts to the Indians. A tart of preserved fruits, served with cream from a cherished cow, found friends all around the board; and a charming dish of Floating Island was so submerged in brandy that Mrs. Annandale opined it might be called—"Half seas over."

One might not have divined that Mrs. Annandale's sharp truculence in orders and admonitions had added wings to the swiftness of the cook and roused him to accomplish his utmost. She looked suave and benign as she presided in festival array over the feast that did the quarters so much honor. All was jollity and genial good fellowship as the three ranged themselves around the table. The two tall silver candle-sticks, with their wax candles, lighted up smiling faces as they looked at one another across the well-spread board, which so definitely belied Mrs. Annandale's pretended solicitude for the state of the commandant's larder.

There was something singularly home-like in the informal little feast, and it appealed gratefully to the sentiment of the young soldier who had seen naught of home for three long years. He laughed at Mrs. Annandale's sallies and made bold to fling them back at her. He explained with long-winded and eager diligence all frontier conditions that seemed to impress Arabella. He talked of his immediate future after his return to England, his plans for the next few years, with an intimate expectation of their responsive interest which sent a glow to the pallid cheek of the wily tactician, for it was as if in his anticipation they shared in these events. She doubted if Arabella perceived this collocation of his ideas—she was sure that he was not aware how definitely he had expressed them to her intuitive comprehension. But she could piece together the thought in his mind with the suggestion in his speech, and the coherence combined in the augury of the fulfilment of her dearest dream. They sat long at table; the candles had burned so low that Mrs. Annandale was fain to cock her head like a sparrow as she peeped around the blaze.

"My certie," she exclaimed at last, "you cannot sit till midnight over your bottle when you come to dine with two lone lorn women. Clear away the dishes, man—" (this to the servant), "and don't let them clatter, if you want whole bones."

And when they were all gone,—disappearing as silently as crockery could,—and the three were about the fire once more, the lute was brought, and Arabella sang the songs of home to the exiles. Out at the door the sentinel, always posted at the commanding officer's quarters, paused on his beat and stood still to listen, spell-bound. The grand rounds, returning along the ramparts, slackened their march to hear the tinkling vibrations and the dulcet, romantic, melancholy voice, that seemed somehow of kinship with the moonlight, a-glimmer outside, on the great bastion; with the loneliness of the vast wilderness; with the vague lilting rune of the river; with the mournful undertone of the wind, rising in the distance.

George Mervyn felt at the blissful portal of an earthly paradise, as yet too sacred to enter, but in his tremors, his delighted expectancy, his tender visions, there was no stir of doubt. He felt her demand of homage; more than once this day he had been sensible of her power intentionally exerted upon him. She desired him to fall at her feet. Now and again her eyes warned him that he should not think less of her than her large meed. And then the wistful sweetness when she had besought his care! It was hers—it should be hers for life! There seemed even now but a word to speak between them. He watched her as she sat glimmering in silver and white, half in the shadow, half in the light, the lute in her hand, her graceful head and neck bent forward, her eyes on the fire. The song ended; the strings ceased to vibrate; the echo stirred and failed and there was a long pause, while the firelight flashed, and the walls glowed, and the white feathery ash shifted lightly in the stronger draught of the fire, for the wind was rushing in at the crevices of the window, drawing with the heated air up the great chimney. The sentinels as they walked their beats outside noted its gathering strength, and glanced from time to time toward the sky, mindful of the sombre, fateful portent of the great cloud in the west that now reached near the zenith, the moonlight showing the tumult and trouble of its convolutions, its densities, its cavernous recesses, the subtleties of the variations of its shoaling tints, from the deepest purple through all the gamut of color to the edges of glistening gray.

Suddenly there came a deafening crash. A vivid white flash flickered through the room. The next moment the loud rote of the echoes of the thunder was reverberating through the mountain defiles; the surging of the wind sounded like the engulfing turmoils of a tidal wave, and the rain beat tumultuously on the roof.

Mrs. Annandale, all unaware of the coming tempest, by reason of the curtained window and her own absorptions, sprang to her feet with a wild little cry of blended terror and temper, and Arabella, pressing her hands to her eyes, let the lute slip from her lap to the floor, where its impact sent out a hollow dissonance. Mervyn had stooped to pick it up when Mrs. Annandale clutched him by the arm.

"Why didn't you tell me a storm was coming?" she demanded.

"Dear madam, I did not know it myself," said Mervyn, gently, yet nevertheless constrained to smile. So does a superiority to the fears of others elate the soul that he did not even shrink from the claw-like grip that the skinny fingers of the little woman was making felt even among the tough muscles of his stalwart arm. "Believe me, there is no danger."

He spoke in the random way in which men see fit to reassure a terrified woman or child. Seldom is the insincerity of this haphazard benevolence so signally exposed as in the next moment when an insupportable, white, sinister brilliance filled the room, a terrific crash stunned their ears, and the ashes and coals from the fireplace were scattered in showers about the apartment, the bolt evidently having struck the chimney.

"Oh!—oh!—you wicked man!—(where's my sal volatile!) to mislead your old friend and neighbor! No danger! No danger! Why, the powers of the air cried out upon your deceits!" she exclaimed, between sniffs at the hartshorn in a little gilded bottle that hung from a chain about her waist.

There seemed a vast incongruity between Mervyn's mild short-comings and the tumultuous rebukes of the thunder as it rolled about the house. Despite his duplicity he was esteemed by the old lady the most reliable support attainable against the anger of the elements, and she clung to one arm, while he held the lute in the other hand. As he turned to note how far the coals had been scattered on the puncheons, the instrument struck the back of a chair and the blow elicited a plaintive susurrus of protest. At the unexpected sound Mrs. Annandale gave a galvanic start so violent that it seemed as if it might have dislocated every bone in her body.

"Man alive!" she exclaimed, irritably, upon observing the cause of the sound, "put the dratted thing down—somewhere—anywhere! Do you think this is a time to go perking and majoring around, like a troubadour!"

One might have thought the lute was hot, so quickly did Mervyn let it slide upon the table. Then with a certain air of importance, for he was not accustomed to be rated in this tone, and infinitely did he deprecate ridicule in the presence of Arabella, he said, "Let me conduct you to a chair, Mrs. Annandale; you would be more comfortable seated."

Despite her nerves and terror the little lady detected the change in his tone, and made haste to insinuate her apology.

"Oh, child—child!" she said, gazing up artfully at him. "You do not know what it is to be afraid—you are the very spirit and frame of a soldier! But me—Lord!—I *am* so timid!"

And with another flash and crash she clung to him anew.

As far as a mere matter of good-nature might go, Mervyn would not have hesitated to sacrifice his comfort or pleasure to the terrors with which he could not sympathize; he would have permitted her indefinitely whatever solace she derived from her painful grip upon his arm. But he had become alert to the idea of ridicule. He was aware that he cut a farcical figure as he stood in the pronounced elegance of his attire,—his brilliant gold-laced uniform, his powdered hair, the delicate, costly lace at throat and wrist, his silk stockings and gold-buckled shoes,—in the custody of the ancient lady, clinging frantically to his arm, and berating him as she would. At all events he had been subjected to the situation in Arabella's presence as long as he had a mind to endure it. Mrs. Annandale felt very definitely the firmness of his intention under the gentle touch as he contrived to unloose her clutch, and holding the tips of her fingers with a courtly gesture he led her across the room and to a seat. She sank down with a sense of luxury amidst the soft folds of the buffalo rug that covered it, but she relinquished his arm reluctantly. She felt the need of something alive to cling to—a fold of the buffalo rug did not answer; something to clutch that could tingle and respond with sympathy. Suddenly she caught at the chain that hung from her waist and supported her fan, her pomander-box, and a bunch of trinkets of more or less utility, and sounded a silver whistle—a dulcet, seductive tone all incongruous with the service to which it summoned. This man was no better than a lay-figure, she said scornfully within herself,—a mere bit of padding, tricked out in the latest military style! He hadn't enough mortality about him to feel the electric thrills in the air. He could not hear the thunder, he could not see the lightning,—and for her own part she wished it might strike close enough to tickle him, and to tickle him well, provided of course it tickled no one else. She wanted her maid; she wanted Norah; who was here on the instant at the door, with very big eyes and red cheeks, smart enough, too, with a blue dimity gown and white cap and apron.

"And why are you genuflecting there at the door, you vixen?" cried the irate lady, as the girl reached her side. "Waiting to see me struck by lightning, eh?"

"Oh, no, sure, mem. God is good!" volunteered the girl, reassuringly.

"Oh," said Mrs. Annandale, fairly rebuked. "Oh—ah—He has that reputation, to be sure!" Then recovering herself and mindful of the presence of Mervyn: "And remember, girl, nobody but the sinner ever doubts it—the depraved sinner! Never—*never* let me hear of your doubting it!"

She tossed up her chin with her head-dress aloft with something of a pose, as if she herself had preached the little sermon. Then she turned smoothly to Mervyn, with her best airy grace somewhat shivered as she quaked before inconsiderable flashes of lightning—"If you will excuse me I will return, after taking a dose of that Indian remedy for the nerves which was recommended so highly to dear Brother."

Mervyn, remembering the curious knowledge of toxicology which the Indians possessed and their extraordinary skill in distilling vegetable poisons, ventured to remonstrate.

"Dear madam," he said, still standing beside the table where he was waiting to hand her to the door, "have a care what you drink."

"I might say that to you—if the decanter were on the table," she retorted, with her customary sparkle and smile, which a sudden flash distorted into a grimace before she had finished speaking.

"True,—only too true, and especially on the frontier," assented Mervyn, showing his susceptibility to her pleasantry by a formal smile, something really in the manner of the lay-figure, "but some acquaintance with the herbal remedies is essential to safety, and—pardon me—the only Indian remedy that Captain Howard uses is bullets."

"For his own nerves—" began the lady.

"The decanter,"—Mervyn laughed, a trifle abashed.

"Dear Aunt," Arabella struck in, somewhat alarmed, "pray be careful."

She had been standing most of the time since the tempest began to rage, one hand resting on the back of the chair beside her, the other lifted to the high mantel-piece. Her face was pale and grave, now and then she shuddered at the sinister white glister of the lightning. She looked tall and stately in her silver-shotted shoaling gray silk, glimmering in the shadow and sheen of the fire, and now and then of a transcendent dazzling whiteness in the fugitive flashes of the lightning. Mervyn had longed to reassure her with a word, a look, for he divined her fright, and even—so does love extend the sympathies—the nervous shock that the mere flarings and uproar of the tempest must inflict on more delicate sensibilities than those of a frontier soldier, but Mrs. Annandale's demands upon his attention had absorbed his every faculty. His heart melted within him at her next words.

"Pray,—pray, dear Aunt, do be careful. Listen to Mr. Mervyn."

"Listen to him yourself!" cried the old lady, who hardly for her life could have forborne the quip and the confusion it occasioned her niece. It gave less point to the moment when she flustered out of the room, and Mervyn, hastily bestirring himself to hand her to the door which her maid ran to open, turned with a sense of infinite relief toward the fire.

He wondered at himself afterward. He knew that he had but a moment; that Arabella's poise was already shaken by the events of the evening; that there were days to come when occasion would offer a more propitious opportunity for solitude *à deux*. He could not resist her aspect; he could no longer deny himself the bliss of merging expectation in certainty.

He crossed the hearth and stood by her side. He saw the surprise in her eyes; the flush flutter in her cheek; the tense lifting of her figure into an added stateliness, an obvious pride. She looked a very queen as she turned her head—and after all, he was the suitor.

"And will you listen?"—he said, catching the phrase. "Will you let me tell you how I worship you—how I worship you, how every glance of your eye and every turn of your head and every intonation of your voice is almost sacred to me? It hardly seems a sacrilege to say I could fall at your feet and adore you. And will you look kindly on my suit? And will you hear my humble prayer? And will you reward my devotion? Will you be my wife?"

He had acquitted himself very prettily, and with a rare interpretation of her state of mind. She had begun to like him well, but it was not enough that she should like him. His phrase-making fed her pride. He had much to offer, and he offered his abundance in great abasement.

As she slowly lifted her eyes they met his; and he went on without waiting for a reply. "I wonder at my courage in speaking at all," he said. "It seems impossible that you should care—or that you should come in time to care for me."

He paused, and in the tenseness of the silence the beat of the rain on the roof had an inimical suggestion as if in its turbulence it might come flying in at them. The thunder rolled and the echoes followed with hollow reverberations hardly less resonant. The lightnings flickered over her face and figure, and she visibly quailed a little, and he drew nearer.

"When you asked me to take care of you—the other day—I could scarcely keep from begging for that privilege forever. It would be my blessed and sacred duty—it would be my life's crown. No behest on earth can be so dear to me as those words. But let it be forever."

There was continued silence.

"You will speak to me," he said with feeling.

She turned her fan in her hand—she was agitated, but inscrutable.

"I know you so little," she faltered, and he was sensible of a sudden reaction of the heart; he had been chilled by the fear that she might actually refuse.

"And I am glad of that," he said heartily, and with a cheery intonation. "While there is nothing in my experience that is dishonorable, still I feel so unworthy of you that I am glad to have the chance of building myself up into something better than I have been, for you to learn to know. I love you for what you are, but I want you to love me for what I shall be for your dear sake." His words were enthusiastic, his heart beat fast, his face flushed with eager expectation.

It was impossible not to be flattered. "Nobody that was *anybody*," quotha! "He held himself so high! So far," forsooth, "above a girl without fortune," the good duenna had said!

Arabella's pride had stormed the citadel, albeit his own fancy had made the breach. Her pride shone in her eyes, held her head aloft, flushed her fair, meditative, dignified face. He thought with exultation how she would grace all he had to bestow—more—far more.

"My love," he almost whispered, "I wish I had a crown to lay at your feet; you look like a queen."

She burst out laughing with pleasure, declaring that Love was indeed a villainous hood-winker, that he should be thus blinded to the aspect of a girl whom he had known all her life, and whom he was now minded to fancy a goddess.

"No fancy—no fancy—it is the truth—the eternal truth!"

"Yes—yes—tell the truth," Mrs. Annandale cried, catching the last word as she entered the room.

"Tell the truth while you can—while you are young. For when you are old your conscience is stiff and you can't. Well, the marplot storm is almost over, and I suppose we may deal the cards for 'three-handed Ombre.'"

She noticed—for what could escape her keen glance—that the young officer, though embarrassed and agitated, had an elated aspect, and the girl's stately carriage impressed her. "*My lady*, that is to be!" she thought, with a glow of triumph. "And yet I departed this place only some three minutes and a half ago."

Still the thunder rolled, but further and further and further away, and only the echoes were near—from the rocks of the neighboring river-banks, the mountains, and the foothills hard by. Still the lightning flashed, now in broad sheets, and now in long zigzag streaks beyond the eastern woods. The tempest had passed over, and the moon was struggling through the rack, now seeming on the crest of waves, again lying in the trough of tossing clouds, like some beaten and buffeted barque, resigned to fate, and riding out the storm.

Mrs. Annandale, seated at the table, glancing over the top of her cards, was annoyed to perceive Norah genuflecting at the door to the inner apartment, now opening it a bit, and as she caught the eye of her irate mistress, closing it hastily.

"You baggage!" called out Mrs. Annandale, with such sudden sharpness that Mervyn, notwithstanding his cast-iron nerves, started as if he had been shot. The door closed instanter, tight and fast, and Norah, leaning against it outside, had the strength to hope that her last hour had not come. "What ails that girl? Are you bewitched, you hussy?"

"Perhaps she wants something," suggested Arabella, whose loyal temperament seldom made question of her aunt's right to her peculiarities; but she was somewhat ashamed of their exhibition to-night—to-night, when she was both proud and happy.

"No, Miss, sit you still. By the time you and George Mervyn would be through with all your bowings, and counter-bowings, and minuet-ings, and handing each other to the door, the besom would have forgot what she wants, or would have run a mile for fear of me. Come in, girl, and speak up. Sure, I've no secrets to keep. Now, minx, what have you to say to this worshipful company?"

Norah, red, miserable, and embarrassed, emerged from the door and stood dropping courtesies of humble placation and twisting with a gesture of apology one corner of her apron between her fingers.

"Please, mem," she said, "I do be hearing that same knocking what went on bangin' an' bangin' in the storm, at the dure agin."

"You ninny!" exclaimed Mrs. Annandale, in scorn. "Do you know that in these colonies they burn folks alive for hearing what they can't hear and seeing what is not to be seen?"

The girl, looking thoroughly wretched, emitted a short, sharp squeal of dismay that she tried a moment afterward to retrieve as a cough.

Mervyn had all an officer's aversion to familiarity with inferiors in rank, but as Arabella leaned back in her chair to be out of her aunt's range of vision, and gazed smilingly, reassuringly, at the maid, blithely shaking her head the while, he thought her as kind as she was lovely, and benignly watched the restoration of Norah's composure.

"Sure, mem, all the time I did hear ut I tould yez av ut incessant, an' yez thought 'twuz but the thunder, an' the wind, an' the rain. But now, mem, it's at the dure agin, fit to break it in, an' onst at that low windy some man climbed up, an' knocked, he did, with his knuckles on the glass."

In the moment's silence that followed her words the sullen sound of a repeated knocking at the outer door was obvious. Mervyn suddenly rose, throwing his cards down upon the table, and dashed through the hallway to the outer door.

"Indians! Indians!" quavered Mrs. Annandale, in a paroxysm of terror. "Indians, I'll wager! Cherokees! Chickasaws, and those devils that wear nose-rings—oh-h-h! and *me*—so timid!"

Then she said something that Arabella did not understand, and only remembered long afterward.

"We might have caught this bird in England. There was no need to lime a twig for him! Oh—why did I come, and leave my good home—and journey over that nasty smelly ocean to this queer distracted country! Indians! Indians! Indians!" she continued to quaver, rocking herself back and forth, and Norah, flying to her side for protection, knelt at her knee and mechanically repeated the word—Indians! Indians! as if it were the response of some curious liturgy they had picked up in their travels.

Arabella snatched a blunderbuss of her father's that swung above the mantel-piece and pressed forward into the hall to make sure what disaster had befallen them.

The outer door was open, and the wind still blowing steadily, had extinguished the lamp. Without there was more light than within. She could see the glistening surface of the parade in the moonbeams, shining like darkly lustrous glass with the rainfall, and beyond, the guard-house, near the gate. Its door stood broadly aflare, and the yellow radiance of the firelight fell on the sodden and soaked ground. But what surprised her at this hour was the number of figures astir.—Could there really be a demonstration of the Cherokees impending? she wondered, with a clutch of fear at the heart, hearing always the ominous chant from within—"Indians—Indians!" as mistress and maid swayed in unison. She knew it behooved the rank and file to be in barracks and in bed at this hour. She glanced toward the long, low building where the soldiers were quartered. To her surprise the lanterns, swinging in the galleries, showed the doors were open; figures were going in and coming out. Then she observed that they moved slowly and at their ease, loungingly, and there seemed to be much loud but unexcited talk amongst them, continuous, as of the details of individual experience. Whatever the sensation had been it was obviously spent now. And thus she marked the conversation at the door.

Mervyn stood on the threshold, and on the step below a non-commissioned officer was punctiliously saluting, his attitude, his uniform, his face, rendered visible by the lantern which one of two soldiers held.

"Lieutenant Jerrold's compliments, sir, hand Hi was to hinform you, sir, that the fire is hout."

"Fire! what fire?" exclaimed Mervyn, wildly, looking out in keen anxiety, as if he expected to see the substantial block-houses, the store-house, the armory, the guard-house, the barracks all vanish like a mirage. The wind tossed his hair, dispersing its perfumed powder backward through the hall, where Arabella scented the fragrance of attar of roses blended with the dank odors of the rain-drenched woods.

"Sure, sir, the granary. The lightning struck it fust volley, and it was blazing like a puffick pyr'mid in ten seconds."

"The granary! Damme! Why was I not informed?"

"Sure, sir, the hofficer of the day sent a detail 'ere, sir, to hammer on the door, but they got no answer, an' the fire 'ad to be fit with all 'ands, sir. Lieutenant Jerrold 'ad 'is fears for the fort."

Mervyn, all unmindful of the dank, wintry air that played round his legs, inadequately protected in silk hose and pumps, felt as if he could faint. The garrison had fought out its battle for the very existence of the little frontier fort, and he, the acting commandant, tucked away in a lady's bower, making love to one and soothing the terrors of another—what did he say in the confidence of his inner consciousness as he heard Mrs. Annandale's patter, "Indians! Indians!" He vaguely fancied there was a relish of the situation in the face of the corporal, but he whirled about, intending to take his hat and go to the scene of action. Then reflection stayed him. This would merely gratify his personal curiosity and interest. Before he should meet the other officers he preferred full official information of so serious a mischance during his service as commandant of the garrison and fort.

"What was saved of the corn? What was done with it?"

"Lord, sir,—nothing! The fire raged like 'ell, and was as tall as a tree, sir. And 'twas hall the men could do, sir, to keep the armory an' store-house from going, too—they both caught fire. Nothing but the tremenjous rain-burst saved the fort. The force 'ere couldn't handle no such fire as this 'ere one."

"I daresay,—I daresay—" Mervyn affected an ease of manner he was far from feeling. Then fury for the dilemma in which he was placed overcame him anew. "It should have been reported to me. Who did he send here?"

"Meself, sir, an' Hi 'ammered with two men. But we was of the gyard, sir, an' the Injuns was right around the counterscarp an' the horficer of the gyard was fearful they'd rush the gate. Sure, sir, he had the guns manned an' fired blank ca'tridges to keep 'em at a distance."

Was ever a commanding officer in so dolorous a plight—and for no fault of his own?

Mervyn suddenly heard the rich stir of a paduasoy skirt in the darkness near him, and with an effort curbed his vexation.

"This is all very well, since it ends well. But, my man, this is the duty of the officer of the guard and the officer of the day. It doesn't concern me. You ought to know that. What is your mission to me from the officer of the day?"

The man hesitated and stammered. He knew that he was detailing news—the most momentous that had befallen Fort Prince George for many a moon. He could hardly accept the statement that it concerned only the officer of the day. He recalled himself hastily.

"Yes, sir, Hi was to mention Ensign Raymond's arrival, sir. He wishes to report to you, sir, and to see if the leddies have any messages for Captain Howard, sir, as 'e is about to start up the river to rejoin 'im."

CHAPTER VIII

MERVYN had not earlier been aware of the presence of Arabella in the dimly lighted hall during the report of the corporal, but it was coercive now. She had not intended concealment, and she broke out with sudden enthusiasm. Her father's absence counted but a few hours, but the thought of it was as heavy as if it had endured for a year.

"Lord,—to be sure we want to send messages. Have Mr. Raymond in at once, Mr. Mervyn, and let us hear what he has to say of papa, and how he weathered the storm."

The rich rustling of her silk dress as she fluttered through the shadowy place, the clear, resonant note of happiness in her voice, her gurgling, melodious laughter, and the striking of the light on her sheeny attire and her golden hair as she flashed into the illuminated room beyond were as unexpected as a supernatural vision to the corporal, standing at gaze with his lantern at the door. Mervyn made haste to dismiss him, hearing all the time the voices of the ladies within raised beyond precedent.

"Not Indians—no Indians have come, Aunt Claudia!" cried Arabella. The words merely added another repetition to the monotonous chant of the two swaying women. "No Indians at all. Ensign Raymond has returned, and is coming in!"

She stood in the centre of the floor, resplendent and joyous, and waved her hand at arm's length with a wide, free gesture to express gratulation and safety.

Mrs. Annandale was suddenly silent, her face more dismayed than when terror had distorted it. One might have thought the presence of Raymond was even less welcome than a raid of Indians. Her jaw fell; her head-dress was awry; her eyes grew troubled and then bright with a spark of irritation.

"Why does the creature have to come here? Has George Mervyn no better sense than to receive official reports in *my* presence?" She drew herself up to her extreme height to express the dignity of her personality and to repudiate the contaminating influences of official reports. But Raymond was already at the door.

A brief conference with Mervyn in the hall had sufficed for business, for he had no official matters to report to the acting commandant. It was merely a form to report at all. Raymond still cherished a proud and wounded consciousness of the false position in which he had been placed because of an exacting whim of his quondam friend. He could not have put his finger on the spot, but he knew he was suffering a counter-stroke for some blow dealt Mervyn's vanity, unintentionally, unperceived, he could not say how.

He had taken his punishment—the commandant's reprimand, a most half-hearted performance—and the matter had passed. But Mervyn, in view of their old intimacy, had an uneasy wonder as to the terms on which they should meet again, and would fain it had been otherwise than under circumstances in which, if not obviously at fault, he was the ridiculous sport of an unsoldierly chance. Raymond, throughout the interview, had deported himself with punctilious formality, saluting with the respect due a superior officer, bearing himself with a null inexpressiveness, phrasing what he had to say with not a word to spare; only when he turned to the door of the parlor, and Mervyn bade him pause, did his impetuous identity assert itself.

"I hardly think," said Mervyn, whose quick senses had caught something of the old lady's protest, which reinforced a jealous folly that grudged even a glimpse of Arabella, "that a visit is in order at present. Mrs. Annandale is not well and the hour is late; the pettiaugre should not be kept waiting within the reach of marauding Indians."

He even went so far as to lay a detaining hand on the door.

"Under your favor, sir," said Raymond, stiffly, his blood boiling, his eyes on fire, "in so personal a matter I shall not consult your pleasure. I shall wait upon the ladies with such news as I can give them of the expedition."

He had lifted his voice, and its round, rich volume penetrated the inner apartment. The door opened suddenly from within and he was greeted by Arabella, herself, in a sort of ecstasy of expectation. The wilderness, in whose vastness her father was submerged, seemed not so formidable when so soon after his departure she might have word how he was faring in its depths.

"Oh, Mr. Raymond!—how good of you to come and tell us the news—"

"I feared I might be intrusive," he hesitated, his ill-humor put to rout at the very sight of her, and feeling a little abashed, a little wistful in having forced his way, so to speak, into her presence.

"Why, no—!" she cried, her voice as fresh as a lark's. "I wanted to see you. I asked Mr. Mervyn to send for you!"

Mervyn flushed, and as she observed it she noticed that the red glow in Raymond's cheeks was deeper and richer than even their florid wont. The eyes of both men glittered, and she had a sudden recollection of the difficulty that had heretofore risen between them touching the guard report,—had there been high words in the hall, she wondered.

Mrs. Annandale was endowed with many a sharp weapon which made her enmity feared and her favor prized, and among these were certain indescribable subtleties of manner which she wielded with great skill and murderous effect. The very glance of her eye as she turned her gaze upon

Raymond might have abased many as sturdy a soul, but Arabella was smiling upon him from the opposite side of the table, both elbows on it and her chin on her clasped hands.

"Well, you here again?" the old lady said, her keen eyes twinkling malevolently upon him as he stood beside a chair, his hand on its back, "we thought—we really labored under the impression that we said farewell to you early this afternoon."

"And you shall have that pleasure again, dear madam, within the next few minutes," he retorted, with a courteous smile and a wave of the hat in his hand.

Her eyes narrowed—he was the very essence of a marplot, so handsome, with such a suggestion of reckless dash about him, yet with such a steady look in his eye. He had, too, all the advantages of birth and breeding, and for these she valued him even less. They placed him where she claimed he had no right to be, among his superiors as wealth would rate them. She was not rich, herself, but she had a sentiment of contumely for the indications of wear in his service uniform, of work in his heavy service sword, of the expectation of danger incident to his profession, and the preparation for it evidenced in the pistols he wore in his belt. His unpowdered hair, just drying off from the soakings of the rain, showed its dark auburn hue. He was all most freshly caparisoned, for the rain had not left a dry thread on him, and he, too, was rather conscious of the shabbiness of his second best uniform, donned since his arrival at the fort. In comparison, Mervyn, hovering about, was but a lace and velvet presentment of a soldier, a travesty of the idea expressed in fighting trim.

Arabella took, as she fancied, a sort of friendly interest in Raymond—she loved that look in his eyes, that gay, gallant, fearless glance; it reminded her of sunlight striking on water, and she knew there were depths far, far beneath. There was something so genuine, so vigorous, so hearty about his mentality; he would not know what to do with a subterfuge. She loved to see his rising anger; she laughed with a flattered delight when she thought of a suggestion of jealousy, for her sake, of Mervyn, that she had noticed even on the first day of her arrival,—things move swiftly on the frontier. She would like to sit down beside him and hear him tell of his troubles,—how he hated, and whom; how he loved, and whom; how he had only his sword to cut his way through the world, and his way was like this impenetrable wilderness, too thickly grown for a knight-errant of to-day to make place. She would care rather to hear of his griefs than the joys of another man. His failures were more picturesque than another man's successes. She would like to take out her little house-wife, and with her crafty needle mend that rent in his white glove as he held it in his hand. She reached for it suddenly, and if ever Mrs.

Annandale could have bitten an unsuspicious hand it was when her niece's jewelled fingers began to take in and out a tiny needle and a fine thread through the ripped seam of the soldier's glove.

"More than a few minutes," she said, archly. "You can't go without this!"

Mrs. Annandale had the merit of knowing when the limit of forbearance was reached.

"And now, my good Mr. Raymond," she said, with a sour smile, "if you are quite ready, and have peacocked about to your heart's content, and have handled your sword and fiddled with your pistols to make Arabella and me see that you have got 'em on and are about to get used to wearing such things, and are no play-soldier, though yesterday in the nursery, we want to say we admire your terrible and blood-thirsty appearance, and tremble mightily before you, and should like to know what brought you back, and if anything ails Captain Howard."

Arabella looked up quickly.

"Oh, nothing! Captain Howard is in fine health and spirits," Raymond hastened to stipulate.

"Then take time to sit down, Mr. Raymond," Arabella said, for Mrs. Annandale had malevolently left him standing. "What brought you back?"

"The sight of the burning granary," said Raymond, sinking into a chair with a goodly clatter of his warlike paraphernalia. "We had made fair headway when we met the storm, and the wind scattered the pettiaugres and drove us ashore. We went into an inlet where a ravine ran down the mountain-side, but the water rose and backed up till we took to the rocks, and emerging upon a high pinnacle commanding the face of the country I spied the bonfire you had started here."

"Did you hear the guns?" Mervyn asked, quietly. He had no hope to delude the ladies with the idea that he had ordered the protective firing. But if Raymond had heard the circumstance of his inopportune seclusion it might foster a doubt in his mind.

Arabella noted that jovial widening of the pupils of Raymond's eyes, an expression as hilarious as a laugh. But he said gravely that at the distance they had not discriminated between the discharge of the cannon and of the thunder.

"Captain Howard was not very uneasy about the Cherokees; he thought the fire was kindled by lightning, and at all events the main part of our force was here. But he sent me to bring certain intelligence, and as I am to rejoin him before dawn"—he was rising—"you will not, Mrs. Annandale, tempt me beyond my strength."

He looked down at her with so sarcastic a gleam in his eyes that for once she was out of countenance.

"Hoity—toity," she exclaimed, "we sharpen our wits in the pettiaugres."

The glove was mended. Mervyn could not judge whether it were a mere *façon de parler*, or whether the girl were a coquette at heart, or whether Raymond had won upon her predilections, but he was seriously disturbed and displeased when, with a pretty gesture of significance, she cast it upon the table.

"I fling down the glove!" she said.

"I lift the glove!" he responded, in his full, steady voice.

And neither Mrs. Annandale nor Mervyn had quite the courage to ask what manner of defiance this gage signified, or whether indeed it were merely one of those vain trifles with which young people are wont to solace their emptiness and lack of thought.

Raymond was bowing over the hands of the ladies, presently, and after the fashion of the time he carried Mrs. Annandale's to his lips. She gave it to him with a touch of reluctance, as if she thought he had some cause to bite it, but he dropped the member uninjured, and then he was gone.

Mervyn lingered, but the fire was low, the geniality spent; Arabella, half lost in one of the great chairs as she leaned far back, seemed pensive, distraite; he, himself, could not raise his spirits to their wonted tone; his mind was preoccupied with the unlucky chances of the evening and the sorry figure he had cut when his rank had placed him in command of the fort, and when he would most desire to deserve his prominence. Mrs. Annandale alone preserved her uncanny, indomitable freshness, and talked on with unabated vigor. But the evening was over; to recur to its tender passages would need more auspicious circumstances. He had few words for leave-taking, and when he had gone Arabella slowly pulled herself out of the depths of the big chair, and said how tired she was, and how long he had stayed. And then she yawned. Mrs. Annandale looked at her sternly, opened her mouth for rebuke, thought better of it, lighted her bedroom candle, and disappeared.

Arabella stood for some moments with her own lighted candle in her hand. The room was otherwise dark now, but for a dull glow of embers; the barbaric decorations on the walls, the swan's wings, the aboriginal pictures, the quivers and fantastic medley of baskets, and calabashes, and painted jugs wavered into visibility and again disappeared as the flame flickered in the draught. She was thinking—she hardly knew of what—she was tired—the evening had brought so much. She had a sense of triumph in the capture of Mervyn, and that was an abiding impression. She was glad to see Raymond—her heart was warm when she thought of him. She fancied they had quarrelled because of her, and this made her lips curl with relish—but they might quarrel again. She must not let Mervyn's jealousy go too far. She had half a mind to tell her aunt of her victory—she, the penniless! But there would be time enough. She took the candle in her hand and started up the steep stairway from the hall. It was of rude construction, and the apartment to which it led was an empty disused place upon which the rooms on either side opened. It was situated in one angle of the house, and when it was built had been intended for defensive service. Its outer sides had a row of loop-holes at the usual height, and its walls projected some three feet beyond the walls below like the upper story of a block-house; a series of loop-holes that pierced the floor close to the outer wall gave an opportunity to its possible defenders of shooting downward at an enemy who should seek to enter or to fire the house below. With all these loop-holes, admitting the air, the place was far too open for occupation, save by soldiers, perhaps, in stress of siege. In peace it had lapsed into simple utility as hallway, and possessed a sort of attraction for Arabella, so different was it from aught she had ever seen in the old country. The commandant's residence, otherwise, a quadrangular building, with an open square in the centre, wherein was a well to insure a water supply in any event of blockade or siege, was reminiscent to her of country granges which she had seen on the continent, but these quaint corner rooms above stairs, each practically a citadel, with its loop-holes both for direct and vertical fire, seemed to be peculiarly of the new world, full of the story and the struggle of the frontier. Her own and her aunt's rooms lay to the south, her father's to the east. The other citadel corners and sides of the quadrangle were appropriated to the officers of the garrison, and, like separate houses, there was no means of communication.

The great strong timbers, capable of turning a musket-ball, the heavy low beams, all clear of cobwebs, for these military wights were great housekeepers, came first into view as she slowly ascended the rude stair; then she caught a glimpse of a star shining through a loop-hole in the wall, and she stood still for a moment in the cavernous place, with the candle in one hand and the other on the rough stair-rail, while she watched its white glister, and listened to the sullen drops falling from the eaves, and the continuous sobbing of the unreconciled wind; then she went on up, up, till she stood at the top and turned to glance about, as she always did, at the place which must have stories to tell if there were any idle enough to listen. The next moment the candle was set a-flicker by a gust of wind through a neighboring loop-hole. She held up one hand to shield it. The flame suddenly bowed again before the errant gust, flickered tremulously and flared up anew, failed, and all was darkness. Before crossing the slight distance to her aunt's door

Arabella stood waiting till her eyes should become more accustomed to the gloom. She knew that the loop-holes in the floor were close to the wall, and that so long as she kept her direction through the middle of the apartment there was no danger of a false step. But a certain direction is difficult to maintain in darkness, as she realized, and she eagerly attempted to discern the small squares of the light outside which should apprize her of the position of the upper row of loop-holes, just above the lower series. She would have called out to Norah to open the door of the lighted room, but that she dreaded her aunt's outcries, and reproaches, and rebukes for the carelessness of allowing her candle to be blown out at peril of a sprained ankle or a broken limb.

Suddenly she heard a voice in the parade; it was near at hand and through the loop-hole at her left she could see that two figures were standing close to the wall below. She had no intention of listening. She would have moved, but for her terror of the pitfalls in the floor. Their words were few, but their voices, though low, carried with unusual distinctness in the dull damp air.

"Split me! but I've laughed myself sick," Raymond was saying. "God-a-mercy, the commandant of a fort smirking in a lady's parlor, while his granaries burn and subalterns fire cannon to keep the Indians from rushing the gates. Oh—ho! oh—ho! I hope I haven't done my chest any serious damage, but I ache fit to kill."

"Lieutenant Jerrold was pretty hot, to have to shoulder all the responsibility," said another voice that she did not recognize. "What will the captain say, do you suppose, when you tell him?"

"I shall not tell him! No—burst me if I will. It wasn't the damn fool's fault. It was just so funny! It was as if Fate had tweaked him by the nose!"

"He was quick enough to report *you*," said Ensign Lawrence. "For something not *your* fault."

"Child, I never try to measure my duty by other men's consciences. I shall tell the captain that all his corn is gone and his horses are inquiring about breakfast already, and the cook has no griddle-cakes for Mrs. Annandale—and Indian meal is the only Indian thing she approves of. And that the guard behaved well and stood off the Indians under the command of a gay little ensign, who shall not be nameless, and that the force from the barracks turned out and dealt strenuously with the fire under the orders of Lieutenant Jerrold, officer of the day, till the rain took up the matter and put it out. But unless he asks point-blank of the acting commandant I shall say naught. Let him have all the credit he can get—"

"And the young lady besides?"

"If she will have him."

But there was a change in Raymond's voice. He was aware of it himself, for he broke off—"I take it mighty kind of you, Lawrence, to let me have these bullets. I had enough moulded, as I thought, but the captain—queer in an old soldier—went off without any, and I left him all I had. But for you I couldn't use these pistols at all."

She could see now in the pallid and uncertain moonlight that they were dividing some small commodities between them, and presently, the transfer complete, she watched them trudge off toward the gates. She stepped cautiously across the loop-holes in the floor and looked through one of the slits high enough for window-like usage. It gave a good range toward the south, and she noted flickering lights at the river-bank. Evidently Raymond was on the point of re-embarkation. Soon the lights were extinguished, there was more the sense of movement on the dark water than visible craft, till suddenly a pettiaugre glided into view in a great slant of white glister on the shining water, with the purple mountains beyond, and the massive wooded foothills on either side, with the tremulous stars, and the skurrying clouds, and the fugitive moon above. And on—and on—and on in this white glister, as in some enchanted progress, the lonely boat glided till it rounded the point, and was lost to view.

CHAPTER IX

IT was dawn when Raymond sighted Little Tamotlee, and the early sunshine, of an exquisite crystalline purity, was over all the world—misty mountain, shimmering river, the infinite stretches of the leafless wilderness—as the young officer's pettiaugre was pulling into the bank, where Captain Howard's boats were already beached. The Indian town on the shore, an oasis of habitation in the midst of the unpeopled forest, was all astir. Columns of smoke were rising alike from the conical-roofed dwellings of the characteristic Indian architecture and those more modern structures which the Cherokees also affected, and which resembled the log cabins of the European settlers in the provinces to the eastward. The population seemed all afoot, as if some event of moment impended. Knots of braves pressed hither and thither, with feather-crested heads and painted faces, arrayed in buck-skin or fur shirts and leggings with floating fringes, and many tawdry gauds of decorated quivers and bows, carried for ornament only, long ago discarded as a weapon in favor of the British "Brown Bess," and powder and lead. The chiefs, the cheerataghe or priests, the political head-men, and the warriors of special note were all easily distinguishable to Raymond, as he stood in the bow of the boat, by reason of their splendor of attire, their feather-braided iridescent mantles, or their war bonnets of vertically placed swan's quills, standing fifteen inches high, above the forehead. On the summit of the tall mound, where the great dome-like rotunda or town-house was perched,—its contour conserved by a thick plaster of the tenacious red clay of the region laid on smoothly, inside and out,—a white flag was flying. Presently a wide sonorous voice sounded thence. The Cherokee town-crier was uttering the "News Hollow." It was strictly an official demonstration, for the arrival of Captain Howard and his escort in the night, now quartered in the "Stranger house," was an event that had fallen under the personal observation of all the denizens of Tamotlee. Nevertheless, every man paused where he stood, as if the sound of that great voice possessed gifts of enchantment, and he were bound to the spot.

Raymond, who had caught up some familiarity with the language, was too distant as he stood in the gliding boat, now swiftly approaching the shore, to discriminate the words, but as the proclamation ceased he perceived that all were pressing toward the "beloved square" of the town, a rectangular space, level, and covered with fine white sand, beaten, and trampled, and worn to the hardness and consistency of stone. There was a commodious piazza-like building of logs and bark, having the whole front open, situated at each side of the square, appropriated to the different branches, so to speak, of the primitive government, and these began to fill quickly with the officials of each department,—the ancient councillors on the east, the cheerataghe on the west, the warriors on the north, clanging with martial accoutrement, and on the south the functionaries that the European traders, called "The Second Men," these being, as it were, "the city fathers," having control of all municipal affairs,—the building of houses, the planting and garnering of the public crops, the succor of the poor, the conduct of negotiations with other towns, the care of the entertainment of strangers. It was in their charge that Raymond presently perceived, with that amusement which the methods of the savages always excited in European breasts, Captain Howard and his escort. Very funny, in truth, they looked, their fresh British faces adjusted to a sedulous gravity and inexpressiveness and their manner stiffened to conform to Indian etiquette, and manifest neither curiosity nor amusement. This was difficult for one of the young soldiers, a raw Irish boy, whose teeth now and again gleamed inadvertently, giving the effect of being swallowed, so suddenly did his lips snap together as his orders recurred to his mind. His head seemed set on a pivot when first he took his seat with the others on the benches in the booth-like place, but a sudden stroke upon the cranium from a drum-stick in the seemingly awkward handling of Robin Dorn, sitting beside him and moving the instrument as if for added safety, was a sufficient admonition to foster a creditable degree of discretion. Captain Howard's typically English face, florid, smooth, steadfast-eyed, evidencing a dignity and self-respect that coerced a responsive respect, was indeed curiously out of place seen above the bar of the booth-like piazza, where he sat on the lower settee, his men ranged in tiers behind him. When Raymond, who was met at the water's edge by a messenger for the purpose, was conducted to a place by Captain Howard, he rather wondered that they had not been given seats beside Rolloweh, the prince of the town, in the western cabin, for it was the habit of the Indians to pay almost royal honors to their guests of official station. He took the place assigned him in silence, and he observed that the occasion was indeed one of special importance, for Captain Howard said not a word, made not an inquiry as to his mission, save by a lifted eyebrow. Raymond answered by a debonair smile, intimating that all was well. Then both turned their eyes to the "beloved square," and this moment the Reverend Mr. Morton was led out in charge of two Indians and stationed before the great white seat of the "holy cabin." Captain Howard flushed deeply and darkly red, but made no other sign, and such proceedings began as Rolloweh had elected should take place.

Mr. Morton was old, and lank, and pallid, and dreary. No affinity had he with the portly and well-liking type of his profession of his day. Such manna as gave them a repletion of self-satisfaction had been denied him. He had an infinite capacity for hardship, an absolute disdain of danger. Luxury affected his ascetic predilections like sin. He desired but a meditative crust to crunch while he argued the tenets of his religion and refuted the contradictions of his catechumen. He was as instant in and out of season as if he were in pursuit of some worldly preferment—one can say no more. He did not need encouragement, and he was so constituted that he could recognize no failure. He had no vain-glory in his courage—to him it was the most natural thing in the world to risk his life to save Rolloweh's soul. He knew it was rank heresy to think it, but he was willing to trust the salvation of Captain Howard and the garrison of Fort Prince George to their own unassisted efforts, and such mercy as the Lord might see fit to grant their indifference, their ignorance, their folly, and their perversity. But Rolloweh's soul had had no chances, and he was bound personally to look after it. He even hoped for the conversion of those great chiefs of the upper towns—Yachtino of Chilhowee, Cunigacatgoah of Choté, Moy Toy of Tellico Great, and Quorinnah of Tennessee Town. He was worldly wise in his day and generation, too. He had fastened with the unerring instinct of the born missionary on the propitious moment. Not while prosperity shone upon them, not while their savage religion met every apparent need, not while facile chance answered their ignorant prayer, was the conversion of a people practicable. But the Cherokees were conquered, abased, decimated, the tribe scattered, their towns in ruins, the bones held sacred of their dead unburied, their ancient cherished religion fallen in esteem to a meaningless system of inoperative rites and flimsy delusions. Now was the time to reveal the truth, to voice "the good tidings of great joy." Hence he had said, "Woe is unto me if I preach not the gospel!"

And the common people had been listening to him gladly. Thus the chiefs feared they would never seek to made head against their national enemies under their national rulers. Simple as he stood there in his thread-bare black clothes and his darned hose,—he was wondrously expert with a meditative needle,—he had the political future of a people and the annihilation of a false and barbarous worship in his grasp. Therefore said the Cherokee rulers to Captain Howard—"Your beloved man must remove himself."

It was an old story to the soldier. He had written to the missionary and remonstrated, for peace was precious. In reply he had in effect been admonished to render unto Cæsar the things that are Cæsar's and unto God the things that are God's. A meek address was not among the merits of the Reverend Mr. Morton. The obvious interpretation of this saying seemed to the commandant a recommendation to go about his business. He desisted from advice for a time. He had known a certain luke-warmness in religious matters to ensue upon a surcharge of zeal, and he had waited with patience for the refined and delicately nurtured old man to tire of the hardships of life in that devastated country among the burned towns and the angry, sullen people, and the uncouth savage association. But he had continued to preach, and the tribesmen had continued in hordes to listen, expecting always to discover the secret of the superiority of the British in the arts of war and manufacture,—the reason of their own deplorable desolation and destruction. They could not separate the ideas of spiritual acceptability and worldly prosperity. The Briton revered his religion, they argued, and therefore he knew how to make gun-powder, and to conquer the bravest of the brave, and to amass much moneys of silver and gold,—for in their enlightenment the roanoke and the wampum were a wofully depreciated currency,—perhaps it was the religion of the British people which made them so strong. Thus the Cherokees lent a willing ear. As they began to discriminate and memorize, certain familiarities in the matters offered for their contemplation were dimly recognized. The archaic figment or fact— whichever it may be—that the ancient Scriptures had once been theirs, and through negligence lost, and through degeneration forgotten, reasserted its hold. The points of similarity in their traditions to the narrations of the old Bible were suggested to Mr. Morton, who accepted them with joy, becoming one of the early converts to the theory of the Hebraic origin of the tribes of American Indians. It was a happy time for the scholarly old man—to find analogies in their barbarous rites with ancient Semitic customs; to reform from the distortions of oral teachings a divine oracle of precious significance; to show in the old stories how the prophecy fore-shadowed the event, how the semblance merged into the substance in the coming of the Christ. In this way he approached their conversion to Christianity from the vantage ground of previous knowledge, however distorted and inadequate, and commingled with profane and barbaric follies. He was convinced—he convinced many— that they were of an inherited religion, into which he had been adopted, that they were descendants of the lost tribes of Israel, that the Scriptures they had had were a part of the Book he revered, and that he would indoctrinate them into the remainder. Perhaps Mr. Morton doubted the account of the teachings of the Roman Catholic captive, Cabeza de Vaca, among the Floridian Indians early in the sixteenth century, or perhaps he disbelieved that any remnants of such precepts had drifted so far to this secluded and inimical tribe, always at war as it was with its southern neighbors and totally without communication with them.

Though this persuasion took hold on the masses it encountered great disfavor among the chiefs, more especially when the valorous and fearless old man thundered rebukes upon their pagan follies and observances, their superstitions, their methods of appeasing the "Great White Fire." He knew no moderation in rebuke; intolerance is the good man's sin. He was especially severe in his denunciation of the pretended powers of necromancy, above all of the supernatural endowment of a certain amulet which they possessed and which by the earlier travellers among them is termed their "Conjuring-Stone."

This was said to be a great red crystal. According to Adair, the historian, it was a gigantic carbuncle; others have called it a garnet—these gems are still found in the Great Smoky Mountains; more probably it was a red tourmaline of special depth and richness of color.

Mr. Morton had never seen the stone, but Cunigacatgoah of Choté had told him triumphantly that he could never captivate his soul, for he held the precious amulet in his hand whenever the missionary preached, and it dulled the speech, so that he heard nothing. As the aged Cunigacatgoah had been deaf these several years, this miracle had involved little strain on the powers of the stone. These days were close upon the times of witchcraft, of the belief in special obsessions, of all manner of magic. This stubborn and persistent paganism roused the utmost rancor and ingenuity of the Reverend Mr. Morton, and at last he made a solemn statement in the council-house of Choté, in the presence of many witnesses, that if they would show him one miracle wrought by the stone, if they could bring positive testimony of one evil averted by the amulet, he would renounce his religion and his nation, he would become an adopted Cherokee and a pagan; he would poll his hair, and dance in three circles, and sacrifice to the "Ancient White Fire" and the little Thunder men.

In the sullen silence that had ensued upon this declaration he had demanded why had the amulet not stayed the march of the British commander, Colonel Grant, through the Cherokee country? Why had it not checked the slaughters and the burnings? Why had it not saved to the Cherokees the vast extent of country ceded for a punitive measure in the pacification and forced treaties of peace? Where was the luck it had brought? Defend all good people from such a possession!

The old missionary owed his life less to any fear that should he disappear the British government might bethink itself of such a subject as a superannuated and pious old scare-crow in the barren field of the Cherokee country than to the hold he had taken on the predilections of the people. There was scant use in burning him—many among themselves would resent his fate. He, himself, would rejoice in martyrdom, and their utmost deviltries would add to his crown.

The savage leaders had a certain natural sagacity. Wiser than they of eld they cried not upon Baal. They would not accept the challenge of the man of God. They would not produce the amulet at his bidding, lest it be discredited—they said the touch, the evil eye of a stranger were a profanation. Yet they feared that the conversion of the people to Christianity was national annihilation. And they clung to their superstitions, their polytheistic venerations, their ancient necromancies, their pagan observances; to them all other gods were strange gods. They realized the hold which the new faith was taking on the tribesmen. Therefore they had told Mr. Morton that he had long plagued them with many words and they desired him to leave the country. When he refused in terms they despatched a delegation to refer the matter to Captain Howard at Fort Prince George, with a most insistent demand that he should return with it and meet them at Little Tamotlee, a village at no difficult distance from the fort itself, and easily accessible by boat, by reason of the confluence of the Keowee and Tugaloo rivers.

This was one of the smaller towns of the Ayrate district, sending only sixty gun-men to the wars and with a population of women and children in proportion. The inhabitants could by no means muster such an assemblage as had now gathered. Visitors whom Raymond, familiar with the people, recognized as hailing from the towns of the Ottare region had crowded in, making the day in some sort a representative occasion. They had arranged themselves around the "beloved square," some standing, some seated, others kneeling on one knee, and the proceedings had well begun before Captain Howard realized what manner of part he was expected to sustain. In noting the number of chiefs ranged in state in the "holy cabin" on the "great white seat," Raymond thought that the lack of space might explain the fact that Captain Howard was not offered a place commensurate with his rank and importance on the frontier. After a few moments, however, he understood that this subsidiary position better accorded with the rôle assigned to the commandant.

The row of chiefs glittered in the brilliant sunlight, in their rich fur shirts, their feather-woven mantles, their plumed crests, their gayly painted faces, their silver bracelets worn above the elbow, their silver head-bands and earrings, their many glancing necklaces of roanoke,—all, however, devoid of any weapon worn in sight. The wind was gentle, yet fresh; the hour was still early,—the Reverend Mr. Morton's shadow was even longer and lanker than his tall, bony anatomy might seem to warrant. His attendants, or guards, had taken off his shovel hat and clerical wig, and his head was bare, save for its wandering wisps of gray hair, blowing about his face and neck,—and whenever Captain Howard glanced toward him he turned as red as his scarlet coat, his eyes fell, he cleared his throat uneasily. He had long been habituated by the exigencies of his military service to the exercise of self-control, and he had need now of all the restraints of his training.

The preacher opened the session, so to speak, by demanding in a very loud voice, with every assurance of manner and in fluent Cherokee, why he was arraigned thus amongst his friends.

Rolloweh, a man of a fierce, hatchet-shaped face, rendered sinister of expression by the loss of one eye, rose and imperatively bade him be silent.

"I will not hold my peace," declared the venerable missionary. "I will know why I am brought here, and why these,"—he waved his hand—"have assembled."

"Because," said Rolloweh, the Raven, craftily, "you have too many words. You weary our ears waking, and in our dreams you still talk on. We have loved you—have we not listened to you? You are our friend, and you have dwelt in our hearts. We have seen you shed tears for our sorrows. You have lent ears to our plaints and you have eaten our salt. You have given of your goods to the needy and have even wrought with your hands in building again the burned houses. You have paid with English money for your keep and have been a charge to no man."

He looked with a steady, observant eye to the right and the left of the rows of eager listening faces. They could but note that he had religiously given the old man his due, for the good missionary was much beloved of the people.

"But your talk is not a straight talk. You have the crooked tongue. You tell lies to mislead the Cherokee people—who are a free people—and to make them slaves to the British. You tell them that these lies are religion—that they are the religion of the British people."

There was absolute silence as his impassioned tones, voicing the musical, liquid Cherokee words, rolled out on the still morning air.

"You say that the tongue is a fire—it kindles about you, for these lies that you have spoken. You are our friend, but you stretch our hearts to bursting. We have besought you to leave the country and mislead our youth no more. You have been stubborn. You say—'Woe!' and you will preach! We have summoned this Capteny Howard, a beloved man of the English king, to question between you and show these men from the towns that what you teach our youth is not the English religion, but a charm to bind the Cherokee."

Through the interpreter these words were perfectly intelligible to Captain Howard, and for one moment it seemed as if this officer—a stalwart specimen of middle-aged vigor—might faint; then, with a sudden revulsion of color, as if he might go off in an apoplexy. To be so entrapped! To be caught in the toils of a public religious controversy dismayed him more than an ambush of warriors. But the old missionary's life might depend upon his answers. They must confirm the "straightness" of Mr. Morton's talk. He must prove that the teaching of the parson to the Cherokee nation was not a snare for Cherokee liberties, but the familiar religion of the British people, known and practised by all.

It was not to be presumed that with these postulants Mr. Morton had delved very deeply into sacerdotal mysteries and fine and abstruse doctrines of theology, but Captain Howard was so obviously relieved when his interpreter, standing very straight and stiff outside his booth,—a man whom he had employed as a scout,—repeated the words flung at him by the interpreter of Rolloweh, who stood very straight and stiff outside the "holy cabin," that Raymond, despite his surprise, and agitation, and anxiety could have laughed aloud.

"Did you ever hear of a man called Noah?"

"Yes—oh, yes, indeed," said Captain Howard, so plumply affirmative and familiar that they might have expected to hear him add that he had served with Noah in the Hastenbeck campaign.

All the eyes of the Cherokees around the vacant square were fixed first upon the questioner, Rolloweh, and then upon Captain Howard, in the incongruous rôle of catechumen. The space was not so large as in the "beloved squares" of towns of greater population, comprising perhaps not more than one acre. Every word could be heard—every facial change discriminated. Mr. Morton stood as if half amused, one thumb thrust in his fob, his grizzled eye-brows elevated, his thin wisps of hair tossed about his bare poll, a smile on his face, listening with an indulgent meditative air to the inquiries of Rolloweh propounded in Cherokee, which, of course, he understood, and the sturdy cautious response of the British commandant. Captain Howard had not thought so much about Biblical matters since he sat and swung his feet in his callow days to be catechised by the nursery governess.

"Did he have a house that could float?" demanded the interrogator.

"Oh, he did,—he did indeed," declared Captain Howard, freely.

There was a certain satisfaction perceptible on the face of Rolloweh, despite the enigmatical cast given it by the loss of his eye. The other head-men, too, assisting at this unique literary exercise, showed an animation, a gleam of triumph, at every confirmation of the ancient Biblical stories found by the early missionaries to be curiously, mysteriously familiar to all the pagan Cherokees, distorted in detail sometimes, and sometimes in pristine proportions. When a sudden blight fell upon the smooth progress of this comparative theology and the question awoke from Captain Howard no responsive assurance of knowledge, Raymond was more sensibly impressed by the gloom, the disappointment that settled upon the faces of the head-men on the "great white seat." He could not understand it. The Indians were very subtle—or did they really desire the verification of what they had been taught by the missionary.

The "beloved square" was absolutely silent. The shadow of a white cloud high in the blue zenith crossed the smooth sanded space; they could hear the

Tugaloo River fretting on the rocks a mile down-stream. The bare branches of the encompassing forests, with no sign that the spring of the year pulsed in their fibres, that the sap was rising, clashed lightly together in a vagrant gust and fell still again.

Captain Howard knitted a puzzled brow, and his men, ranged in tiers of seats back of him, who had been startled and amazed beyond expression by the unexpected developments, gazed down upon him with a ludicrous anxiety lest he fail to acquit himself smartly and do himself and the command credit, and with an *esprit de corps* wholly at variance with the subject-matter of the examination.

"Why, no," the officer said at last, "I don't think I ever before heard of the dogs."

He cast a furtive glance of deprecation at the missionary, who still stood, listening unmoved and immovable, fixing his eyes with a look of whimsical self-communing on the ground as if waiting, steeling himself in patience till this folly should wear itself out of its own fatuity.

"Never heard of the Dogs of Hell?" Rolloweh at last asked with a tone insistently calculated to jog the refractory memory. Raymond marked with a renewal of surprise his eagerness that the officer should retract. Captain Howard frowned with impatience. What an ordeal was this! That the life of a blatant and persistent preacher—yet an old and a saintly man—should depend upon the accuracy of his recollection of Scriptural details to which he had not given more than a passing thought for thirty years. What strange unimagined whim could be actuating the Indians? He might have prevaricated had he but a serviceable phrase to fill the breach. He could not foresee the result, and he dubiously adhered to the truth.

"I have heard of Cerberus, the three-headed classical dog, you know, Mr. Morton. But I don't remember any religious dog at all."

There was silence for a time. Then Rolloweh began to speak again, and the voice of Captain Howard's interpreter quavered as he proceeded to instruct his sturdy commander.

"You surely know that as you go to hell you reach a deep gulf full of fire. A pole is stretched across it, with a dog at each end. The beloved man of the king of England must know that pole right well?"

Captain Howard doggedly shook his head.

"Never heard of the pole."

Rolloweh persisted, and the interpreter quavered after.

"The wicked—the great Capteny, precious to the hearts of the Cherokees, cannot be considered of the number—the wicked are chased by one of the dogs on to this pole, and while crossing the fiery gulf the dog at the other end shakes the pole and they fall off into Hell. Now surely the great Capteny remembers the Dogs of Hell?"

Surely Captain Howard's face seemed incapable of such a look of supplication as he sent toward Mr. Morton, who was gazing smilingly straight at him, as if the whole session were an invented diversion for the day. The clergyman gave no intimation as to how to meet the situation, and Captain Howard reiterated sturdily—"Never heard of any religious dogs," and lapsed into silence.

He was beginning to grow extremely disquieted, to doubt his wisdom in coming in response to their summons, and sooth to say if he had dreamed of the intention animating it he would have considered twice ere he consented. He had thought only of soothing their rancors and smoking the "friend pipe." The freakish fierce temper of the Cherokees could not be trusted, and they felt aggrieved in a certain sort that they were not left to such solace as they might find in their polytheism, or Great Spirit worship, or the necromancy of their Conjuring-Stone, but must needs be converted or regenerated on the plan of salvation which the missionary set forth with such ruthless logic. It was evident that they had found it necessary to discredit the preacher, and with this view the assemblage had been gathered as witnesses. Albeit Captain Howard did not understand its trend, he saw the investigation was going amiss,—Mr. Morton's life would prove the forfeit. He trembled, too, for the lives of his escort—they were but a handful among some hundreds of vigorous braves. His were troops flushed with recent victories, and if he had found it hard to witness unmoved the venerable missionary before such a tribunal, how must the scene strike the young, ardent, impulsive soldiers? Some thoughtless action, some inconsiderate word or look, and the lives of all would not be worth a moment's purchase.

The investigation fared little better when it quitted the infernal regions. Captain Howard, troubled, flushed, with an unsteady eye and an uncertain manner, watched disconsolately by his whole escort, knew nothing about a multiplicity of heavens.

He had heard the phrase "seven heavens" in ordinary conversation, but he had never been taught it was Scriptural. He was prompted, urged, goaded to a modification of this statement. Did he not know that the first heaven was little higher than the tops of the Great Smoky Mountains, but this proved too warm—therefore God created a second heaven, and then others until the ideal temperature was reached in the seventh heaven, where the Great Spirit dwelt, which was the reason that in prayer all should raise the hands seven times before speaking? No, the Capteny knew none of these things. And Rolloweh's eye, resting on him with an access of rancor, suggested a doubt of the officer's ignorance of such simple and obvious lore. He was found deficient, too, in any knowledge of a statement made by Rolloweh that one of the most significant warnings given rebellious man before the Deluge was the unprecedented fact that several infants were born with whole sets of teeth.

This ignorance vanished in the meeting with Moses. The officer knew him well and was even able to recognize him under the name of Wasi. In the wilderness Captain Howard, in the phrase of to-day, was "all there." Never did pilgrims so gayly fare through benighted wastes as he and Rolloweh, while they traced all the consecutive steps toward the Promised Land and lived anew the familiar incidents of the wanderings. True, he gave a lamentably uncertain sound as to the tint of the standards, and did not believe that the Holy Scriptures stated that one was white and one was red, but Rolloweh so slurred this matter that it was obvious to all observers that the two men were practically of one mind and one source of information thus far.

The escort had taken heart of grace at perceiving their commander's feet once more on solid ground—so to speak—in fact, they waxed so insolently confident as to grow drearily tired and absent-minded, as if at prolonged Sunday prayers in garrison or a lengthy sermon, but the attention of the Indians never flagged. Suddenly the crisis came when Rolloweh demanded:—

"The Capteny is a Christian?"

Captain Howard stanchly declared that he was.

"If a man should strike you on one cheek, Capteny, would you turn the other?"

The blow had fallen—the bomb had burst. Yet Captain Howard, somewhat blown, perhaps from his brisk jaunt through the wilderness, did not realize its full significance. He sat silent for a moment, blankly staring.

There was a stir in the great white seat of the "holy cabin," sinister, inimical. An answer must be forthcoming. Captain Howard hesitated, a vicarious fear in his eyes—a fear for the missionary who suddenly called out—"Oh, man of blood! Would you forswear yourself?"

"No," he said, glad to rely on his sturdy veracity; "I would not turn the other cheek."

"And this," cried Rolloweh, addressing the assemblage with sudden passion, "the forked tongue of this old serpent of the provinces"—he waved his hand at arm's length toward the missionary, "teaches is religion for the Cherokee. Not for the British! The religion that has been the same road till now branches with a white, smooth path for the British, and a bloody, rocky, dark path for the Cherokee."

A visible sensation swayed the crowd. The Indians exchanged glances of doubt, surprise, excitement, or triumph as the individual sentiment of congratulation or disappointment or indignation predominated. The soldiers looked at one another in dismay. Captain Howard, fairly ambushed, hardly knew which way to turn. Only the missionary stood unmoved, still gazing smilingly, indulgently, at the officer who had begun to fear that he had unwittingly compassed the old man's ruin.

"Did the Capteny ever see any other Christian Briton who was struck and who turned the other cheek?"—Rolloweh demanded, pushing his advantage. Even the interpreter's voice faltered as he put the query into English.

Captain Howard was minded to vouchsafe no reply. He had already been entrapped, it was true, through too anxious a desire to placate the savages, to conserve the peace of the frontier, and save the life of the old missionary. He might have done harm, rather than good, so impossible was it to forecast the event under circumstances so unprecedented. Then he resolutely swallowed his pride. The safety of his men was his primal consideration.

"No," he replied, albeit a trifle sullenly, "I never saw a Christian struck who turned the other cheek."

Rolloweh rose, with a fierce smile, bending to the crowd, waving both arms with the palms outward.

"If a man took your cloak, O Christian Capteny, would you give him your coat also?" he demanded.

"No," snarled the Christian captain, "I'd give him a beating."

There was a guttural sarcastic laugh around the square, ceasing as Rolloweh resumed:

"But this is the religion for the Cherokees—that they may be meek and broken, and after the land fling the weapon, and wear the yoke and drag the chain. Men and brothers, the spirits of the dead will rise against you if you suffer this. It is not agreeable to the old beloved rites that we tolerate this serpent of the forked tongue to scoff at our ancient worship and bring in a new religion, manufactured for the free and independent Cherokee, which means British rule."

There is something strangely daunting in the half-suppressed tumult of an angry crowd. It was not merely that an imprecation was heard here and the sibilance of whispered conspiracy there, or that restless gestures betokened a rising menace,—it was that a total change had come upon the aspect of the assemblage, as unmistakable as if a storm-cloud had blighted the day. The people were convinced. The work of the missionary was annihilated in this masterstroke of craft. To him it was only a reason for a renewal of his labors. When Captain Howard, tearing a leaf from his note-book, wrote a few words upon it and sent it into the "beloved square" by the interpreter, the clergyman merely glanced at it with a shaking head, and tossed it aside, saying with a smile, "No—my place is here. Woe is unto me if I preach not the gospel!"

Rolloweh had watched the communication with jealous disfavor, but as the familiar words resounded on the air his eye glittered, his long, cruel, flat lips were sternly compressed; he glanced over to the booth where the English officer so incongruously was stationed, and enunciated the fatal words,— "Your beloved man will be removed."

The attentive crowd caught the phrase, and a keen, savage cry of triumph suddenly broke forth, unlike anything ever voiced by civilized man—an utterance blended of the shrill exultation of a beast of prey, and the guttural human halloo, indescribable, nerve-thrilling, never to be forgotten, once heard. The transformation was complete. They were no more men—not even savages; they had entered upon that peculiar phase of their being which seems to those of different standards absolutely demoniac and demented. There was no right reason in some of the faces gazing at the impassive, unmoved old man in the centre of the square. They were waiting only the word for an act from which the imagination shrinks appalled. Captain Howard's fears were intensified for his stalwart young soldiers, despite the terrors of the retributive power of England which the recent Cherokee war against the British government had served to induce in the tribe. As the swaying of the crowd and the gaudily decorated figures of the head-men in the "holy white cabin" betokened the breaking-up of the assemblage, he ordered a young sergeant to have the men fall in quietly and keep them together. Captain Howard's attention was suddenly bespoken by the appearance of two or three chiefs who claimed a personal acquaintance, and who were approaching across the square to meet him. They were wreathing their harsh countenances into sardonic smiles, but they called out: "How! How!" very pleasantly by way of salutation.

Constrained to await their greeting, he bethought himself that perhaps some new influence, a fresh urgency, might avail with the stubborn old missionary.

"Raymond," he said in a low voice to the ensign, "do you go to the Reverend Mr. Morton and use your best endeavors to persuade him to embark with us. If he remains here after our departure I fear me much these damn scoundrels will burn him alive."

"I think I can persuade him, sir," said the capable and confident ensign.

Captain Howard looked hard at the dashing and debonair young officer, erect, stalwart, alert, clear-eyed, as he lifted his hand to the brim of his cocked hat and turned away, jostled considerably in his movements, and perhaps intentionally, by a dozen or more contumacious looking tribesmen, who were awkwardly crowding about the booth assigned to the soldiers.

"Take three men with you, Ensign," added Captain Howard. He had a positive fear that alone the subaltern might be attacked in the press, throttled, whisked away, tortured on the sly, and mysteriously disappearing, be lost to the service forever. "A trio of wide red Irish mouths," he thought, "could not easily be silenced."

And with this preparation for the graces of social intercourse he turned to greet the three chiefs who now came up with acclamations of pleasure, desirous of showing their companions the degree of consideration they enjoyed on the part of the commander of his Majesty's fort.

CHAPTER X

TO a man whose life is regulated on a basis of a difference in rank, a part of whose training is to conserve the respect due his military station and his social supremacy, who is habituated to stiff formalities of address, both in phrase and bearing, the familiarities of an inferior have a grossness which a custom of lenient condescension, or kindly indulgence, or careless indifference does not as readily perceive. But no man, however little fastidious, would have relished the peculiar impediments to Raymond's progress across the limited space of the "beloved square" to the spot where he thought—he could now no longer see for the press—the old missionary was standing. Indeed, Raymond might have better exerted tolerance had he not perceived that the demonstration was actuated by a rancorous spirit. The contact with the blanketed shoulders of the braves intentionally thrust against him to impede his progress; a peering, painted face stuck almost against his own, the survey followed by a wild cackle of derision; a feathered crest of a man, not so tall as he, jerked into his eyes, were incidents calculated to try the self-control of an ardent, impetuous young soldier to the extremest tension. He set his teeth and held hard to his composure, though his cheek flushed and his eye glittered. Naught that was personal should jeopardize the success of the forlorn hope of his appeal to the fears of the old missionary. The sturdy soldiers at his heels marked his demeanor and emulated his self-restraint. Presently, he almost ran against the old man, still bare-headed, still between his guards, replying in Cherokee to the jeers or reproaches of his recent converts as they gathered about him, upbraiding for double-dealing, and threatening as if with the just wrath of the deceived. He had a wistful, pained look as he sought to justify himself, to explain the misunderstanding, and it cut Raymond to the heart. He was of the temperament which throws itself with ardor into the joys and griefs of others—especially he deprecated infinitely the sight of sorrow in the aged. Let the young wrestle with the woes of life—not when strength, and hope, and illusion are all gone! He accosted the old man in a cheery voice, speaking in English, that the crowd might catch no chance word of offence.

"Captain Howard presents his compliments, Reverend sir, and wishes me to say that we have a place in our boat, which is at your service, and we shall feel much honored if you will occupy it," he said.

The old man, turning from the revilings and the insults heaped upon him by the savage rabble, must have felt an attraction toward the young, spirited face, and have softened to the sympathy in the ensign's eyes, the respect that vibrated in every inflection of his voice.

"I thank you, my young friend," he said in a kindly tone, "but my station is here. I cannot desert my post. I am a soldier of the Cross."

"Under your favor, Reverend sir, we are taught that we have no right to throw away our lives in desperate emprises, to the loss and detriment of the British service. And it seems to me that the rule ought to hold in the service of the Cross that sorely needs good soldiers."

The argument struck home, and the old missionary made haste to justify his position.

"There is not more danger than usual," he declared, "I have often heard such threats. I have weathered many such storms. My place is here. I must recall these troubled and wandering sheep that have believed in the truth and trusted in me, and whose faith has this day been so rudely jostled."

"Troubled and wandering—wolves!" Raymond could not help exclaiming, as he noted the furious faces, the menacing gestures of a group here and there colloguing apart, their feathered heads almost touching each other, their drapery of coarse blankets intermingled as they stood together, an absorbed brow lifted now and again to glance at the subject of their conference. The dispensation that the sun shall shine alike upon the just and the unjust seemed more an insensate process of nature than a divine ordinance at that moment as he looked about mechanically in the pause, noting the pellucid brilliance of the noontide splendor that lay over all the wrangling crowd of braves, the huddled huts of the town, the vast stretches of leafless woods that had yet the aspect of winter, the blurred violet tones of the hills hard by, the far-reaching of the myriads of azure ranges, the differing blue of the sky as it bent to meet the horizon. So unwontedly still had been the town during the morning that a drift of white swans lay asleep in the river, close to the moorings of Raymond's pettiaugre. Now, warned by the tumult on shore, they had lifted their heads and were beginning to glide imperceptibly along. A deer, approaching the town on the hither side, had taken sudden affright, and, plunging into the water, was swimming the river so near at hand that its head presented a fair target to the short-range rifles of the day and even for an arrow. No marksman sought the opportunity. The minds of the braves were all intent, undivided. The dogs of the town caught the scent and sight, and half a dozen hounds raced to the water-side, lustily yelping excitement. But there was no human cry of encouragement, no command to hie them on, and though one plunged in and swam twenty yards in the wake of the fleeing animal, he lost heart in thus proceeding on his own initiative, and turning about, came splashing in to the bank, all unnoticed. Significant incidents these trifles seemed to Raymond, showing an absorption that betokened no gentle fate to the old missionary. He marvelled that the old man could be so mad. He determined on a renewed effort.

"You could return at a more propitious time, dear sir. And permit me to express my wonder, Mr. Morton," he said, with gentle reproach, "that though you do not entertain fears for yourself, you have no consideration of the fears of your friends for you. Captain Howard, who is a man of great experience on the frontier, thinks your life is not worth an hour's purchase after our departure, and I, myself, who am no alarmist, feel that if we leave you here I look upon you for the last time."

Despite Raymond's self-control, he was greatly harried during this speech by the antics of a young tribesman, who had taken up his position on the other side of Mr. Morton and was reproducing in grisly caricature every word and gesture of the British officer—even to the motions of the cocked hat in his hand. The ensign had uncovered in token of his respect and as he talked he gesticulated, in his earnestness, with the hat. In the florid imitation of mockery the Indian permitted Mr. Morton's hat, which he himself held, to sharply graze, in one of his flourishes, the pallid cheek of the aged minister. It was in effect a buffet, and Raymond gave a quick audible gasp, recovering with difficulty his impassive demeanor.

"My dear young sir," said the old man, "I have stanch friends among these good people, who will not see me evilly entreated. I cannot put aside—I cannot postpone the Lord's work to a more convenient season. I must remain—I must repair the damage to the faith of these new Christians done by their chief's crafty cross-questioning of the commandant to-day. I must not leave my sheep to the lion, the weaklings of all my flock to the ravening wolves of doubt. I must be with them—but have no fears for me. I have twice been bound to the stake, and yet came safely off."

Raymond was at his wits' end. There was a shifting in the crowds. They were converging down the sunny slope toward the river-bank. Beyond their heads he caught a gleam of scarlet against the shining current, near the white flashing of the swans' wings as the great birds rose in flight. The soldiers were embarking. There came to his ears the loud, guttural voice of the chief of the town, Rolloweh, pronouncing the sonorous periods of his official farewell to Captain Howard. Time pressed. The response of the captain would be curt and concise,—there was scant utility to mint phrases for Rolloweh,—and Raymond could well divine that the commandant was sick at heart. On the smooth spaces of the "beloved square" there lingered those inimical plotting groups, still whispering, still casting speculative glances at the missionary and the ensign, still waiting, Raymond faithfully believed, to seize the old man and bear him to his doom, before the English boats should be a furlong down the river.

The ensign's patience, never a formidable endowment, gave way suddenly. He clapped his hat on his head with a nonchalant flap. He turned a burning eye on two stalwart young soldiers of his escort and spoke but one short phrase, with a significant gesture. The intelligent fellows comprehended the extraordinary order in an instant. With light willing steps they ran forward, bent down, seized the Reverend Mr. Morton in their strong young arms, lifted him bodily, and at a swift, sure, steady run they set out with their captive for the river-bank, their young officer close on their heels calling out in Cherokee, with glad bursts of laughter, "The 'beloved man' shall be removed!"

The whole community was in an uproar. The culmination came so suddenly, with no sort of warning, that the crowds by the water-side, remembering the urgency of the chiefs that the "beloved man" should be removed, fell in with the apparent spirit of the exploit and shouted and laughed as at some rude jest and boisterous horse-play. The conspirators of the "beloved square" did not catch the significance of the incident for one brief moment of stunned surprise, roused as they were from the absorptions of their secret plottings, but though they came howling their baffled rage and vengeance and frenzied protests hard upon Raymond's party, that one moment saved the life of the Reverend Mr. Morton. Their voices were overborne in the joyous clamors of the populace, not yet admitted into the plans of revenge, and chorusing the ensign's jocular mockeries. Raymond, himself standing in the bow of the pettiaugre and urging his crew,—"Push off—Let fall—Back oars—Row—Pull, lads, pull for your lives!" in a half-stifled undertone of excitement, did not feel that the return trip was a possibility till the pettiaugre reached the centre of the shining stream, then turning southward caught the current and began to slip and glide along as fast as oar could ply, and the momentum of the stream could aid. Even then a rifle ball came whizzing past.

"It is nothing," said Captain Howard, reassuringly—"some lawless miscreant. The head-men intend no demonstration."

The plans of the conspirators, divulged in that moment of embarkation, had mightily caught the fancy of the "mad young men" of the assemblage—that class on whom the Cherokee rulers charged the responsibility of all the turmoils and riots, those who fought the battles and endured the hardships, and carried out the treacherous enterprises and marauding massacres which the head-men secretly planned and ordered and abetted. Some who had just been rollicking with laughter came running after the boats along the bank, their breath short, their features swelled with savage rage, their eyes distended with futile ferocity. Some were crying out mockeries, and blasphemies, and furious maledictions on the head of the old missionary, and others, among whom were the conspirators of the "beloved square," were protesting craftily that the missionary was abducted against his will and was to be carried as a prisoner to Fort Prince George—adjuring the commandant to permit him to return and threatening force to stop the boats if he were not immediately set ashore.

"We shall meet them, sir, when we round the bend," said Raymond, in a low voice to Captain Howard, for the river made a deep swirling curve around a considerable peninsula, and a swift runner cutting straight across this tongue of land would have little difficulty in anticipating the passing of the pettiaugre, although the men were bending to the oars with every muscle stretched, and the iterative impact of the strokes was like the rapid ticking of a clock.

As the boats came shooting with an arrowy swiftness around the peninsula, an Indian, the foremost runner, was already there, standing high on a rock. His figure on the promontory, distinct against the blue sky with his hands up-stretched, the palms together, ready to spring and dive, was visible from far off. He looked back over his shoulder to make sure that other Cherokees were following, then timing his adventure with incredible precision, he sprang into the water with a great splash, was invisible a few seconds, and came up alongside the pettiaugre, with a hand on the gunwale, near the bow.

A hundred braves, almost all armed, stood at gaze on the lower banks, a trifle blown by the swift pace, a score or two laying aside their weapons, apparently preparatory to entering the water. The soldiers, well within rifle range, all frontier veterans, young though they were, as obedient and as unmoved as parts of a mechanism, rowed steadily on, disregarding their muskets, stowed in the bottom of the pettiaugre. Only the man nearest the Indian, hanging to the boat, contrived in a lengthened stroke to hit the pendulous legs some heavy covert blows with a feathered oar, which, sooth to say, might have broken less stalwart limbs.

"Ensign," suggested Robin Dora, in the bow, plaintively, "wad it fash your honor gif I dinged that fist a clout wi' ae drum-stick? It's gey close to my shoulther."

"Be silent," said Raymond, severely, and Robin Dora subsided, even ceasing to glance over his shoulder at the uncanny hand so close to his arm.

Captain Howard, in the haste of embarkation had taken his place in Raymond's boat, and his own had fallen under the conduct of the adjutant. It followed like a shadow the craft in the lead, as silent as a shadow, as swift. Captain Howard had not by virtue of his rank assumed command, the crew being already organized. He earnestly desired to provoke no attack from the Indians, but he expected it momently, and fingered his pistols in his belt as he eyed the gathering tribesmen on shore; under these circumstances he was in doubt as to his wisest course; the impunity of the figure clinging to the boat invited recruits, yet to it Raymond gave not a glance. Captain Howard was moved to a comment.

"You give transportation to passengers, Ensign?" he queried.

"It seems so, sir," Raymond replied, succinctly.

It had evidently been the plan of the Indians to send out swimmers to the boats, and demand and secure the return of the missionary on the pretext that he was torn from them against his own desire, and if the crew dared to refuse, despite the coercion of the rifles of the hundreds on shore, the swimmers were to upset the craft, seize their prey, and make for the main body. The leader had far out-stripped his following, and his zeal had jeopardized the practicability of the feat. He had given the little British force the opportunity to make a great display of coolness and indifference. The contempt with which their demonstration was treated disconcerted the Cherokees, who relished naught so much as the terrors their presence was wont to inspire,—the surprise, the agitation, and commotion that were the sequence of their sudden attacks.

The crowd on shore stood at gaze, watching the unexpected scene—the Indian clinging like a reptile to the boat, while its keel cleft the clear brilliant waters, and the silent crew rowed like men spurting for a prize. Suddenly the Indian, belabored possibly beyond endurance by an eccentric oar, made a movement as though he would spring into the boat. Raymond swiftly leaned forward, and with a courteous manner, as of offering aid, caught the Cherokee's arm with a grip like steel, and fairly lifted him into the pettiaugre.

The Indian stood for a moment, staring at the calm faces of his enemies. Had he been fifty instead of one the matter might have resulted far more seriously, but his fellows had not followed; their plans had not matured; they stood doubtful, watching the results of his effort and its futility, for he was going straight down the river as a prisoner to Fort Prince George. He looked bewildered, agitated, glanced wildly from one to another, then as if fearing detention leaped high into the air, fell into the water, and struck out for the shore as fast as his limbs might carry him, while the tribesmen on the bank, whom he had expected to lead, burst into derisive cries, and laughter, and gay buffoonery.

It was the turn of the tide; it was the trifle that so often broke the designs of the inconstant Indians. The two officers knew that the game was played out when they heard, far up-stream, so fast was their progress, the shouts of raillery and ridicule as the adventurous wight waded ashore.

"Very well managed, Ensign Raymond," said Captain Howard, laughing with comfortable reassurance. "It might have been much more serious."

"But is this well, Captain Howard?" said the deep melancholy voice of the missionary. "I am a British subject. I have done naught to forfeit my independence of action, my liberty. I am made a prisoner, and torn from my sacred work and my chosen habitation against my will. I am in no sense within your jurisdiction or under your control as commandant of Fort Prince George, and I protest against this infringement of my rights as most unwarrantable tyranny."

Captain Howard, who happened to be standing in the pettiaugre, and being a landsman had no sea legs to speak of, toppled to and fro in his surprise and agitation, and had he not fallen instead against the bulk of a tall and burly oarsman he might have fallen overboard. He hastened to place himself on a seat, and then, red-faced, dumbfounded, and sputtering with half a dozen phrases that tumbled over each other in his amazement he exclaimed:—

"My God! sir, do I understand you? Can I believe my ears? Are you not with us now by your own free will, the exercise of your own mature judgment?"

"Indeed, no, sir, as I have already stated," said the old man, with dignity. "Did you not see, sir, that I was literally carried to the boat in the arms of soldiers under the command of your own officer?"

"By God Almighty, sir," declared the agitated commandant, "I swear when I saw you carried in the arms of the soldiers I supposed it was in a measure to shield you from the fury and malevolence of the Indians. Ensign Raymond," he turned upon the young officer, who was calm enough to stand steadily, "you shall answer for this. I empowered you only to invite, to persuade Mr. Morton to come with us."

"And I did persuade him, sir," Raymond stoutly averred.

"Do you define 'persuasion' as the kidnapping of a minister of God? Damme, but you shall answer for this!"

"I am more than willing, sir, to endure any punishment that I may have deserved," Raymond replied, downcast and dreary. It seemed to him that he was now always under the ban of reprimand. "But to leave Mr. Morton there was to my mind like committing murder on a minister of God when I have the means to bring him away."

Captain Howard had a sudden recollection of the faces of hate and craft, the frenzied foolish reasoning, the fateful ferocity of temperament. He shuddered even yet for the old man's sake.

"You ought to have had the reverend gentleman's consent," he said more mildly.

"It is hard to be old and poor, and of no earthly consideration," plained the old man. "My consent was very easily dispensed with. But—I *am* a British subject!"

"He ought to have *given* his consent," Raymond boldly replied to Captain Howard, "and saved one who only sought to do him kindness from the necessity of incurring ignominy for his sake. But I care not," he continued, doggedly, tossing his head in its cocked hat. "I should liefer have taken his life, old and gray as he is, than have left him where he stood, if art, or force, or persuasion failed to get him away. No—no, I could not leave him there—if I am to be broke for it!" he declared with passion.

The generous temper of the old missionary was reasserted, although the smart in his heart for his deserted Indian sheep was keen. He looked up wistfully, anxiously, at the young officer who stood in the shadow of discipline, of professional ruin, perhaps, on his account. Oh, it was not his mission to wound, to drag down; but to bind up, to assuage, to save. He spoke suddenly and with a different intonation.

"You intended a benefit, doubtless, young sir. You urged me first with every argument in your power, I admit. You found it hard and not without danger to yourself to persist so long, till indeed the very moment of departure. You shall incur no rebuke nor ignominy on my account. Your methods of 'persuasion,' it is true, are somewhat arbitrary," he added with a wintry smile. "But, Captain Howard, I call you to witness—and soldiers, bear witness, too—I accompany this expedition of my own free will, for doubtless the commandant, after what he has said, would put me ashore if I so desired. I am going to Fort Prince George on the invitation of the commandant very thankfully, and I am grateful to this kind young man for 'persuading' me."

He held out his hand to Raymond, who was still standing. The ensign was startled by this sudden change, and touched by the look in the old man's face. He made haste to offer his hand in response, and sank down on one knee beside the seat to obviate the distance between them. Suddenly Raymond became aware of that which in the stress of the embarkation and the unusual excitement of their progress down the river had escaped the notice both of officers and soldiers—the fact that in the rapid progress across the "beloved square" some heavy missile unnoticed in the mêlée had inflicted a severe bruise and cut on the face of the old man; a livid line, ghastly and lacerated, extended almost from brow to chin. It had bled freely, and wisps of the thin gray hair were matted upon the wrinkled brow, even more pallid than its wont, for the shock had been severe, inducing for some little time a state of semi-insensibility.

At the sight of this Raymond cried out sharply, as if he, himself, had been struck; the blood surged swiftly into his face; his heart beat almost to suffocation; he looked piteously into the faded, gentle eyes, full of that sanctity which hallows a stainless old age. The sense of sacrilege and horror overcame him.

"Those fiends have wounded you!" he exclaimed, in the low, appalled, staccato tones of intense excitement. Suddenly his eyes filled, and hiding his face against the worn sleeve of the old clergyman's coat, he burst into a flood of tears, his shoulders shaking with his sobs.

Captain Howard stared in blunt and absolute amaze, but Mr. Morton, better accustomed to ebullitions of emotion, only gently patted the soldier's scarlet coat as if he were a child.

"I hope you will be more careful how you persuade people after this," said the commandant, with the manner of improving a moral lesson. Now, however, that Captain Howard had recovered somewhat from the shock of the interference with the liberty of a British subject, he was disposed to congratulate himself on the fact that he had the missionary hard and fast in the boat, and to think that Raymond had conducted himself in a dilemma almost insoluble with extraordinary promptitude, resource, and nerve, and to be rather proud of the subaltern's ready aplomb.

As to the tears—they were incomprehensible to Captain Howard, and by the rank and file they were deemed a disgrace to the service. The soldiers could not enter into Raymond's complex emotions, and they were at once the source of wonder and disparagement.

When the discipline which had prevailed at the outset was somewhat relaxed, and the men at the rowlocks, still pulling steadily down the river, were free to talk in subdued voices, the events of the day were canvassed with much spirit. The personality of various Indians was discussed, certain parties from the upper towns were recognized by soldiers who had seen more than one campaign in this region, the jeopardy of the occasion was argued, individual experiences narrated, threats that had been overheard were repeated, and it was agreed that the ensign's little party had been in great danger during the progress of the "persuasion"—they all grinned at the word. Then one of the young giants who had performed the feat of abduction, remarked—"But I always feel safe with the ensign. Somehow he allus gits the short cuts."

"I did too—*thin*; more fool, me! Begorra, I niver dhramed he was such a blasted babby!"

They giggled at the word, and when their rations were served, it was pleasant to old Mr. Morton and the officers to see such hilarity among the honest fellows. They could not divine the men were badgering the quarter-master-sergeant from time to time to know why no "sago-gruel" or "sugar-sops" had been provided for the nourishment of the "babby" they had in command, and threatening to report the deficiency to Captain Howard.

Raymond had recovered his serenity. He had snatched up the hat of the old missionary, when the mimicking Indian had tossed it on the ground, and now he tenderly helped him to adjust it. As the boat glided on into the sunset waters, enriched with the largess of the sunset sky, and the tranquil evening came on apace, and the shadows leaned far across the western bank, the subjects that allured the old man's mind reasserted their fascination, and he talked on with placid pleasure of the Hebraic origin of the Indians, their possible identity with the "Lost Tribes," the curious similarity of certain of their religious observances with the rites of the Mosaic dispensation, and cognate themes, while Raymond punctiliously listened, and Captain Howard dozed and nodded with no more compunction than if he were in church.

CHAPTER XI

GREAT were the rejoicings at Fort Prince George when the two pettiaugres pulled in with the tidings that as yet the peace of the frontier was unthreatened. The handful of troops that had garrisoned the British fort on the verge of the Cherokee country had endured their exile, the hardships of savage warfare, the peculiar dangers that menaced them, the rude conditions of their environment with a sturdy fortitude, a soldierly courage, and a long patience. But now that their return to the provinces was imminent, preparations under way for the evacuation of the post, marching orders expected by every express, they could scarcely await, day by day, the approaching event. They jealously scanned every current incident lest a reason for a postponement lurk therein; they canvassed every item of news from the Indian country for signs of uprising; they took cognizance of the personal traits of the men of influence among the Cherokees, and in the guard-room and the galleries of the barracks theorized and collogued together on their mischief-making proclivities,—all as these tended to affect the liberation from the wilderness. Some of the soldiers were pathetically pessimistic, and thought death or accident would frustrate their participation in the joyous exodus. "I'm feared *something* will happen," one protested. "I'm fairly feared to cross the level parade, lest I fall down on it and break my neck." And a forlorn wight in hospital, who had known serious wounds, and the torture of the small-pox, and the anguish of a broken limb, suffering now from a touch of malarial fever, earnestly besought the chirurgeon daily to be frank with him and let him know if his early demise would keep him here forever.

Mervyn did not share the general eager anticipation of the return of the expedition, and he deprecated greatly that Raymond should have been at the commandant's ear before he, himself, should have the opportunity to report the destruction of the granary. That the ensign would make the most of his supposed dereliction in the matter he did not doubt. Since he had regained his composure and recouped his self-esteem by the favorable reception of his suit by Miss Howard, he had begun to realize that he had let his wounded vanity carry him too far in his antagonism toward Raymond. In the vexatious little contretemps on the occasion of the dinner of welcome, when, like an egregious coxcomb, he had seemed to expect that her next words would be a practical avowal of her preference for him, he had detected both divination and ridicule in Raymond's eyes. But this was an untenable cause of quarrel. He had fallen, instead, upon the omissions of the guard report, and he began to be painfully aware that if Captain Howard knew that this information, on which he had based his report, had come to him merely through the gossip of his groom, *he* would have received the reprimand instead of Raymond. He was particularly pleasant to Jerrold, with that gracious unbending of the rich and highly placed, as if in the main values of humanity these fortuitous conditions count not at all. But Lieutenant Jerrold was well aware that as officer of the day he had fought the fire and saved the fort in the absence of the acting commander, and he had none of the fine-spun generosities of Raymond's character to induce him to disregard either a nettling fact or an actual fault. He, too, was bland and inscrutable, and Mervyn could not for his life divine whether Captain Howard would be satisfied with the cursory report of his captain-lieutenant, or would he scan the reports of each tour of service during his absence on the expedition.

To Mervyn's amazement, the commandant met at the gates of Fort Prince George the first intimation of the burning of the granary, and the spirit in which Captain Howard received it might indicate that he expected to live exclusively on Indian meal for the rest of his life. His quick, keen glance as entering, he paused under the archway of the gate, taking a cursory view of the whole place, fell upon a vacancy where the gable of the granary used to show from over the sheds of the stables. His eyes widened, the blood surged up into his cheek, he stepped forward two paces.

"My God!" he cried. "Where's the granary, Mervyn?"

The face of the captain-lieutenant flushed. Jerrold and Innis were both standing by, and it was indeed hard that through no fault of his he should be put at so gross a disadvantage.

"The granary is burned, sir," he replied.

"Burned!" volleyed Captain Howard. "Who burned it? Was this negligence?" he demanded, sternly.

Mervyn had a sudden monition that Jerrold and Innis were secretly commenting on the fact which he, himself, was now contemplating with stunned amazement, that Raymond had not made the most of his opportunity to decry the captain-lieutenant with a very valid cause.

"Raymond should have told you," he began.

"Raymond has been busy." Captain Howard nodded his head succinctly.

"I thought he came here expressly for information about the fire."

"I am not asking you why Ensign Raymond did not give me the information he was sent to gather. I happen myself to know why. I ask you how that granary came to be burned?"

"The lightning, sir," said Mervyn, greatly offended by the tone of his superior officer.

"And was it a total loss?" asked Captain Howard.

"A total loss, sir."

Captain Howard set off at a resolute trot toward the charred remains and stood gazing dolorously down at the blackened, fallen heap of timbers and the pile of ashes.

The sound of his familiar voice elicited a responsive whinny of pleasure from within the stables close at hand, where his own charger stood at the manger, unconscious of the possibilities of famine that hung above his high-bred head.

"What are you doing for feed?"

"Buying from the Indians of Keowee Town—paying six prices."

Captain Howard shook his head disconsolately. During the late war the public granaries of the Cherokees had been destroyed by the British commands as punitive measures and the people reduced to the verge of starvation. The scanty crop of the past summer by no means replaced those great hoards of provisions, and in his report as to the store of corn he would have remaining at the time of his departure he had expressed his intention, entirely approved, to bestow it as a parting gift upon the neighboring town of Keowee. Now he, himself, was destitute, and how to forage his force on the march through the wilderness to Charlestown he could not yet imagine.

Suddenly—"How did the horses stand it?" Mervyn thought the ordeal would never end. To answer in his capacity as captain-lieutenant, temporarily in command, these strict queries in the presence of men who knew that he had seen naught of the event tried his nerve, his discretion, his ingenuity to the utmost. He revolted at the mere simulacrum of a deception, and yet he desired to report the matter to Captain Howard when they should not be at hand to hear his superior officer's blunt comments. He felt that the unlucky chance owed him this slight shield to his pride.

He had naturally expected that his report would be made at the usual time and in the usual manner, when he could explain properly the details and account for his absence with seemliness and dignity. He said to himself that no one could have foreseen that instead of making the official inspection at the regulation time the commandant would be struck on the instant of his arrival by the absence of the granary and fly over the whole place, peering into every nook and squawking with excitement like some old house-keeping hen of a woman. The sight of the vacant place where the granary should have stood seemed to affect his nerves as an apparition might have done. He could not be through quaking over it. Mervyn, however, gave no token of the perturbation that filled his mind as he turned to Jerrold.

"You were at the stables, lieutenant."

"I had considerable trouble with the horses," said Jerrold. "They were terrified, of course, by the noise and glare. I had them led out of the stalls, thinking the stables might take fire."

"Casualties?" sharply asked the captain.

"Oh, none, sir," replied Jerrold, with dapper satisfaction. He had managed with much address an infinite number of details, depending on scanty resources and urgently pressed for time—"Only one horse, a good blood bay, became restive and kicked down his stall and caught his off hind leg in the timbers; somehow, in the mêlée it was broken, and he had to be shot."

"*Only* one horse," Captain Howard commented rebukingly. "Are we on the eve of a march? And the war has left hardly a hoof in the whole Cherokee country! Do you expect to foot it to Charlestown?"

Lieutenant Jerrold asserted himself. He wished to marry no one's handsome daughter, and he cared to play Piquet with no one's clever sister. He would be particular not to exceed the bounds of military decorum, and that was his only consideration. He knew that he had exerted himself to the utmost to save the situation, succeeding almost beyond the possibilities, the responsibility of which devolved on another man. "I might well have lost them all, sir. The rain had not begun. The store-house and the armory were both on fire, I had no help at first, for I dared not call off the main guard—you had twenty stout fellows in the boats—and the rest of the men were asleep in barracks; some of them were pulled out of bed by the heels. By your leave, Captain, one horse is a small tribute to pay to such a lordly conflagration as that."

The commandant, open to conviction, nodded his head meditatively. Mervyn wondered if he had not noticed the personal pronoun so obtrusive in Jerrold's account of the measures he had taken. Mervyn had an ebullition of indignation against himself as he recognized his own inmost thought. He was so proud a man he would fain stand well with himself. Had he not been so cautious a man, so self-conscious, he would at the moment have blurted out the fact of his absence, instead of steeling himself against the waiting expectation, the cynical comment in the eyes of Jerrold and Innis, and postponing the disclosure till he was sure it could come with a good grace. And then the blunt captain! He could not submit his pride to the causticities of Howard's unprepared surprise and brusque comments. He would say things for which he would be sorry afterward, for which Mervyn would be more sorry, and particularly that Jerrold and Innis should hear them. He was angry with himself, nevertheless, that he should give a galvanic start as

Captain Howard's voice, keyed to surprise and objection, struck smartly on the air.

"Why, that gun, there," he said, waving his arm toward one of the cannon on the nearest bastion—"that gun has been fired!"

For the piece was run back on its chassis and stood as it was left after the alarm. Jerrold made haste to explain that the men who were detailed to the service of this gun—there were only a few regular gunners in the garrison—were with the expedition. Mervyn stipulated that as the absence of a score had left extra duty for the rest of the garrison the position of this gun had happened to be neglected, although it, as well as the rest, had been cleaned and reloaded.

"Reloaded! But why were they discharged?" demanded Captain Howard, with wide eyes.

The sight of the fire naturally attracted the attention of the Indians—Jerrold explained. They came over from Keowee in canoes by scores. He was afraid that they would seize the opportunity of the disaster while all were so busy with the fire to rush the gates. He ordered the sentinels to disperse them, saying the cannon were to be fired to appease the storm gods. Any lie might be excused—there was such a great crowd gathered as near as the counterscarp in front of the gates. "How many Indians had assembled there, do you think, Mervyn?" Jerrold asked with a touch of mischief or malice.

"I don't know; I didn't see them," Mervyn responded, shortly.

Captain Howard was meditating on the details.

"You must have had a devil of a time," he said with emphasis. "Do you know if the ladies were much frightened?"

Mervyn was silent, but Jerrold with his crisp, fresh, capable air was ready to take the word.

"I think they knew nothing of the fire and the Cherokee demonstration till everything was over," he said.

"You did well—you did well!" the commandant declared, addressing no one in particular, and Mervyn, who could hardly say, "It was not I," saw him, with infinite relief, turn presently from the scene of these incidents and take his way toward his own quarters, with a belated monition that it was now in order to greet his waiting family.

There the news met him of the notable capture in his absence, for Mrs. Annandale had learned the particulars from her niece and was herself blissful enough to be translated. In fact, so beaming, so softened, so benign was she, that Captain Howard, more gratified than he would have cared to acknowledge, could not forbear a gibe at her vicarious happiness.

"One would think you were to be the bride, Claudia," he said, laughing in great good-humor.

"With the handsome young husband, and Mervyn Hall, and the Mervyn diamonds! But it's none too good for my treasure—the brightest, the best, the most beautiful and winsome creature that ever stepped!" She put her handkerchief to her eyes, for those sardonic little orbs were full of tears.

"She is—she is indeed!" cried Captain Howard. He felt that no man could be worthy of Arabella.

"But now, *you* must be careful—don't speak as if it is absolutely settled. You know dear Arabella is a bit freakish—"

She would have said—"perverse like you," but for the bliss that curbed her thoughts. But indeed Captain Howard took the alarm on the instant.

"Now, Claudia," he said with earnest, remonstrating eyes, "you are not persuading that child into this rich marriage against her inclinations?"

Mrs. Annandale looked for a moment six feet high—so portentous was her dignity as she drew herself up. "*I*" she said, in freezing accents, "*persuade!*" with an infusion of contempt. "My good sir, *I* knew nothing whatever of his proposal of marriage, till Arabella saw fit to confide in me!"

"I beg pardon, I am sure—" began Captain Howard.

"*I* disregard her inclination—*I* who have sought nothing but her happiness since her mother's death!" said Mrs. Annandale.

"True, true, my sister. And I always gratefully remember this."

He crossed the room, sat down beside her, and took her hand. It was a tiny wrinkled hand, soft and unsubstantial, suggestive of something uncanny,—a mouse or a young chicken, that does not lend itself to hearty pressure. Captain Howard's gingerly touch was more as if he felt her pulse than clasped her hand.

She permitted herself to be reconciled, so benign was her triumph.

"They settled it between them. *I* knew nothing of it. It was during the storm. I was not in here. I went to my room for my sal volatile partly, and partly because I could not, without screaming, see the lightning capering about like a streak of hell turned loose on earth, and when I had done with my vocalizes,"—she could afford to laugh at herself on a fair day like this—"and came back, lo! here were Corydon and Phyllis, smiling at each other, as sentimental as you please!"

Captain Howard laughed with responsive satisfaction. It was a relief to him to know that his beautiful daughter would be so safely settled in the world—that her path would be smoothed by all that wealth and station could give. He had known Mervyn all the young man's life, and his father and grandfather before him, and liked him well. He thought him safe, steady, conservative, of good parts, and a capable officer. Doubtless, however, he would sell out of the army when he should come into the title and estate, and Captain Howard was not sorry for this, despite his own military predilections. He was glad that Arabella's lot should be cast in the pleasant paths of English country life, instead of following the British drumbeat around the world. He was sensible, too, of a great pleasure in the fact that her beauty, her cleverness, her careful education,—for learning was the fad of the day among women of fashion, and Miss Howard added to considerable solid acquirements musical and linguistic accomplishments of no mean order,—would all be conspicuously placed in a setting worthy of their value and calculated to enhance their lustre. She would embellish the station as no Lady Mervyn heretofore had ever graced it. As he sat gazing, half-smiling, into the fire, he could hear echoes from the future—"The beautiful and gifted Lady Mervyn," she would be called; "the clever Lady Mervyn,"—"the fascinating and accomplished Lady Mervyn!" Life had been good to her; the most extravagant wishes would be fulfilled—wealth and station, love and beauty, grace and goodness would all be hers. The father's heart swelled with gratification and paternal pride.

"How is she freakish?" he asked, suddenly.

"She will not let it be spoken of as if it were absolutely settled. She says she does not know him well enough. She has every opportunity to make his acquaintance. He is at her feet all the day long."

Only when his daughter herself spoke to him was Captain Howard's satisfaction dashed. He was a blunt, straightforward man, and he did not comprehend subtleties. He only felt them.

"Did Mr. Raymond tell you about the fire?" she asked, apropos of nothing.

When he replied that he had learned of the incident only after he had returned to the fort, she looked at him searchingly, silently, her hazel eyes grave and pondering as she sat beside him on the settle, her hand in his. Then she edged closer and began to pull and plait the bullion fringes of his nearest epaulet, the clumsy decoration of those days, while the white lids and long dark lashes drooped half over her pensive eyes, and a slight flush rose in her cheek.

"Did he really tell you nothing of Mr. Mervyn's dispositions during the fire?"

"He did not mention Mervyn's name," Captain Howard answered, and he was thinking this silence significant—it intimated a sort of professional jealousy on Raymond's part, which was certainly an absurd sentiment to be entertained by an ensign toward the efficiency of a captain-lieutenant—for the management of the fire and the interdependent details had been admirable in every way. It gave Captain Howard special pleasure to commend this management, for he thought that surely if she cared for Mervyn such commendation would please her. Certainly, as he doubtless would leave the army soon, it mattered little now, whether or not he were a capable officer, but the commandant had enough feeling for his profession as the art of war to greatly value efficiency in the abstract, and he had a martinet's stern conviction that whatever a man undertakes to do should be a manly devoir, strictly rendered.

"Mervyn's management of the fire and the demonstration of the Indians was most excellent," he said. "It was an exceedingly difficult and nettling incident. I really should not have been surprised if a band of Cherokees had forced their way into the parade while practically the whole force was busy fighting the fire, and even if the Indians had been actuated by mere curiosity in coming in, serious consequences might have ensued, the place being at their mercy. He showed excellent conduct—excellent."

She stared at him with wide eyes, then her face fell unaccountably.

"And Mr. Raymond said nothing," she faltered.

He did not understand it at the time, and afterward he pondered on the matter in futile irritation. When the formal reports had been presented and Mervyn had stated that in the clamors of the storm he had heard naught of the uproar in the fort, and the officer of the day had met the emergency as best he could, Captain Howard, deeply mortified and greatly disillusioned, cared less for the facts than that they had been so long withheld. It was the business of the officers on duty to deal with the difficulties as they were presented. But he asked Mervyn why he had not mentioned the true state of the case in the presence of Jerrold and Innis, when the matter was being canvassed, since they must have perceived the misunderstanding under which the commandant was permitted to labor, and would draw most unflattering conclusions. "You give those fellows a hank over you," he said, curtly.

He realized this even more definitely afterward when he made his acknowledgments to Jerrold, as he felt bound to do.

"I was under the impression that Captain Mervyn had the conduct of the emergency," he said, in much embarrassment. "You managed it with excellent discretion."

"The men responded with so much good will and alacrity, sir," replied Jerrold, waiving the commendation with an appropriate grace. "We needed hearts and hands rather than a head. They deserve all the credit, for they worked with superhuman energy. And I want to ask you, sir, now that the subject is broached, for some little indulgence for those who were burned in their exertions. No one is much hurt, but I thought some little extra, to show appreciation—"

"By all means—by all means," said the commandant, glad to be quit of the subject.

Captain Howard perceived now that it certainly was not jealousy of Mervyn's exploits which had kept his name from Raymond's lips, and he returned unavailingly to his daughter's strict questions as to the young ensign's silence on the subject, and her look of pondering perturbation at his answer. He wondered, too, why Raymond should have maintained this silence on a theme calculated to be of most peculiar relish to him, considering the acrimonious disposition which Mervyn had shown in reporting so trifling an omission in the guard report, necessitating a reprimand, while Mervyn's own lapse, without being his fault in any way, was of a semi-ludicrous savor, which was not in the least diminished by his own self-conscious efforts to ignore it. He sent a glance of covert speculation now and again toward Raymond in the days that ensued as the young man came and went in the routine duties of garrison life, but saw him no more in his own parlor, and several times Arabella openly asked what had become of Ensign Raymond.

Despite the fact that she had imperiously declared she would let nothing be considered settled, Mervyn had contrived to give the impression to the officers of the garrison that his suit had won acceptance with Miss Howard. Thus it came about that when these two walked on the ramparts together on a fair afternoon, or when lights began to glimmer from the parlor windows in the purple dusk, there was a realization in the mess-room that the welcome might be scant even for well-meaning intruders, so in those precincts the cards were cut for Loo, and the punch was brewed, and the evening spent much as before there was ever a lovely lady and a lute's sweet vibrations to gladden the air at Fort Prince George.

Mrs. Annandale artfully fired the girl's pride. Her lover with a mingled delicacy and fervor expended his whole heart in homage. With a dutiful throb of pleasure she marked the tender content in her father's face, and these quiet days in the citadel of the old frontier fort ought to have been the happiest of her life—but yet—she wondered at Raymond's silence! It was too signal a disaster in the estimation of a military man—that a garrison should fight for their lives and shelter while their commander, for whatever cause, was perdu—for the ensign to have forgotten to mention it. Was he so magnanimous? Her eyes dwelt on the fire wistfully. This was not a grace that Mervyn fostered. Why did Raymond come no more? Sometimes she looked out of the window on the parade to mark when he passed. Once in a flutter and a flurry, when she would not take time to think, she threw a fur wrap about her, drawn half over her head, and stole out with Norah, wrapped in a blanket shawl, and stood in a corner of the bastion beside the ramp that ascended to the barbette, and watched him as he put the troops through the manual exercise on the parade. He noticed neither of them. He was absorbed in his work—they might both have been the laundry-maids. Arabella was afraid of her aunt's keen questions that night in Mrs. Annandale's bedroom when Norah broke forth with her gossip of the garrison and her comments on the drill.

"Oh, faix, mem, an' it would gladden the heart av yez ter see how nimble the men do sthep when the drum rowls out so grand! I wonder yez don't come wid me an' our young leddy to look at them, sure!"

"It will do *you* no good to look at the men, and for me to look at them will do *them* no good. And a sure way to make them step nimble is to set a mob of red-skins after them—push up that stool, girl. Art you going to set my silk stocking on the rough stone?"

"An' shure it's that hot," declared the plump, good-natured Norah, trying its temperature with her hand, "it might bur-rn the wee, dilikit fut av yez, mem."

She adjusted the stool and recommenced.

"Shure, mem, I doesn't belave thim gossoons would run fur red-skins at their heels—the lave of 'em are Oirish!"

"And they haven't got sense enough to run," commented the mistress. "What d'ye peel my hose that way for, you vixen—you'll take the skin as well as the stocking!"

"An' they does the goose-sthep mos' beautiful, mem, an' mark time illigint. But that was for punishment,—caught in Keowee Town, gambling wid the Injuns. Larry O'Grady an' a shquad war kep at ut, mem, for hours by Ensign Raymond's ordhers, Pat Gilligan tould me, till they wuz fit to shed tears."

"Shed tears—the hardened wretches!" said Mrs. Annandale, interested nevertheless, *faute de mieux*, in the simple annals of the garrison. For the days were monotonous, and even Arabella, who one might deem had much to think of, were it only to join George Mervyn in planning the alterations at Mervyn Hall and the details of her future reign, lingered to listen beside her aunt's fire, lounging in a great chair, dressed in faint blue, and slipping languidly from one hand to the other her necklace of pearls, her beautiful eyes a little distrait, a little sad, it might seem, fixed on the glowing coals.

"Shure, mem, weepin' is all the fashion in the garrison now. Since Ensign Raymond shed tears in public the tale of it tickles the men so that if a finger be p'inted at one of 'em a whole shquad av 'em 'll bust out sobbin' an' wipin' their eyes,—but Sergeant Kelly says if they don't quit ut, be jabbers, he's give 'em something to cry fur."

"You insolent wretch!" squealed Mrs. Annandale, "how dare you say 'be jabbers' in my presence?"

"Shure, mem, 'twuz Sergeant Kelly shpakin'—not me," said Norah, well frightened.

"Sergeant Kelly 'shpakin' here in my room, you limb!"

But Mrs. Annandale could not divert the inquiry—she would fain expunge the very name of Raymond from the rolls.

"How did Ensign Raymond happen to shed tears?" demanded Arabella, stiffly.

"Shure, Miss Arabella, the sojer bhoys does say that whin the ould jontleman preacher-man wouldn't lave the Injuns,—an' it's a quare taste in folks he have got, to be sure,—an' the captain, with the soft heart av him, cudn't abide to lave him there, this young ensign,—though if he didn't hould his head so high, an' look loike he thought he was a lord or a juke, he'd be a most enticin'-faced young man,—he was ordered to pershuade the missionary to come. An' he just shwooped down on the riverend man of God and bodily kidnapped him. I am acquainted with the men that he ordhered to carry the ould jontleman to the boat."

"I think you are acquainted with the whole garrison," snapped Mrs. Annandale.

"Shure, there's but foive other white women in the place, an' they are mostly old and married, an' though I'm not called of a good favor at home I'll pass muster on the frontier," and Norah simpered, and actually tossed her head.

Mrs. Annandale would have preferred dealing with this insubordinate levity, and vanity, and disrespect on the spot to returning to the subject of Raymond, but the question had been Arabella's, and the maid did not wait for its repetition.

"An' when they had got the cr-razy ould loon in the boat—savin' his honor's riverence, but to want to stay wid thim Injuns!—he shpake up pitiful an' said he was ould, an' feeble, an' poor—or they wouldn't have dared to thrate him so! An' Ensign Raymond axed his forgiveness, an' whin he giv it, Ensign Raymond drapped down on one knee, an' laid his head on the ould man's arrm, an' bust into tears! Think o' that, mem! The men all call him now—Ensign Babby!"

Norah lifted a fresh, smiling, plump face and Mrs. Annandale sent up a keen, high cackle of derision. Then she stole a covert glance at her niece. Arabella, too, was smiling as she gazed into the fire—a soft radiance had transfigured her face. Her beautiful eyes were large, gentle, wistful, and—since emotion was the fashion of the hour—they were full of limpid tears, so pure, so clear, that they did not obstruct the smile that shone through them.

Mrs. Annandale was not sentimental herself, but she was familiar with sentiment in others, and its proclivities for the destruction of peace. Aided by the fortuitous circumstances of the man's absence and Mervyn's monopoly of Arabella's society, she had been as thoughtful, as far-sighted, as cautious as if she had custody of the treasure of a kingdom, but she determined that she would be more on her guard hereafter, and never let the mention of the man's name intrude into the conversation. She fell into a rage over her disrobing on slight provocation, and hounded and vilified Norah to her pallet with such rancor that the girl, who had been in high spirits, and felt that she had contributed much this evening to the entertainment of her employer, followed the lachrymose tendencies of the mode, and softly sobbed herself to sleep.

CHAPTER XII

THE next day only it was that, George Mervyn being on duty as officer of the day, Arabella felt a dreary sort of freedom in being alone. A realization that this lassitude, yet sense of relief, was no good augury for her future oppressed her. She said to herself that doubtless when she should be married to him she would soon have less of his society. She knew few marriages in which the devotion was so constant as to grow wearisome; she thought it was because of the intensity of his affection that she felt it a drag. She declared with a sigh that she liked him—she liked him well. She did not realize how much her pride had predisposed her to entertain his protestations, her aunt's artful goadings, her own ambitions, and her inherited disposition to persist, to press forward against resistance, to conquer.

She wanted to be out—away, far from the scenes with which he was associated, apart from the thought of him. She wanted to regain her old identity—to be herself—to feel free.

She was in haste as she donned her bottle-green rokelay, for the weather was keen, and she had a calash of the same dark tint, bordered with brown fur that made a distinct line along the roll of her fair hair above her brow. She went out alone upon the ramparts, walking very swiftly, catching a glimpse through the embrasures, as she severally passed the cannon, of the cold, steel-gray river, the leafless woods bending before the blast, the ranges of mountains, all dull brown or slate-gray save far, so far they hardly seemed real, mere pearl-tinted illusions in the sombre north. She caught her breath in deep quick respirations; she heard how rapidly her footsteps sounded on the hard-beaten red clay. She said that it was exercise she had wanted, the fresh air, to be out, the privilege every creature enjoyed—that bird, an eagle, cleaving the air with his great wings; a party of Indians on the opposite bank, going into the woods in a regular jog-trot, single file; the very garrison dogs; a group of men at the great gate. And suddenly she threw up her arm and hailed this group, for she had recognized her father among them.

She had recognized another—it was Raymond, and she wondered that she had identified him at the distance. The sentinel first perceived her gesture and called Captain Howard's attention. The party paused, stared at the approaching, flying figure on the ramparts, then as she reached a ramp and rushed down the steep incline to the parade they came forward at a fair pace to meet her.

"Lord, papa!" she cried breathlessly, "where are you going? Let me go with you, sir, wherever it is. Truly, sir, I am perishing for a breath of change. I feel as if I have lived in Fort Prince George since America was discovered. Let me go, sir!"

She had him by the arm now, and he was looking down leniently at her.

"You are a spoil-sport, Arabella. You cannot go where we are going, child."

"Then go somewhere else," she insisted. "Sure, sir, I'm not a prisoner of war. Let me through that gate, or I shall die of Fort Prince George."

"We are going to speak to one of the chiefs of Keowee Town about an important matter—feed for the pack animals; we must have feed, you know, or we shall never get away from Fort Prince George."

"Across the river! Oh, bless us and save us, papa, I *must go*. I could sit in the canoe while you bargain, or confer, or what not. You would be near at hand and I should not be afraid."

"It is under the guns of the fort, sir," suggested Raymond.

"Oh, thank you, Mr. Raymond, for the word!" she cried. "Papa, I am going! All for Keowee, follow me!"

As she whisked through the gates the sentinel presented arms ostensibly to the party of officers, but so promptly that it had the savor of a special compliment to her as she passed in the lead. The frozen ground was so hard beneath her flying feet, the wind struck so chill on her cheek, the sparkle in her eyes was so bright, the timbre of her clear, reedy, joyous tones was so youthful, so resonant, that she seemed indeed like some liberated thing. Mervyn's monotonous discourse of himself, his views, his hopes, his experiences, recurred with a sarcastic suggestion to Raymond's mind, albeit he, himself, had entered into these subjects with a fraternal warmth and interest in the days of their devoted friendship, and he reflected that an affectionate feeling for an egotist blunts the sharp point of the obtrusive pronoun.

He was suffering a blended poignancy of pain and pleasure in this unexpected meeting. He had already discovered the depth of his feeling for the commandant's daughter before the expedition to Tamotlee. On his return he had heard the gossip as to the engagement, and realized that his love was hopeless. It had taken a strong hold upon him, and he needed all his courage to sustain the disappointment, the disillusionment, for he had dreamed that he might have found favor, the despair. He told himself sternly that he had been a fool from the beginning. She looked higher, naturally, than an ensign of foot, who had scarcely any resources but his commission,—the meagre pay of a subaltern. The very idea, reasonably considered, was a death-blow to any hope of speedy marriage. As the ensign was of good birth his lowly estate seemed only to illustrate his unworthiness of his distinguished lineage. All the remote ancestral splendors that the Heralds' College could show were of scant worldly utility to an ensign of foot. Nevertheless, he relished the fact that Mervyn had paid him the compliment to be bitterly jealous of him, and he saw in Mrs. Annandale's disingenuous little face that she feared him and his attractions, whatever she might esteem these endowments, beyond measure.

He had told himself that he ought to rejoice in the young lady's good fortune, that she should be so worthily placed; that if Mervyn's wealth and station could serve her interest this would demonstrate a purpose in his creation, hitherto doubtful. He did not deny himself the illogical grudging of this fair creature to Mervyn with an infinite rancor. He had never seemed so unworthy of her as now, failing even in fair words, just dues, which most men contrive to pay. Raymond had held his peace, however, when Mervyn had been bitterly disparaged among the little cluster of brother officers in the mess-hall, and kept away from the commandant's parlor, denying himself even the pleasure of a formal call. It was not well that he should see her, for his own sake—the mere recollection of the contour of her face, the pensive fall of her eyelash, the clear lustre of her eyes, broke his heart, and shook his nerve, and half-maddened his brain. He did not think that she might miss him, might care for his coming. She loved Mervyn, or thought she did, and he, himself, loved her so well as to hope that she might never wear out that illusion. Now, however, that he was with her again, through no volition of his own, mere chance, his heart plunged, his cheek flushed, his poor, denied, famished love renewed its tremors, its vague, vain hopes, its tumultuous delight in her mere presence.

As they crossed the bridge, and passed the counterscarp, and took their way toward the glacis, he hastened to offer his arm to support, after the fashion of the day, the young creature, bounding on so lightly ahead of them, for no woman of quality was esteemed stalwart enough to dispense with man's upholding strength. Reminded thus of etiquette Miss Howard accepted the proffer, and leaning graciously upon him, she somewhat slackened her pace as they crossed the glacis and turned down the slope toward the river.

The animation of the expedition seemed suddenly monopolized by Captain Howard and his colleagues—the quarter-master and the fort-adjutant, discussing loudly ways and means, the respective values of varieties of forage, the possibility of caches of corn among the Indians, their obvious relish of the commandant's destitution when he most needed feed for his pack-trains, and his march in the evacuation of the fort. He had been told more than once how they wished they had now the vast stores burned by the British commander, Colonel Grant, in his furious forays through the Cherokee country two years previous—they would bestow it on the Capteny without money and without price.

Scarcely a word passed between the young people. Arabella, to her amazement, felt her hand so tremble on Raymond's arm that she was constrained to furnish an explanation by a shiver and an exclamation on the chill of the day. She could not understand her own agitation. She felt the silence to be awkward, conscious, yet she dared not speak, lest her voice might falter. He, the dullard, had no divination of her state of mind. It never occurred to him to doubt the truth of the reported engagement. The smug satisfaction which the face of the captain-lieutenant now wore, despite the blight which his military laurels had suffered, was a sufficient confirmation of the truth of the rumor he had set afloat. It never occurred to Raymond that undue persuasion had been exerted upon her—he never dreamed that Mrs. Annandale's meagre little personality stood for a strategist of a subtlety never before seen in the Cherokee country, that she was capable of making the young lady believe herself in love with George Mervyn, and her father accept the fact on his sister's statement. Raymond could but mark the flushed, conscious look now on Arabella's face, the sudden timidity in her downcast eyes, the tremor of her daintily-gloved fingers on his arm. A sudden gust blew a perfumed tress of her waving golden hair over the brown fur and the dark green cloth of her calash, whence it escaped, and thence across his cheek for a moment. Its glitter seemed to blind him. He caught his breath at its touch. But the next moment they had reached the rocky declivity to the river-bank, and he was all assiduity in finding a practicable path amongst the intricacies of ledges and boulders, over which she could have bounded with the sure-footed lightness of a gazelle.

The long stretches of the still, gray river, flecked with white foam, wherever an unseen rock lay submerged beneath its full floods, reflected a sky of like dreary tone. One could see movement above, as the fleecy gray folds, that seemed to overlay a denser medium of darker shade, shifted and overlapped, thickened and receded noiselessly, a ceaseless vibrating current, not unrelated to the joyless, mechanical rippling of the waters. The leafless trees on the banks looked down at their stark reflections in the stream that intensified the riparian glooms—here and there a grim gray promontory of solid rock broke the monotony with an incident not less grave. Mists hung in the air above the conical roofs of the Indian town on the opposite bank, not easily distinguished from the smoke issuing from the smoke-holes, for chimneys they had none. No sound came across the water; the town might have been asleep, deserted, dead. As the party reached the bank a gust came driving through the open avenue of the river, damp with the propinquity of the body of water, shrill with the compression of the air between the wooded banks, and so strong that it almost swept Arabella from her feet, and she clung to Raymond for support. Her father renewed his protests against her venturing forth upon the water—it might rain, if indeed it were not too cold for this,—

and urged her to return to the fort, and await a fair day for an excursion on the river.

In reply she pertinently reminded him that this was no time to deny her whims, when she had come out all the way from England to visit him. Indeed, she did not wait for a denial. She stepped instantly into the boat as soon as the soldiers who were to row had taken their oars and brought it alongside, and as she seated herself in the stern, Captain Howard could only console his fears for her safety by wrapping her snugly in a great fur mantle and listening to her feats of prowess as she was good enough to detail them.

Apparently she had suddenly found all her facility in words, mute as she had been during the walk, and it seemed to Raymond, as he wistfully eyed her from the opposite seat, that she had said nothing then because she had nothing to say to him.

"Sure, papa, I'm neither sugar nor salt. I shan't melt, except into tears for your cruelties. I am not such a dainty, flimsy piece of dimity as all that comes to. Why, when we crossed the sea every soul on board was sick—except *me* and the men that worked the ship. And there was wind, no capful like this, but blowing great guns—and water! the waves went all over us—the water came into the cabin. Aunt Claudia said she hoped we would sink; she would give all she possessed to be still one moment on the bottom of the ocean. And while she was helpless I staid on deck and advised the ship's captain. He said he had *heard* of mermaids, but I was the first he had ever *seen*! Oh, he was very gallant, was the sea-captain, and made me a fine lot of compliments. And did I expect to be cooped up in Fort Prince George, as if it were in blockade!"

Captain Howard rather winced at the word, and thought ruefully of the lack of corn, and the coming of his marching orders.

"I expected to ride, papa. I thought you might lend me a mount some day—"

"Permit me to offer you a horse of mine that might carry a lady fairly well—" Raymond began, for among his few possessions he owned several choice animals which he had bought very young from the Indians. The Cherokees boasted at that day some exceedingly fine horses, supposed to be descendants of the Spanish barbs of De Soto's expedition through that region. Raymond was an excellent judge and had selected young creatures at a low valuation at one of the sales when the Indians had driven down a herd to barter with the ranchmen of the pastoral country further to the south. His cheek flushed, his eye flashed with a sudden accession of joyful anticipation—but Captain Howard shook his head. He was not so secure in the peace of the frontier as he had earlier been. Certain incidents of the expedition to Little Tamotlee were not reassuring. He would hardly have trusted his daughter out for a canter along the smooth reaches of the "trading-path," as the road was called that passed Fort Prince George to the upper country, or the trail the soldiers made in the forest for fuel supplies, even could he have detailed half the garrison as her escort. Only the guns of Fort Prince George he now considered adequate protection—not because of their special efficiency, but solely because of the terrors of artillery which the Indians felt, and could never overcome.

"Why, papa—when I have ridden cross-country to hounds, and twice in Scotland I was in at the death! Papa—*why, papa*! are you afraid I would fall off the pony?" she demanded, with such a glance of deprecation and mortified pride that it was hard for her father not to express the true reason for his withheld consent. But as commandant of the garrison he could not acquaint the two soldiers who rowed the boat, and through them the rest of the force, with his fears for the permanence of the peace on the frontier, and his doubts as to their speedy departure. Now that the period of their exile had been placed, and that they were in sight of home, as it were, they could hardly wait a day longer, and trained and tried and true as they were, he might well have feared a mutiny, had an inopportune suggestion of delay or doubt grown rife amongst them. He hesitated and cleared his throat, and seemed about to speak, then turned and glanced over his shoulder at Keowee Town, still lying apparently asleep. If the approach of the boat had been noted, the municipality gave no sign, whether from some queer savage reason, or disfavor to the visitors, or simply a freak of affectation, he did not care to think. He was acutely conscious of the face dearest to him in the world, downcast, deprecating, and flushed, appealing to him when he could not speak.

"Oh, I know you are a monstrous fine horsewoman—" he began extravagantly, "but there is no road."

"And now I know you are laughing at me, papa," she said, with dignity, "and I thought you were proud of my riding so well,"—with a little plangent inflection of reproach. "But I left the whole field behind in Scotland—I *was* in at the death, twice—I *can* ride"—with stalwart self-assertion. "And I can shoot—I won the silver arrow at the last archery meet at home!"

"There can surely be no objection to archery, sir," Raymond glanced at the captain, aware in some sort of the nature of his difficulty, and seeking to smooth his way.

"No—no—" said Captain Howard, heartily,—then with a sudden doubt— "except a bow and arrows of a proper size; but I can have these made for you at once—if the Indians are not too lazy, or too sullen, or too disaffected to make them. I will see if I can order a proper weapon at Keowee."

"I have the very thing," exclaimed Raymond, delightedly, "if Miss Howard will do me the honor to accept it. When we were at Tuckaleechee last year, Captain," he said, turning to the commandant, "I secured, for a curiosity, a bow and quiver of arrows which had been made for the Indian king's nephew, who had died before they were finished. Otherwise they would have been buried with him, according to Cherokee etiquette. They are as fine as the Indians can make them, for he was the heir to the throne, following the female line. You know, Miss Howard, here among the Cherokee chiefs the nephew has the right of succession, not the son. This boy was twelve or fourteen years old, and the weapons are of corresponding weight."

"Just the thing," said Captain Howard, cordially,—then with an afterthought,—"but this deprives you of a handsome curiosity, ornamented for royalty. You may *borrow* it, Arabella."

"Oh, but I'd love to *own* it," cried Miss Howard, joyously, with a charming frankness that made the color deepen in Raymond's cheek. "I'll carry it home and shoot with it at the next archery meet. I hope it is very barbaric and splendid in its decorations, Mr. Raymond."

"I think it will not disappoint you," replied Raymond, in a glow of enthusiasm, for it was a choice bit of aboriginal art; the Indians often spent years of labor on the ornamentation of a single weapon. "It carries all the gewgaws that it can without impairing the elasticity of the wood, but the quiver is more gorgeous; the arrows are winged with flamingo feathers, and tipped with crystal quartz."

"Oh," began Arabella—

But her father's admonitions broke in upon her delight. "Those arrows are deadly," he exclaimed, "as hard as steel. And you must be careful how you place your target; you might shoot some animal, or a soldier; you must be careful."

"What a forlorn fate for a soldier—to die by a lady's hand!" she exclaimed.

"Ladies usually shoot by proxy," Raymond said, with a conscious laugh, "and first and last they have done woful execution among soldiers."

"They never shoot by proxy at our club," declared Arabella, densely.

"That's mighty good of them," said her father, laughing a little, as he turned to look at the shore. He ordered the oarsmen to pull in, despite the fact that no signs of life were yet visible about the town.

When, however, the keel grazed the gravelly bank and Captain Howard and his quarter-master and fort-adjutant stepped on shore, there appeared as suddenly as if he had risen from the ground the "second man" of Keowee

Town, attended by three or four of inferior rank, a trifle sullen, very silent, and when he spoke at last, after he had led the way to the municipal booth, or cabin, he was full of ungracious excuses for the non-appearance of the chief to greet the English Capteny. He had thought the boat held only the quarter-master, the fort's "second man"—"Confound his impudence!" interpolated that officer, an observation which the discreet interpreter did not see fit to repeat,—the fort's "second man," come to beg for corn. The British, he continued, were pleased to call the Indians beggars, but no mendicant that he had ever heard whine could whine as the fort's "second man" whined when he begged for corn.

It was well for the fort's "second man" that he was already seated on a buffalo rug on the ground, his legs doubled up, tailor-wise, in front of him, or he might have fallen to the earth in his sputtering indignation. His rubicund, round face grew scarlet. Portly as he was already he seemed puffed up with rage, and his features visibly swelled as he retorted.—Had he not offered the Frog to pay the town in golden guineas for the corn—he had not begged; he had asked to purchase.

Walasi, the Frog, shook his head. Of what good were English guineas to people who had no corn. Corn was more precious than gold—could he plant those golden guineas of the fort's "second man," and make corn? Could horses eat guineas?

"No," said the fort's "second man," "but asses could, and did."

Whereupon the Keowee "second man" said the fort's "second man" spake in riddles, and relapsed into silence.

Thus brought to a dead-lock the quarter-master looked appealingly at the commandant, who, albeit sensible of the discourtesy offered him by the non-appearance of the chief, and his derogation of dignity in conferring with a "second man," came to his subordinate's relief.

The British officer did not wish to inconvenience the town of Keowee in any manner, he said, and regretted much that their visits were not welcome. Whereupon the Frog showed visible uneasiness, for with the Cherokees hospitality was the very first and foremost virtue, and for it to be impugned was a reflection upon the town. He hastened to say volubly that the beloved Capteny was much mistaken; the chief's heart was wrung not to take him by his noble hand. But they had feared—they much deprecated that the British Capteny had come, too, to *beg*—to beg for corn; and it would wrench the very soul of the chief of Keowee to refuse him aught.

"The chief is fortunate to be so well furnished with gold as to throw it away," said Captain Howard.

That the Frog had learned somewhat in his intercourse with the commercial French who, with covert strategy, had plied a brisk trade with the Indians despite their treaty with the British, was evidenced in the shrug with which he declared he could not say. The Indian wanted little—he wanted his own corn—that was all. It belonged to him—he asked for no man's gold.

Captain Howard was at a loss. The military resource of the seizing of supplies was impracticable since the treaty of peace. The British government owned merely the ground on which Fort Loudon and Fort Prince George stood, and a right of way to those works. Moreover, with his small force the measure was impossible. Therefore it was indeed necessary to beg for corn at six—nay, ten prices, in English gold. He sat for a few moments, gazing absently at the prospect, the austere wintry mountains under the gray sky, the illimitable, leafless wilderness, the shining line of the river that caught and focussed such chill light as the day vouchsafed, the bastions and flying flag of Fort Prince George on the opposite bank, and close in to the hither side the brilliant fleck of color that the scarlet coats of the oarsmen and Ensign Raymond gave to the scene, as sombre, otherwise, as a sketch in sepia. He noted that the rowers had thrust out from the shore five or six oars' length, perhaps, and that they now and again gently dipped their oars to keep the craft at a fixed distance and obviate drifting with the current. The people of Keowee Town were not altogether proof against curiosity. From the vantage ground of the second men's cabin Captain Howard could see stealthy figures, chiefly of women and children, peering out from doors or skulking behind bushes, all eyes directed toward the shallop rocking in a steely gleam of light aslant upon a steely ripple of water, the only vivid chromatic tone in the neutral tinted scene.

There is a certain temperament which is incapable of sustaining success. It may cope with difficulty or it may endure disaster. But a degree of prosperity destroys its values, annuls good judgment, and distorts the perspective of all the world in the range of vision. The British Captain was at his wits' end. He had no corn, and if none were to be bought he could get no corn. Few people have shared the Frog's pleasure of seeing their victorious enemies the victims of so insoluble a problem. The declination of the chief of Keowee to receive the magnate from across the river was in itself a blow to pride, an insult, a flout, as contemptuous as might be devised. But as a matter of policy it was an error. If it had been a question of crops, a démêlé with a neighboring town, a matter of boundary, the selection of timbers for building purposes, no man could have acted with finer judgment than Walasi, the Frog. But he was a Cherokee and he hated the British Capteny with rancor. He must twist the knife in the wound, already gaping wide with anguish for the famishing stock. He assumed an air of reproach, and knowing even as he spoke that he transcended politic monitions, he stipulated that it was but the accident of the Capteny's absence at Tamotlee which had precipitated disaster. When the Indians at Keowee had beheld the flames of the granary they had rushed to the assistance of their neighbors, the soldiers. Many hands do much work. But the great gates were closed against them, and when the Cherokees approached, he declared, the cannon were fired upon them from the fort, and many great balls rolled along, and popped hissing hot into the river. And it was only on account of the defective aim of the garrison that any were now left alive. And their hearts had become very poor because of their despised friendship. But cannon there were in the Cherokee nation!—and, he boasted, some day the garrison of Fort Prince George would hear, and shake with fear to hear, the loud whooping from out their throats, and the deep rumble of their howls; and would see, and be dazzled with terror to see, the fire come whizzing out of their muzzles with red-hot balls—but—but—

Walasi, the Frog, suddenly became aware that it was a very intent and steadfast gaze in the commandant's eyes, as he sat and listened, spell-bound. And he, Walasi, who dealt only with crops, and houses, and town politics, who had never been either warrior or councillor, was conscious that he had gone too far in a position of trust beyond his deserts, and above his condition. The insult to Captain Howard in setting a second man to confer with him had developed a double-edged sharpness.

"But—but," the Frog continued, "the good Capteny whom all loved would not be among them. None wished to harm the beloved Capteny."

He paused again, staring in anxiety, for the intent look on the good Capteny's face had vanished. He was shaking his head in melancholy negation.

"No, my good Walasi, no one here loves the Capteny. I am gone to visit my friend, the chief of Tamotlee, and my mad young men burn my granary and fool with my cannon—you have cannon, you say? But no,—I cannot stop to talk of cannon! I think of corn—corn—corn! And for gold you will let me have no corn. And the chief of Keowee will not see me!"

The eye-lashes of Walasi, the Frog, rose and fell so fast that he seemed blinking for some moments. He had said too much, but to obliterate the recollection in the British Capteny's mind it might be well to interest him anew in corn—to keep him anxious and returning; he would not then have time or inclination to recur to the question of cannon—the unwary Frog felt that he had indeed said too much—but he was only a "second man," and should not be set to deal with a capteny of the British.

The policy of sharing their corn had been doubted by the head-men. But he would take the responsibility to send—say a laden pettiaugre.

"Damme, Walasi! *one* pettiaugre!" cried Captain Howard, reproachfully.

"For to-day—another time, perhaps. But the heart of Keowee is very poor to deny the British Capteny, whom it loves like a brother, *one* pettiaugre."

There was a great telling out and chinking of gold in the second man's sanctum, and presently a dozen stalwart tribesmen were carrying the corn in large baskets to the pettiaugre, coming and going in endless procession in this slow method of loading. Captain Howard, resolutely mustering his patience, watched the last bushel aboard that the pettiaugre would hold—the craft, indeed, was settling in the water when he signed to the Indian boatmen to pole it across. Then he took a ceremonious, almost affectionate leave of Walasi, and walked down to the water's edge with so absorbed and thoughtful a mien that he hardly looked up when his daughter called out to him from the canoe, which was rapidly rowing in to take him aboard; as he stepped over the gunwale and caught her eye he had a dazed look as if just awakened from a revery, or some deep and careful calculation, and he said, bluntly,—"Bless my soul, child, I had forgotten you were here!"

CHAPTER XIII

THOSE with whom life deals liberally are often less grateful than exacting. Any failure of the largest of fate is like withheld deserts or a wanton injury. It is as if they had an inalienable right to expect better usage. It never seems to occur to these favorites of fortune that others have as fair a claim upon the munificence of circumstance, and that but for a cloaked mystery of dispensation they would share equally with their fellows. Thus a disconcerting chance or a temporary obstacle rouses no disposition to measure strength with adversity, or to cope with untoward combinations, but an angry amazement, an indignant displeasure, a sense of trespass upon one's lawful domain of success and happiness that result in blundering egotistic self-assertion, which often fails in the clearance of the obstruction to the paths of bland and self-satisfied progress.

Mervyn, chancing to glance down from the block-house tower whither he had repaired shortly before sunset on his rounds, to see that the sentinels were properly posted and that they had the countersign correctly, was not only dismayed but affronted to perceive walking briskly up the slope from the river-bank Captain Howard, the quarter-master, the fort-adjutant, and following them at a leisurely pace Ensign Raymond, with Miss Howard on his arm. They were conversing earnestly; her face was full of interest as he spoke. Now and then she glanced up at him, as if with a question; the glow of the west rested in a transfiguring halo about her head, her golden hair showing beneath the dark green calash. In the setting of the bleak, cold day her face was as illumined as a saint's. A band of dull red was about the horizon above the sombre wooded mountains, promising fairer skies for the morrow, and now and then, through some translucence of the clouds a chill white sheen spread over the landscape less like sunlight than moonbeams. Still gazing at the two Mervyn marked that Arabella noted this aspect, and called her companion's attention to the abnormal quality of its glister.

"That is like 'the sleeping sun,'" she said. "How quaint is that idea of the Indians—how poetic, that the moon is but the sun asleep!"

"This, though, is 'the sun awake in the day.' *Nu-da-ige-hi!*" he explained.

She repeated the phrase after him. "And 'the sleeping sun'?"

"*Nu-da-su-na-ye-hi,*" he replied.

She paused to repeat both phrases anew, smiling like a docile child, learning a lesson.

At the distance, of course, Mervyn could not hear the words, but the responsive smiles, the obvious mutual interest, the graceful attitudes of the two as she once more took Raymond's arm and they walked slowly on toward the gate—each phase of the scene was charged with a signal irritation to his pride, his nerves, his intense self-consciousness. He was angry with her; why should she seek solace for his absence in jaunting abroad? He was angry with her father for granting her this opportunity. He could not imagine why her aunt had not been more insistent in duty—he would have thought it well that she should be penned up in the commandant's parlor sewing her sampler until such time as it was practicable for him to rejoice the dulness by his endless talk of himself—which, indeed, those who loved him would find no burden. He was angry more than all and beyond expression with Raymond, who profited by his enforced absence, and whom he had feared from the beginning as a rival. He knew well the character of the comments of the mess upon his course in pushing the immaterial omission in the matter of the guard report to an extreme limit, and his own reticence afterward concerning his absence from the scene of the fire till it was no longer possible to conceal the circumstance. Captain Howard, himself, had opened his stubborn, reluctant eyes to the repute among his brother officers that this had inflicted upon him. He feared Raymond would acquaint Arabella with their estimate of his part in the incident. He was wild when he thought of the duration of his tour of duty. Till to-morrow he was caught fast, laid by the heels, held to all the observances of the regulations as strictly as if the little frontier mud fort were a fortress of value, garrisoned by thousands of troops. He knew, nevertheless, the special utility of routine here, where the garrison was so weak,—scant a hundred men. The enemy—conquered, indeed, but only by the extraneous aid of a special expeditionary force—was still strong and rancorous, able to throw two thousand warriors against the ramparts in a few hours, but he argued it was farcical to detail the officers to this frequent recurrent duty, albeit appropriate to their rank, when sergeants, corporals, even intelligent privates might be trusted in their stead.

He had been a good soldier, and ordinarily his pulse would have quickened to the partial solution of the feed problem, evidenced shortly by the issuance of the quarter-master's contingent to the unloading of the pettiaugre at the river-bank. The stable men were riding down the horses, harnessed to slides in default of wagons, to bring in the provender; some of them carried great baskets like those of the Indians, but disposed upon the beasts pannier-wise. The loud, gay voices made the dull still dusk ring again. Raymond avoided the great gate whence now and then a horseman, thus cumbrously accoutred, issued as suddenly as if flung from a catapult and went clattering boisterously down to the river-bank. An abrupt encounter under the arch with these plunging wights might not discommode Captain Howard and the quarter-master, but with his fair charge Raymond sought the quieter precincts of the sally-port. There he was detained for the lack of the countersign, and while the sentinel called the corporal the two young people stood, apparently quite content, still softly talking, now and then a rising inflection of their suave tones coming to Mervyn's ear as he lingered in the block-house tower and watched them. They were taking their way presently across the parade to the commandant's quarters, and as Mervyn's eyes followed them thither, he perceived the face of Mrs. Annandale at the window. She looked as Mervyn felt, and as he noted it he winced from the idea that perhaps the chaperon cared for him only for his worldly advantages. He had no mind to be married for these values, he said to himself, indignantly. Then he had a candid monition that he was not in great danger of being married at all—whatever Mrs. Annandale's convictions might be, the young lady had stipulated that nothing was to be considered settled till she knew her own mind—she was yet, she had protested, so little acquainted with him. He had one natural humble impulse, like a lover, to hope that she might never know him better to like him less. The thought cleared the atmosphere of storm. Mrs. Annandale naturally preferred him—why should she not?—and if she had wished to stimulate his devotion she would have set up Raymond, and encouraged him as a rival. He could not imagine that she considered Raymond too formidable for a fictitious lover. A fascinating semblance might merge into a stubborn fact.

Mrs. Annandale met the two excursionists at the door with a most severe countenance of disfavor.

"And where have you been junketing, Miss?" she demanded.

"I have been finding corn for the garrison," Arabella replied, demurely. "I have brought in a whole pettiaugre load."

Mrs. Annandale lifted her gaze to the animated aspect of the parade. A fog hung low, but through it was heard the continual tramp of hoofs, and now and again a laden animal passed swiftly, more than one sending forth shrill neighs of content, obviously aware of the value of this replenishment of the larder and recognizing it as for their own provision. Across the parade and beyond the barracks in the stable precincts lights were flickering and lanterns swaying. One of the large sheds was to serve as granary, and the sound of hammers and nails gave token of some belated arrangements there for the provender.

"And did you think I should be satisfied with that bit of a message that your father sent me through the sentinel at the gate—that he had taken you with him amongst the Indians! Sure, I have had fits on fits!"

"'Twas but to keep in practice, Aunt Claudia," Arabella retorted. "Sure, you could not be afraid that papa is not able to take care of me!"

Mrs. Annandale, in doleful eclipse, looked sourly at Raymond.

"With this gentleman's worshipful assistance," she snapped.

"I am always at her service—and at yours, madam," said Raymond. He bowed profoundly, his cocked hat in his hand almost swept the ground. Mervyn still watching, though the dusk strained his eyes, had little reason to grudge his rival the colloquy that looked so pretty and gracious at the distance.

He contrived to meet Raymond that night in the mess-hall. The dinner was concluded; the place almost deserted, the quarter-master being at the improvised granary, and Jerrold and Innis both on extra duty, the ensign having charge of the pettiaugre still lying half unloaded at the bank, and the lieutenant keeping a cautious surveillance on the parties sent out and their return with the precious commodity.

Raymond had taken down a bow and gayly decorated quiver from the wall, and was examining them critically by the light of the candles on the table. There was a glow of satisfaction on his face and the bright radiance of gratulation in his eyes, for the weapons designed for a royal hand were even more beautiful, and curious, and rare than he had thought; the bow, elastic and strong, wrought to the smoothness of satin, the wood showing an exquisite veining, tipped at each end with polished and glittering quartz, the arrows similarly finished, and winged with scarlet flamingo feathers, the quiver a mass of bead embroideries with dyed porcupine quills and scarlet fringes.

Mervyn stared at him silently for a time, thinking this earnest surveillance might attract his attention and induce him to speak first. But Raymond, thoughtfully murmuring, *sotto voce*,—"'Tell me, maidens, have you seen,'" took no notice of his quondam Damon, save a nod of greeting when Mervyn had entered and sat down on the opposite side of the table.

"What are you going to do with those things?" Mervyn asked. No one can be so brusque as the thoroughly trained. A few weeks ago, however, the question would have savored merely of familiarity, as of boys together. Now, in view of the strained relations subsisting between them, it was so rude as to justify the reply. Raymond lifted his head, stared hard at his brother officer across the table, then answered:—

"What do you suppose?"

Mervyn put his elbow on the table, with his chin in his hand, speaking between his set teeth.

"I will tell you exactly what I suppose. I suppose you are insufferable enough to intend to present them to Miss Howard."

Raymond was obliged to lean backward to be rid of the intervening flame of the candle in order to see his interlocutor, face to face, and the action gave added emphasis to the answer,—"Why, bless me, you are a conjurer!"

"I want you to understand distinctly that I object."

"I shall not take the trouble to understand any objection of yours," declared Raymond.

"I have a right to object to your presumption in offering her any gift. She is engaged to be married to me."

Raymond paled visibly. Then with a sudden return of color he declared, hardily:—

"I should send them to her even if she were already married to you."

"You are insolent and presuming, sir. I object. I forbid it. It will be very unpleasant to her to refuse them."

"I should suppose so," cried Raymond, airily, "since she has already accepted them—this afternoon, in her father's presence."

Mervyn sat dumbfounded. He had not dreamed that she would continue to exercise such free agency as to act in a matter like this without a reference to his wish. And her father—while the distinctions of rank in the army did not hold good in outside society or even in the fraternal association of the mess-room, he could not easily upbraid the commandant of the fort, in years so much his senior, for a failure in his paternal duty, an oblivion of etiquette, of his obligations to his daughter's fiancé and undue encouragement of a possible rival. But why had Captain Howard not given her a caution to refer the matter to his, Mervyn's, preference,—why had he permitted the offer and the acceptance of the gift in his presence. To be sure the weapons were but curios, and of only nominal cost in this region, but to receive anything from Raymond! And then the pitfall into which Mervyn had so resolutely cast himself—how could Raymond do aught but send the gift which the lady had so willingly, so graciously accepted. Raymond's eyes were glancing full of laughter at his sedate objection, his lordly prohibition. The things were already hers!

Not a syllable of speech suggested itself to Mervyn's lips; not a plan of retraction, or withdrawal from the room. He felt an intense relief when Jerrold and Innis came plunging into the hall, full of satisfaction for the accomplishment of the proper bestowal of the corn in the makeshift granary, and their computations of the length of time the quantity secured might by economy be made to last.

"What beauties," said Jerrold, noticing the weapons. "You got these in Tuckaleechee last year, didn't you?"

"And I have presented them to Miss Howard," said Raymond.

"Good! Just the right weight, I should judge. Does she shoot?"

Mervyn sat boiling with rage as he heard Raymond interrogated and answering, from the vantage ground of familiar friendship, these details, all unknown to him, concerning his fiancée.

"Won the silver arrow recently at an archery competition, she tells me."

"Gad! I'd like to see her draw this thing!" And Jerrold pulled the taut line of deer-sinews, noting admiringly the elasticity of the wood as the bow bent and he fitted an arrow in place.

He laid it aside, presently, and turned to the table. "And what is this?" he asked, picking up a bag of bead embroidery, rich and ornate, with long bead fringes, and a stiff bead-wrought handle, like a bail.

"Oh, that's for Mrs. Annandale—I think it must be intended for a tobacco pouch, but it occurred to me she might use it for a knotting-bag, and as a souvenir of the country."

Mervyn silently cursed himself for a fool. Possibly Raymond had naught in mind other than the ordinary civil attentions incumbent in such a situation. He was merely making his compliments to the two ladies, members of the commandant's family, visiting the post under circumstances so unusual. Jerrold evidently thought the selection and presentation of the curios very felicitous, and was obviously racking his brains to devise some equally pretty method of expressing his pleasure and interest in their presence here.

Even the acute Mrs. Annandale viewed the incident in much the same light. The simultaneous appearance of the bow and quiver with the gorgeous little "knotting-bag" seemed only well-devised compliments to the ladies,—guests in the fort,—and she thought it very civil of Mr. Raymond, and said she was glad to have something worth while to take back to Kent to prove she had ever been to America,—she apparently did not rely on her own word.

In truth it was not every day that such things could be picked up here. The Cherokees were growing dull and disheartened. The cheap, tawdry European trifles with which the Indian trade had flooded the country had served to disparage in their estimation their own laborious ornaments and articles of use. When a pipe or a bowl of a kind turned out by millions in a mould, strange and new to their perverted taste, could be bought in an instant of barter, why should they expend two years in the slow cutting of a pipe of moss agate, by the method of friction, rubbing one stone on another; when a bushel of glass beads was to be had for a trifle how should they care to drill holes through tiny cylinders of shell, with a polish that bespoke a lifetime of labor? There could be blankets bought at the traders in lieu of fur robes and braided mantles. Now-a-days, except grease, and paint, and British muskets,—the barrels sawed off as the Indians liked them,—there was little to choose for souvenirs in the Cherokee country.

Arabella was unaccountably disappointed. Not in the weapons, themselves—she cried out in delighted pleasure and astonishment on beholding them. Then, certainly, she did not grudge Mrs. Annandale the trophy of her knotting-bag. But she had felt that he had not intended the present as a mere bit of gallantry, a passing compliment. She had valued the gift because of its thoughtfulness for her pleasure; he had noted the need it filled; it contributed to her entertainment; it came as a personal token from him to her. But now since it was relegated to the category of a compliment to the ladies, along with the knotting-bag which was already blazing in considerable splendor at Mrs. Annandale's side, and lighting up her black satin gown with a very pretty effect, Arabella felt as if she had lost something. A light that the skies had not bestowed on that dark landscape was dying out of the recollection of the day on the river,—she remembered it as it was, with its dull sad monotone of the hills, the gray sky, the cold rippled steel of the waters, and the cutting blasts of the wind. She had returned home all aglow, and now she was cold, and tired, and dispirited; and she wondered that Raymond did not come to play "Whisk" or Quadrille if he desired to make a general compliment to the ladies—and why her father had grown to be such dull company.

For Captain Howard did naught but sit after dinner in his great chair, with his decanter on the table beside him, and his glass of wine untouched in his hand, and stare at the flaming logs in deep revery, agreeing with a nod or an irrelevant word to all his sister might say while she detailed practically the whole history of the county of Kent, not merely since his departure thence, but since indeed it was erected.

Captain Howard, tall, bony, muscular, stout of heart, rude of experience, seemed hardly a man to see visions, but he beheld in the flames of the fire that evening things that were not there.

Cannon in the Cherokee country! How they volleyed and smoked from between the logs of the commandant's fire. Here and there in the brilliant dancing jets he beheld a score of war bonnets. He could see quick figures circle, leap, and turn again in the lithe writhings of the protean shadow and blaze. The piles of red-hot coals between the fire-dogs were a similitude of the boulders, the cliffs, the rocky fastnesses of those almost inaccessible wilds. Above a swirling current of blazes bursting forth from a great hickory log he beheld a battery planted on a commanding promontory, harassing with its scintillating explosions, the shadowy craft that sought to escape on the turbulent stream below.

Cannon in the Cherokee country!

Naught could so extend the power of the Indians. Always they had longed for artillery. How many times had the crafty delegations sought to represent to him that "one little piece" would do much to strengthen them against the advance of the perfidious French,—whom, in truth, they loved, and they rallied continually to the standard of the "great French father." But even though the French were in their aggressions successful beyond all precedent in detaching the Cherokees from their compact with Great Britain, and setting them in arms against the government, they never dared to trust the tribe with cannon. So easily is a swivel gun turned, and with the fickle Indians it might be against the foe to-day and the friend to-morrow. With the comparative long range of the arm of that time, a few pieces, well placed in commanding situations, might hold the defiles of the Great Smoky Mountains against all comers.

Cannon in the Cherokee country!

How could Walasi's words be true! Captain Howard meditated on the difficulty of their transportation amidst the stupendous upheavals that made up the face of the country,—the steep slopes, the tremendous heights, the cuplike valleys, hardly a plot of twenty acres of level ground in the whole vast region. For his own part in expectation of the evacuation of Fort Prince George he was thankful that the currents of the Keowee and the broad Savannah would serve to bear its armament to the forts in the lower country. He continued to canvass this theme with a soldier's interest in a problem of transportation. To the civilian the glories and honors of war are won or lost on the fenced field of battle, but to the military expert the secret of victory or defeat is often discovered in the mobilization of the force. He was returning with unappeased wonder to the problem,—and to this day it is a matter of conjecture,—how the twelve cannon of Fort Loudon, more than one hundred miles to the northwest, had ever been conveyed to that remote inaccessible post. The blockade of the fort, its capitulation, and the massacre of its starveling garrison were events that befell before his detail to Fort Prince George, and much of mystery still environed the catastrophe. He knew that after the Cherokees were punished, and subdued, and practically disarmed by the British force sent into the country to reduce them to submission, the treaty of peace provided for the return of the cannon which the Indians had seized. They brought them as far as they could on the Tennessee River, then with infinite labor dragged them through the wilderness, an incredible portage, to the Keowee. Suddenly Captain Howard sprang to his feet; his glass of rich old port, falling from his hand and shivering into a thousand fragments on the hearth, sent up a vinous white flame from the coals that received the libation.

For the Indians had brought eight guns only! One piece was known to have burst, overcharged and mishandled by the Cherokees in their experiments in gunnery after the reduction of the fort. The others, it was declared, had been spiked, or otherwise demolished, by the defenders, in violation of the terms of their capitulation—it was claimed that they had sunk each piece as they could in the river. The fact which had been established that they had hidden large stores of powder, in the hope and expectation that the government might soon again reoccupy the works, was not consistent with this story of the destruction of the guns and might serve in a degree to discredit the statement of the Indians that all the cannon they had captured were delivered to the British authorities. And now this boast of cannon in the Cherokee country! He well believed it! He would have taken his oath that there were three pieces—all part of the armament of the ill-fated Fort Loudon, withheld by the Cherokees, awaiting an opportunity and the long-delayed day of vengeance for the slaughter and the conflagrations that marked the track of the British forays through their devastated land, when for lack of powder they could oppose no effective resistance, and were fain to submit to the bullet, the knife, the torch, till the conquerors were tired out with their orgies of blood and fire.

He became suddenly conscious of his daughter's hazel eyes, wide and lustrous with amazement, lifted to his, as he stood, alert, triumphant, tingling with excitement, on the hearth, and heard in mingled embarrassment and laughter his sister's sarcastic recommendation that he should throw the decanter into the fire after his bumper of port wine.

"Upon my word you frontier fanfarons are mighty lavish. In England we picture you as going sadly all the day wrapped in a greasy blanket, eating Indian meal, and drinking 'fire-water,'—and we come here to find you all lace ruffles, and powdered wigs, and prancing in your silk hose, and throwing your port wine into the fire to see it blaze!"

"The goblet slipped from my hand—it was a mischance, Sister."

"My certie! it shows you've had too much already; 'twas ever the fault of a soldier. Had I my way in the old times you should have been none."

"I would seem more temperate under a table, after a meet, like one of your home-staying, fox-hunting squires," suggested the captain.

"Well, but 'tis a pity a man should have no resource but the army. Faith, I'm glad George Mervyn is not to be forever marching and counter-marching."

She glanced slyly at Arabella, who looked pale in faint blue and a little dull. She did not respond, and Mrs. Annandale had a transient fear that she might say she did not care how George Mervyn spent his future. The girl's mind, like her father's, was elsewhere, but with what different subjects of contemplation! Captain Howard was saying to himself that he could never leave the Cherokee country with British cannon in the hands of the Indians. Even without this menace the evacuation of Fort Prince George seemed a trifle premature, in view of their inimical temper. How far this was fostered by the expectation of securing an adequate supply of powder to utilize the guns to the destruction of the British defences, which could not stand for an hour against a well-directed fire of artillery, and the massacre of the garrison, none could say. The French, now retiring from the country on every hand, might, as a Parthian dart, supply the Indians' need of powder, and then indeed the Cherokee War would be to fight anew,—with much disaster to the infant settlements of the provinces to the southward, for the stalwart pioneers were hardily pushing into the region below, their "cow-pens," or ranches along the watercourses, becoming oases of a rude civilization, and their vast herds roaming the savannas in lordly promise of bucolic wealth.

Cannon in the Cherokee country!

Captain Howard could but laugh, even in his perplexity, when he thought of the resilient execution of the insult offered him by the chief of Keowee Town in declining to receive the military mendicant and setting a "second man," Walasi, the Frog, a commercial man, so to speak, to deal with the soldier.

"Tell us the joke," said his sister, insistently, with no inclination to be shut out of mind when she was aware it was closed against her.

"Only reflecting on the events of the day," he said evasively, and Arabella, brightening suddenly, declared with a gurgling laugh, "Yes, we had a fine time on the river."

CHAPTER XIV

MANY an anxious perplexity had harassed Captain Howard's repose in the night watches during his tour of duty at Fort Prince George. Never one like this, he thought. Try as he might, the problem seemed to have no possible solution. Every plan bristled with difficulties. Every chance seemed arrayed against his eager hopes. The British cannon were in the Cherokee country, withheld, in defiance of the terms of the treaty, capable of incalculable harm both to the garrison as matters now stood, and to the frontier settlements in the future. The moral effect of supinely permitting the Indians to overreach and outwit the government was in itself of disastrous possibilities, reinstating their self-confidence, renewing their *esprit de corps*, and fostering that contempt for the capacities of their enemy, from which the Cherokees always suffered as well as inflicted so many futile calamities. The cannon must be surrendered in accordance with the terms of the treaty, or he would be obliged to call down the retributive wrath of the British War Office upon the recalcitrant and perfidious Cherokee nation. But while with his handful of troops he awaited British aid,—an expeditionary force sent out to compel compliance with the treaty and to discipline the Indians,—he must needs expect to sustain the preliminary violence of such wars. Fort Prince George might well be razed to the ground by the very cannon in contention, the settlers to the southward would certainly be massacred as of old, and all the dearly-bought fruits of the late terrible conflict would be lost and brought to naught. If it were only possible to secure the cannon without an appeal to the government, without jeopardizing the peace of the frontier!

Captain Howard held himself no great tactician, but when he rose in the morning from a sleepless pillow he believed he had formulated a scheme to compass these ends which might possibly stand the strain of execution. True, it had its special and great dangers, against which he would provide as far as he was able, but he feared nevertheless it would cost some lives. And then a new and troublous doubt rose in his mind. It would not be consonant with his duty to again absent himself from Fort Prince George at this crisis. He must needs delegate the active execution of his scheme, and somehow the material on which he could depend impressed him as strangely unavailable when it came to such a test. Mervyn, by virtue of his rank, might seem best fitted for the enterprise, and he had been considered a steady and capable officer. The matter was extra hazardous. It necessitated a clear judgment, an absolute obedience to orders if possible, great physical endurance, and a cool head. In many respects he thought Mervyn filled these requirements, but a mistaken appraisement of his qualities by his commanding officer would be an error of fatal results, and somehow Captain Howard found on sifting his convictions that he had, albeit for slight cause, lost confidence in Mervyn.

To be sure, Mervyn had in his formal report rectified the false impression under which he had permitted the commandant to rest for a time, but Captain Howard was a straightforward man himself and he could not easily recover from the impression created by the captain-lieutenant's duplicity in standing by and receiving commendations for the acts of another man—the fact of being in that other man's presence made it a futile folly, which implied a lack of logic. Oddly enough, logic was one of the essential requisites on an expedition among the Indians. Such emergencies might arise that the officer could only act on his own initiative, and Mervyn seemed not capable of striking out the most effective course and holding to it at all odds.

Captain Howard groaned under the weight of responsibility. He was compelled to trust the lives of a score of his men to the wisdom or unwisdom of his selection of an officer to command them. While Mervyn, by virtue of his rank, had the first claim to the conduct of an important matter requiring tact, discretion, mental poise, he was ruled out of the possibilities. He was too self-conscious, too uncertain, too slack in judgment, too obtuse to fine distinctions. Ensign Innis also was out of the question. He was too young, too inexperienced, and Ensign Lawrence was too young, not only in years, but in mind,—a mere blundering boy. It would be suicidal to match his unthinking faculties against the subtle wiles of the sages of the upper towns. Lieutenant Jerrold then it must be,—but Jerrold was the most literal-minded of men! He was absolutely devoid of imagination, of speculation, of that capacity to see through the apparent fact to the lurking truth beyond. He was a very efficient man in his place, but his place was a subordinate station. He would do with thoroughness the obviously necessary, but he would not be conscious of an emergency till it was before his feet as a pitfall, or immediately in his path as an enemy. He would take the regulation precautions, but he would not divine a danger, nor detect duplicity, nor realize a subtlety which he did not share. He was the predestined victim of ambush. He was a martinet on the drill ground and a terror at inspection. He laid great stress on pipe-clay and rotten-stone, and whatever the stress of the situation the men of his immediate command always showed up preternaturally smart. Captain Howard was no prophet, but he felt he could view with the eye of accomplished fact the return of Jerrold in ten days with the calm announcement that there were no British cannon in the Cherokee country, for he had been given this solemn assurance by no less a personage than Cunigacatgoah.

Captain Howard did not even consider Bolt for the enterprise; he was a military machine, incapable of devising an expedient in emergency or acting on his own initiative. Besides, his duties as fort-adjutant were particularly pressing just now in view of the preparations for the early evacuation of the post and they could not be delegated. Therefore there remained only

Raymond,—Captain Howard was in despair as he thought of Raymond and his interpretation of his orders to "persuade" the missionary to return. Impulsive, headstrong, eager, quick, indefatigable, emotional, imaginative,— what room was there for prudence in this fiery temperament! Still, he had shown a degree of coolness at the encounter of the boat with the Tamotlee Indians, and had given the soldiers an excellent example of imperturbability under the stress of exciting circumstances. But this was his element,—the contact of actual contention,—the shock of battle so to speak. How would he restrain himself when outwitted,—how would he gather few and feeble resources and make the best of them,—how might he see fit to tamper with his instructions and obey or not as he liked,—or if a right judgment found those orders based on fallacious premises, unknown to the commandant, how should he have discretion to modify them and act on his own initiative, or would he, like Bolt, persist in following the letter if it destroyed the spirit of his instructions? Oh, it was hard to be reduced to a choice of a madcap ensign, in this matter of paramount importance? He could not, he would not, send Raymond—his impetuosity was enough to bring the whole Cherokee country about their ears.

He shook his head, scowling unwittingly, as he chanced to catch sight of Raymond while crossing the parade, and still uncertain and morosely cogitating, he took his way to the commandant's office and disappeared from vision.

On the space beyond the parade Raymond and Arabella were greatly exercised in marking out a course for her archery practice. The promise of a fair day had been joyously fulfilled. The breeze was fresh, but bland and straight from the south; despite the leafless forests the sun shone with a vernal brilliance; a flock of wild geese going northward passed high over the fort, the cry, unfamiliar to Arabella, floating down to her ears, and she stood as long as she could see them, her head upturned, her hat fallen on the ground, her eyes following their flight as the wedge-shaped battalion deployed through the densely blue sky: there seemed even a swifter movement in the current of the river, and through the great gate one could from the parade catch sight of a white glister on the face of the waters where the ripples reflected the sun.

So soft was the air that the young lady wore no cloak. Her close-fitting gown of hunter's green cloth, opening over a vest and petticoat of sage-tinted paduasoy, brocaded in darker shades of green, was not out of keeping with the woodland suggestions of the bow which she held in her hand and the quiver already slung over her shoulder, its gorgeous polychromatic tints rendering her an object of mark in the brilliant sunshine from far across the parade. But she paused in her preparations to lament the lack of the uniform of the archery club which she had left in the oak press of her room at home, and Raymond listened as she described it, with her picture, thus arrayed, as vivid in his mind as the actual sight of her standing there, her golden hair glimmering in the sun, her white hands waving to and fro as she illustrated the features of the uniform and recounted the contentions of taste, the cabals and heart-burnings, the changes and counter-changes which the club had shared before at length the triumph of costume was devised, and made and worn before the acclaiming plaudits of half the county.

"Faint green," she said, "the very shade for a Diana,—"

"I like a darker green,—Diana wears a hunter's green," he interrupted.

"Why do you think that?" she asked, nonplussed, her satisfaction a trifle wilted.

"I know it," he said, a little consciously; and as she still stared at him, he went on: "hunter's green is the shade of the forest verdure,—it is a tint selected not only for beauty but to deceive the keen vision of game. It stands to reason that Diana should wear a hunter's green."

She meditated on this view for a few moments in silence, and the eyes of Lieutenant Jerrold, as he loitered in the door of the mess-hall, noted their eager absorption as they stood in the grassy space between the commandant's quarters and the block-house in the bastion, in which was situated the mess-hall. There were a few trees here, still leafless, and a number of the evergreen shrubs of the region, either spared for shade where they originally grew, or transplanted by some earlier commandant, voicing as clearly as words a yearning homesickness for a colonial or an English garden, and now attaining a considerable height and a redundant spread of boughs. An English rose, now but leafless brambles, clambered over the doorway of the commandant's quarters, and along a hedgerow of rhododendron, which reached the proportions of a wind-break, protruded some imported bulbous plants of a simple sort, whether crocus or hyacinth, one could hardly judge from so slight a tip piercing the mould. The bare parade was quiet now; earlier in the morning there had been roll-call and guard-mounting; and Mervyn, released from duty as officer of the day, could also see from where he sat in the mess-hall the interested attitudes of the two as they paused in their preparations for target practice to enjoy the pleasures of conversation.

"The benighted ninny!" Mrs. Annandale, commenting on Mervyn, said to herself in pettish despair, watching the *tête-à-tête* from the window of the commandant's parlor,—she had promised Arabella to witness her proficiency from this coigne of vantage, for the outer air was too brisk without the off-set of active exercise, "Why *doesn't* George Mervyn join them?" For she had observed Mervyn as he had quitted the orderly room, and marked his start of surprise and relaxed pace as his eyes fell upon the two,—then his dogged affectation of indifference as he briskly crossed to the block-house in the bastion.

"Hunter's green is the wood-nymph's wear forever," Raymond declared, eying Arabella as she stood in distinct relief against the darker green of the rhododendron hedge, in the flickering sunshine and shade under the branches of a balsam fir. "But I have no doubt," he continued, with a sudden courteous afterthought, "that the archery uniform, though not designed with a strict view of sylvan utility, was very smart in faint green."

"Oh, it was,—it was,"—she acceded, with ready good-humor. "It was relieved with white—"

"Oh, another tone of green, by all means," he blurted out impulsively, and now he had some ado to catch himself in this inadvertence—was he dull enough, he asked himself, to openly worship in set phrase the gown she now wore? "Was the relief a dead white,—like our pipe-clay gear?" he critically demanded.

"No-o—what they call a white silver cloth, now-a-days, and with a little cap of white silver cloth, with a tinsel half-moon."

"Oh, a lady is so fair,—the caps ought to have been a dark green to set off an exquisite fairness,—and a broad hat, a furry beaver hat, would have been prettier in my eyes than a cap."

Oh, fool! seeming much confused now, and just remembering that it is her hat—her broad furry beaver hat—in your mind, lying there in the sand, with its drooping feather and its long strings of wide sage-green ribbon to tie under her delicate chin. No wonder you turn deeply red, and begin to try the bow-line of a great unstrung Indian bow with all your strength.

"But all ladies are not fair," she protested. "That white silver cloth cap was Eva Golightly's selection to set off her black hair,—she wears no powder,—that is, not on her hair!"

He laughed gayly at the imputation, and the roguish glance of her eyes encountered in his a candid mutual enjoyment of the little fling.

"But it is a charming costume," she went on, "and so convenient,—with no hanging sleeves, nor lappets or frills to catch at the bow and arrow as one shoots,—everything laid on in plain bands,—I wish I had not left it at home, but of course I did not dream I should have any such lovely chance to shoot here."

"And why not, pray?—the land of the bow and arrow!"

"How could I imagine I should be furnished with these adorable toys—just the proper weight and size. I could not handle a real bow like yours, for instance. It is a weapon in truth!"

She suddenly held out her bow to exchange for experiment, and lifting the long, straight, heavy weapon, she sought to bend it from the perpendicular to string it. The stout wood resisted her force, and she paused to admire its smooth grain, which had a sheen like satin. He did not think its history worth telling,—a grewsome recollection for so fair a day! He had taken it from a Cherokee warrior whom he had slain during the late war in a hand-to-hand conflict—a desperate encounter, for the Indian had held him half doubled by a clutch on his powdered and perfumed hair, and the scalp-knife had grazed his forehead before he could make shift to fire his pistol, twice flashing in the pan, into his captor's heart. He had no time to reload, and snatching up the bow of his adversary he had fitted and shot an arrow with fatal effect at a tribesman who was coming up to his comrade's assistance; then Raymond made good his retreat, carrying the bow as a trophy.

It was indeed a weapon. "Terrible was the clanging of the silver bow" as he strung it and then drew back the cord to try it, and then let it fly again. Arabella exclaimed with a shrilly sweet delight at the unexpected resonance of the taut bow-line. He fitted an arrow and drew back, sighting carefully at the target. This was a board painted white, with several dark circles about a bull's-eye, affixed against a tree, beyond which was the blank interior slope of the rampart, and above, the red clay parapet surmounted by the long line of the stakes of the tall stockade. Captain Howard, himself, had selected the spot. In common with all regulars he believed—and fire cannot scorch this faith out of them—that only the trained soldier can fight, or shoot, or acquire any accuracy of aim. He had therefore placed the flower of the archery club where her quartz-tipped arrows, if wide of the mark, could only pierce the heavy clay embankment and endanger the life and welfare of neither man nor beast. Suddenly Raymond let fly the shaft, testing the wind. It had fallen now to the merest zephyr, and did not swerve the arrow a hair's breadth from the mark. It struck fair and full in the bull's-eye, for these frontier officers often were called upon to defend their lives with their own hands, and sought skill in marksmanship, a steady hand, a trained eye, and a cool head as zealously as did the rank and file.

The youthful Diana, her draperies flying in the motion as she sped through shadow and sheen, gained the target as quickly as he. As he recovered his arrow he was laughing with flattered pleasure noting her eagerness to assure herself of the accuracy of his aim, while she uttered little exclamations of wonder and delight at his efficiency.

"Wouldn't you make them stare in Kent?" she cried breathlessly, as the two raced together swiftly to the starting-point.

Then she selected an arrow from her gorgeous little quiver, hanging over her shoulder, and fitted the shaft to the bow. It was the prettiest attitude imaginable as she stood in the mingled shadow and sheen, her golden hair glimmering in the sun, and drawing the cord took careful aim. Her arrow sprang smartly from the string, sped through the air, and entered one of the circles so close to the centre as to justify Raymond's joyous cry of congratulation, echoing through the parade.

"Gad! I think I'll see this thing through!" Jerrold exclaimed, as he still stood in the mess-room door. He turned to the wall, and took down a bow that had been used there for ornament rather than a weapon. As he approached across the parade he noticed that the face of every passer-by was turned with smiling eyes toward the spirited and handsome young couple, and when he came up and was greeted genially by Raymond, and with a gracious word of welcome by the lady, he thought sagely that the best archer on the ground was invisible, and that the prettiest shots were not registered on the target.

The absence of Mervyn seemed the more significant now, since the other young officers not on duty were occupied in the gallant endeavor to make the archery practice of the young lady more interesting and exciting by competition. As he dully sulked in the deserted mess-hall, he had the cold comfort of perceiving that his presence was by no means essential to the young lady's enjoyment of the occasion. Her musical, ringing laughter, now much heartier than either Mrs. Annandale or Mervyn thought becoming or consonant with the simpering ideals of the times, was blended with the very definite merriment of the young officers, who by no means had been taught to "laugh by note." Jerrold's entrance to the pastime had added greatly to its gayety. He was a fair shot with fire-arms, but he entertained, of course, great contempt for the bow and arrow as a weapon. He had no sort of appreciation of its grace in usage nor interest in the romantic details of its archaic history, either in civilized countries of eld or in this new and savage world. In his literal mind the mighty bow-men of whatever sort were a set of inefficient varlets, whom a pinch of gun-powder might justly put to rout. Hence he scarcely knew how to take hold of the weapon. He had not even taxed his observation with its methods, although he had often seen Indian hunters use it in shooting at game, and more than once, since the scarcity of powder among the Cherokees, a forlorn destitute wight seek to defend his life with its dubious and precarious aid. Therefore there was much glee on the part of the two experts when Jerrold claimed his turn; after several efforts he awkwardly contrived to draw the bow and sent an arrow feebly fluttering through the air to fall to the ground a few paces distant. Arabella clapped her hands like a child as she burst into melodious peals of laughter, and

Raymond's amusement at this travesty of archery was hardly less spontaneous. Though vastly superior, they showed themselves not grudging of their proficiency; they undertook to instruct Jerrold in correct methods, one standing on either side of him and both talking at once. Suddenly Raymond called out sharply to Arabella, cautioning her lest she pass between the archer and the target. "For heaven's sake,—for mercy's sake," he adjured her solemnly, "pray be careful!"

She flushed deeply at the tone; it thrilled in her heart; the next moment her heart was aching with the realization that it was of no special significance. Any one might caution another with a reckless exposure to danger.

"I fancy the safest place is between the archer and the target when Mr. Jerrold shoots," she said laughing.

Then again ensued the farce of Jerrold's efforts, the faltering shaft falling far short of the mark,—with such wide divergence, indeed, even from the line of aim, that Captain Howard's disposition of the target in so remote a spot was amply justified. As once more the joyous laughter rang forth in which Jerrold, himself, readily bore a sonorous part, Mervyn suddenly joined the group. He had gained nothing by his absence, and indeed he could no longer nurse his anger in secret to keep it warm.

"What is all this?" he asked curtly, glancing about him with an air of disparagement.

"Can't you see?" returned Jerrold. "It is archery practice."

"Will you shoot?" Raymond suggested, civilly offering him the bow which he had used himself.

Mervyn hesitated. He thought himself a fair bowman, but he fancied from the state of the target and what he had heard of the acclaim of success that Raymond had made some very close hits. He feared lest he might come off a poor second. He was not willing to be at a disadvantage in Arabella's presence even in so small a matter. He resented, too, the sight of her use of Raymond's gift,—the beautiful bow in her hand, the decorated quiver, with its crystal-tipped arrows, hanging from its embroidered strap over her dainty shoulder. He could not refrain from a word that might serve to disparage them.

"No," he refused, "I don't care for archery. It is a childish pastime."

"I am beholden to you, sir!" exclaimed Arabella, exceedingly stiffly.

She really was so expert as to render her proficiency almost an accomplishment, and she was of a spirit to resent the contemptuous disparagement of a pastime which she so ardently affected.

"I mean, of course, for men and soldiers," Mervyn qualified, with a deep flush, for her tone had brought him suddenly to book.

"The bow-men of Old England?" she said, with her chin in the air.

"They had no better weapons," he reminded her, with an air of instruction. "And their victories were not child's play. It was the best they could do."

"And this is the best that I can do!" she said, fitting an arrow to the bow and throwing herself into that attitude of incomparable grace.

Whether it was an accident, whether she had made an extraordinary effort, whether the discord, the nettled displeasure, the roused pride, served to steady her nerves, as self-assertion sometimes will do, the arrow, springing from the string, cleft the air with a musical sibilance that was like a measure of song, and flying straight to the mark struck the bull's-eye fairly and stuck there, rendering the feat absolutely impossible of disallowance.

Raymond's delight knew no bounds. He sympathized so in her pleasure. They looked at each other with wide, brilliant eyes full of mutual joy, and ran together to the target to make sure of what was already assured. As they came back both were laughing excitedly, and Raymond was loudly talking. "Let us leave it there to show to Captain Howard. He will never believe it else. Let not another arrow be shot till then, lest somebody strike the target and the jar bring this arrow down."

"Except Mr. Jerrold!" Arabella stipulated, with a gush of laughter. "There is no danger of his hitting the target, far or near."

"Yes,—yes,—" exclaimed Raymond, adopting the suggestion. "Here, Jerrold, value your special privileges! You only may draw the bow."

Jerrold braced himself to the endeavor, good-naturedly adopting the advice of each in turn as they took up their station, one on either side.

"Slip your left hand lower!" Raymond urged.

"Oh, you *must* hold the arrow steady!" Arabella admonished him.

"Now aim,—aim,—man!" Raymond prompted.

"Why don't you take sight, Mr. Jerrold?" Arabella queried.

Mervyn, looking on disaffectedly as all were so merrily busy, noticed that two or three soldiers who passed near enough to see down the little grassy glade among the trees sensibly slackened their pace in their interest in the commotion, and, indeed, the whole scene was visible to the sentries at the gate, the warder in the tower, and to a certain extent from the galleries of the barracks.

"Don't you think it is injudicious, Jerrold," he remarked, with distant displeasure, "to make yourself ridiculous in the eyes of the men of your command?"

"Oh, no!" said Jerrold, lightly. "They know it is capital punishment to ridicule me. Make your mind easy."

"It must lessen your influence!" Mervyn persisted. He hardly knew what he wanted in this argument. He did not care a fig for Jerrold's influence over the men. He only desired some subterfuge to break up the merry-making in which he did not choose to share.

Jerrold did not even answer. Arabella on one side was offering a dozen suggestions tending to improve his aim, and Raymond was by precept and example endeavoring to get him into the right posture.

"Now,—hold steady for a minute before you shoot," said Raymond.

"If you only could count ten in that position without moving," suggested Arabella.

"Or better still, repeat the Cherokee invocation for good aim," Raymond proposed. "Might improve your luck." And he continued sonorously: "*Usinuli yu Selagwutsi Gigagei getsu neliga tsudandag gihi ayeliyu, usinuliyu. Yu!*" (Instantly may the Great Red magic arrow strike you in the very centre of your soul.)

"Oh, repeat it! repeat it!" cried Arabella. "Try it, and see if it will really mend your aim! What strange, strange words!"

Jerrold was haltingly repeating this after Raymond when Captain Howard came out of his office, and seeing the group took his way toward it. Raymond's back being toward him, he did not perceive the commandant's approach and continued the invocation, delivering it *ore rotundo* in imitation of the sonorous elocution of the Indians.

It sounded very clever to Captain Howard, who always declared he envied the facility with which the young officers picked up the colloquial use of the Indian languages. He took no trouble himself to that end, however. In his adoption of the adage with reference to the difficulty of teaching an old dog new tricks, he did not adequately consider the disinclination of the dog to the acquisition of fresh lore. The younger men were more plastic to new impressions; they exerted a keener observation; and felt a fresher interest, and few there were who had not some familiarity with the tongue and traditions of the tribe of Indians about the fort, and those among whom their extensive campaigns had taken them.

"What does all that mean?" Captain Howard asked curtly.

Raymond translated, and explained Jerrold's predicament and his need of luck in default of skill. Then he turned with animation toward the target, to celebrate the famous hit of Miss Howard's arrow in the bull's-eye while she stood flushing and smiling and prettily conscious beside him. But Captain Howard laid a constraining hand on his arm and looking at him with earnest eyes, demanded, "Where did you get all that Cherokee stuff?"

"Oh, in the campaigns in the Cherokee country," Raymond answered, "I picked up a deal of their lingo." For Raymond had served both in Montgomery's campaign and Grant's subsequent forays through this region two years ago, and his active mind had amassed much primitive lore, which, however, he had never expected to use in any valuable sort.

"Were you ever in Choté, Old Town?" queried the captain.

"I was there on one occasion, sir" said Raymond now surprised and expectant.

"Then go there again,—take twenty picked men,—your own choice,—and set out to-morrow at daybreak. Report for final orders this evening at retreat."

Arabella, dismayed and startled, felt her heart sink. She turned pale and tremulous; she did not know if a cloud passed over the sun, but for her the light of the day was quenched. She could not understand Raymond. His face was transfigured with a glow of delight. She could not imagine the zest of such an employ to a young officer, brave, ardent, eager to show his mettle, ambitious of any occasion of distinction. This was his first opportunity. A distant march,—a separate command of experienced soldiers,—even if only twenty! The dignity of the prospect set Raymond all a-quiver. What cared he for the jungles of the wild mountains, the distance, the toils, the danger! As to the Indians,—it behooved the nations to look to their safety when he was on the march with twenty men at his back! His cheek was scarlet; his eyes flashed fire; he responded with a staid decorum of acquiescence, but it was obvious that in his enthusiasm for the opportunity he could have fallen at the feet of the commandant and kissed his hands in gratitude.

CHAPTER XV

TO Arabella's amazement the other officers looked nettled, even resentful, as if disparaged in some sort. Mervyn indeed wore an expression of blank dismay as if he hardly knew how he should interpret this setting aside of himself in favor of his subordinate. He could not altogether restrain himself, and with a cold smile and a stiff dignity he said presently, "We have all learned more or less of the Cherokee language."

"Well,—well,—it is no great matter, for of course the official interpreter goes with the party." Captain Howard, so to speak, shouldered the affair aside. He could well understand, however, the mortification of Mervyn and Jerrold that they should be passed over for a younger officer and only an ensign in rank. But he had had the evidence of his senses to Raymond's knowledge of the Cherokee language, and this confirmed him in the selection which he had already considered. He was glad to discover this particular fitness in the man of his choice for this delicate and diplomatic mission, one who would be keenly alive to all he might hear or see on festive or informal occasions when no interpreter could be on duty.

Raymond now had not a word to say, and presently he excused himself with a look of importance and the plea that he desired to glance over the roll and select the men for the expedition, to make sure that all were fit, and properly equipped for the march.

When he had quitted the group a silence ensued, heavy with the unspoken reproach of the captain-lieutenant. The commandant felt constrained to some casual comment: "The trouble with very young men is that they are too disposed to underestimate difficulties,—too cock-sure. Raymond would be as well pleased with the assignment if the march were five hundred miles instead of one hundred and fifty!"

"And so should I," said Mervyn, suggestively.

"Tut! Tut! You young men shouldn't be so grudging," said Captain Howard, making the best of the untoward situation. "Give a man a chance to show that he holds his commission for some better reason than the purchase money. Gad, sir, don't grudge him so!"

As he turned away Jerrold, recovering himself from his disappointment as best he might, thinking it a matter which he could more fittingly deplore in secret and seclusion at another time, sought to obviate the awkwardness of the discussion by inviting Captain Howard's attention to his daughter's fine shot, the arrow still sticking in the bull's-eye. Captain Howard responded alertly, grateful indeed for the opportune digression, and walked briskly down to the target with the fair Arabella hanging on his arm, Jerrold at his side, and

Mervyn still sullenly preoccupied, following slowly. But the pleasure of the day for Arabella was done and dead. Her father's outcry of surprise and approbation and commotion of applause, she felt was fictitious and affected,—the kind of affectionate flattery which one offers a child for some infantile conceit. It was a matter of supreme inutility in his estimation whether she could shoot with a bow or not, and his mind was busied with more important details. Jerrold's phrases of commendation as the group stood before the target and commented on the position of the arrow were of no value, for he knew naught of the difficulty of the achievement. Mervyn could really appreciate the exploit itself, but Raymond valued it adequately, more than all because it was hers, and he took pride and pleasure in her graceful proficiency. She had had a glow of satisfaction in a good thing in its way well done; she had been proud and pleased and well content with such honestly earned admiration, but now her satisfaction was all wilted; and when her father said, "There now, daughter, run away,—enough for this morning,—run into the house, dear," she was quite ready to obey, and grateful for her dismissal and the breaking-up of the party. Mervyn, to her infinite relief, did not offer to follow her. His mind was all on the expedition to Choté, which Ensign Raymond was to command, and he walked off with Jerrold and the captain, thinking that even yet something might befall to induce the commandant to countermand his orders and make a change in the personnel of the force.

Arabella was sure she was not tired, for a little exercise such as she had taken was hardly enough to tax her buoyant, youthful vigor, but she felt as she reached the stairs that she had scarcely strength to ascend the flight. She turned back to the room that served as parlor, rejoicing to find it vacant. She sank down in one of the great chairs before the fire, which was dull and slow this bland day; the wood was green, the sap had risen and was slowly oozing out at the ends of the logs and dripping down on the ash below. It had a dulcet sibilance in the heat; it was like some far-off singing, which she could hear but could not catch the melody. As she vaguely listened to this elfin minstrelsy she wondered if Raymond would go without a word of farewell,— she wondered if the expedition were of special danger. She pressed her hands against her eyes to darken her vivid imaginings. Oh, why should such risks be taken! She wondered if he would ever return,—and then she wondered if her heart had ceased to beat with the thought.

Never, never had she imagined she could be so unhappy,—and here, where she had so longed to come. She gazed about the room with its rude construction metamorphosed by its barbaric decorations of feathers, and strange weapons, and curious hangings of aboriginal weavings, and rugs, and draperies of fur, and thought how often she had pictured the place to her mind's eye in England from her father's letters, and how she had rejoiced when her aunt had declared that now that the war was over they would visit the commandant in his own fort. And what a tumult of anxiety, and fear, and doubt, and desolation had whelmed her here!—and would he go without a word?

It seemed just and fitting that the sky should be overcast as the day wore on,—that clouds should gather without as the light had failed within. The air continued mild; the fire dully drooled; and when she asked her father at the dinner-table if the expedition would set forth if it should rain, he laughed with great gayety and told her that frontier soldiers were very particular never to get their feet wet—a not altogether felicitous joke, and indeed he was no great wit, for Mrs. Annandale tartly demanded why if they were allowed to be so particular were they not furnished with pattens. This Captain Howard considered very funny indeed, seeing doubtless in his mental vision the garrison of Fort Prince George thus accoutred; he laughed until Arabella admonished him that he should not be so merry when perhaps he was sending a score of men to a dreadful death at the hands of savages, who were eager and thirsting for blood, in a wilderness so dense and sombre and drear that she thought that Milton, or Dante, or anybody who had sought to portray hell, might have found a new expression of desolation in such mysterious, impenetrable, trackless forests. Then truly he became grave.

"Raymond's mission is not one of aggression," he said. "I have thrown what safe-guards I could about him. I trust and I believe he will be safe if he conducts properly."

"And what is his mission, sir?" asked Arabella.

"Do you expect me to tell you that when he does not know it himself?" said her father, laughing. "He is not to open his sealed instructions till he reaches Choté, Old Town."

Arabella's eyes were wide with dismayed wonder. To her this seemed all the more terrible. To thrust one's head into the lion's jaws, not knowing whether the beast is caged or free, ravenous or sated, trained or wild. She said as much to Ensign Raymond himself, when after candle-light he came in to pay his devoirs and take a formal farewell of the household. He was in great spirits, flushed and hilarious—very merry indeed when he found that Arabella was in much perturbation because he, himself, was in the dark as to the tenor of his mission, and would be one hundred and fifty miles distant in the heart of the Cherokee country ere he discovered the nature of his duty.

"Suppose it proves contrary to your own views and wishes," Arabella argued.

"A soldier must have no views and wishes contrary to his duty," he laughed.

"But suppose you find it is impossible!"

"I have too much confidence in the commandant to believe he would set me an impossible task."

"Oh, don't be too sure of that," interpolated Mrs. Annandale, who was benign, almost affectionate in her manner toward him, now that she was about to be rid of this handsome marplot, who did as much damage to her darling scheme by the unholy influence his presence exerted on Mervyn's temper as by his own magnetic personality. "Poor dear Brother was always a visionary."

Raymond burst out laughing at the idea of the commandant as a dreamer of dreams. "I have such faith in whatever visions he may entertain as to be certain they will materialize at Choté Great!"

"Will you be sure to come back?" Arabella asked, as they stood at the last moment near the table where the candles threw an upward glow on his red coat, his laughing eyes, his handsome, spirited face, and his powdered hair. He held his hat in his left hand and was extending his right hand toward her.

"Will you be sure to come back?"

"Oh, my dear, don't be so solemn,—your tones might summon a man from the ends of the earth or a spirit from the confines of being!" cried Mrs. Annandale.

Once more Raymond's joyous laughter rang through the room. "I shall come alive if I can conveniently, and all in one piece. If not I shall revisit the glimpses of the moon! I shall return—" and then in a more serious tone, seeing her seriousness, "I shall return, God willing."

Mervyn himself entertained considerable doubt of this happy issue of the expedition. He thought Raymond far too young, too flighty, too inexperienced to be trusted at such a distance, unhampered by authority, subject to strange untried conditions which could not be foreseen and provided against. It was necessary that all the details should be confided to his own unaided judgment, and it would not have greatly astonished the captain-lieutenant if none of the party should ever be seen again alive. In the dense jungles of the mountain wilderness, in the power of an implacable, aggrieved, and savage people, the fate of this handful of soldiers might ever remain a mystery and unavenged. The thought softened his heart toward his quondam friend. Mervyn was of the temperament rarely consciously at fault; so little did he admit dereliction in his relations with the outside world that he was often self-deceived. But in this instance his conscience stirred. He realized that for his offended vanity, for an unspoken fleer in a man's eyes which his own coxcombry had provoked, he had in revenge caught at an immaterial matter in the guard report and contrived to wreak his displeasure on Raymond in a sort most calculated to wound him, subjecting him to a reprimand, unwilling though it was, from the commandant. After that event ensued an alienation as complete as their friendship had formerly been close. At the time he winced to discover that Raymond had the magnanimity to refrain from retorting in kind, and had not held him up to ridicule in the commandant's eyes by gossiping on the expedition to Tamotlee of his unlucky absence from the scene of the conflagration. To be sure, Raymond knew that fact would be elicited in the regular channels of the reports, but he had not gone out of his way to further his false friend's mortification. Mervyn wished now that he had been less morose, less intractable. He had, he thought, no reason to be jealous of Raymond's station in Arabella's esteem. He was a dashing, attractive, handsome man, well calculated to entertain and amuse a young lady who was not used to spend her time in so dull a place as a frontier fort. Mervyn had no serious fault to find with the encouragement which she had vouchsafed his own suit. Therefore why should he let the breach yawn and widen between himself and his former friend. He did not linger in the commandant's parlor after Raymond had made his adieus, but followed him to his quarters, where he found the ensign with his servant busily packing his effects for the march.

"Just as I expected," said Mervyn, ignoring Raymond's stare of surprise, and perching himself on one end of the table as of old in the scarcity of chairs; he carelessly eyed the confused medley of articles spread over the bed, the chairs, the floor. "Making ready for the march, are you? I came to see if you wouldn't like to borrow my otter fur great coat and my heavy lynx rug for the trip. There is a change in the temperature impending,—freezing weather,—and you might need them."

Raymond hesitated. He would not wish to churlishly refuse an overture for renewed friendship or, as he rightly interpreted this, a covert apology. But he had that fibre of sensitiveness which winced from a favor bestowed—not from one he loved; a month ago he would have welcomed the offer, but more because of the feeling indicated than the utility of the proffered gear, although doubtless the furs would have stood him in good stead. Now, however, his estimate of Mervyn had changed and his heart had waxed cold toward him. He said to himself that he would be willing to risk the chance of freezing, if his own provision were insufficient, rather than be beholden to Mervyn for aught under the circumstances.

"I am already taking as much weight as I can afford to carry," he replied. "And besides your furs are too costly and delicate to drag through such a march as this,—thank you, just as much."

After some words of fruitless insistence Mervyn's talk digressed to details of ways and means. He was graciously disposed to supplement the younger officer's presumably inferior knowledge by his more mature advice, a senior in rank, years, and experience. Unrestrained by any subtle considerations of feeling on such a theme, Raymond did not scruple to flout this unsolicited counsel with a frank abandon which bespoke a self-confidence expanded to a prideful jubilance by the importance of the mission with which he had been intrusted. But this cavalier reception of the suggestions tendered him did not impair Mervyn's urbanity nor hinder the ostensible renewal of pleasant relations, or rather the ignoring of the fact that such relations had ever been interrupted. He offered his hand at parting with many good wishes, and Raymond, whose quickened intuition had come to comprehend his mental processes, was glad to see the door close upon his well-bred dissimulation.

"He does not want to feel at all uncomfortable in his conscience if I should be unlucky enough to be scalped, or frozen, or devoured by wolves, or lost in the wilderness," he thought, with a bitter insight.

And was this a seemly lover for Arabella Howard? He wondered how she could tolerate the dissembler who was not even frank with himself. He wondered how her father, an epitome of stout-hearted candor, her aunt, the cleverest of keen-sighted women, would permit this sacrifice of her. But there were inducements,—rank, fortune, station,—all powerful to embellish ugly traits, to obliterate unworthy actions, to place the most creditable construction on selfish sentiments. Raymond, however, had not time to rail at Fate according to her perverse deserts, for the hour was late, and his departure imminent.

He was gone on the morrow by the time the garrison was fairly astir, marching out of the gates as the bugle sounded the reveille. The day broke clouded and drear; the wind veered to the north; the temperature fell, and then ensued a long interval of suspense, of gray monotony. The air became still; it was perceptibly warmer; the dense clouds hung low and motionless; it was impossible to prognosticate the character of the change when it should terminate the indefinite uncertainty. Occasionally as the cheerless afternoon wore on, a vague brightening over the landscape gave a delusive promise of fairer skies, and then the sullen day lowered anew. The morrow brought no flattering augury. Now and then Captain Howard, looking at the heavy clouds, portending falling weather, meditated anxiously on the difficulties of the expedition. The temperature was unusually uncertain considering the season. He did not, however, expect a recurrence of cold weather, with spring already astir in the warm earth. But with the fickleness of the southern climate, on the third day after the departure of the little force, a freeze set in at dawn, and as the temperature moderated toward noon the threatened falling weather made good its menace in whirls of snow-flakes.

Captain Howard felt that he could not have been expected to foresee these climatic changes, and least of all he anticipated snow, which, most of all, he dreaded. The mission had already been unduly postponed, and time pressed sorely. The emergency was urgent and this he did not doubt, but with the complication of wintry storms in the wilderness he began to seriously question the wisdom of his selection of the officer to conduct the enterprise to a satisfactory conclusion. He wondered if Raymond would have the prudence to turn about should the route prove impracticable through the snowy tangled forests and across a score of precipitous high mountains and retrace his way to Fort Prince George.

He felt sure that at the first flurry betokening now in the trackless mountain defiles either Mervyn or Jerrold would have ordered an "About-face" movement. His heart misgave him as he reflected on Raymond's pertinacity. He knew in his secret soul that if ever he saw the ensign again it would be after he had accomplished his mission to Choté Great.

"Will he really freeze himself and his twenty men first?" he asked petulantly,—"or lose his way in the storm?"

Mervyn, albeit somewhat anxious himself after the flakes had begun to whirl, could but experience a little relish of the discomforts of his superior, who had apparently passed him over without reason, and had conferred a duty of difficulty and danger on a very young officer, probably incapable of executing it with requisite discretion. He had no inclination to stay and condole with the commandant before the fire in the orderly room. Here Captain Howard sat and toasted his spurs half the morning, having a mind himself to ride out on the trail of the expedition, if its route could be ascertained. There was the usual routine,—the reports of the orderly room, guard-mounting, drill,—all the various tours of duty to be observed as rigorously as if the fort held ten thousand men, instead of its complement of a scant hundred. Mervyn went about these details with a military promptness and efficiency and apparent content which commended him much to the morose commandant, who wished a hundred times that day that he had Raymond here and that Mervyn were in Raymond's place, thirty miles away,—nay, fifty by this time.

"He will have those men off their feet," muttered Captain Howard. "He'll race them through these drifts as if they were sunshine."

He looked out drearily at the snow now lying trodden and criss-crossed in devious paths on the parade. It was untouched, unsullied on the ramparts, where it had lodged in the clefts between the sharp points of the stockade. It hung in massive drifts on the roofs of the barracks, the guard-house near the gate, the block-houses; icicles wrought by an arrested thaw depended from the tower, in which the sentinel was fain to walk briskly to and fro, beating his breast the while, although the relief came at close intervals. The flakes were altogether hiding the contiguous woods, and it seemed that noon had hardly passed before there were suggestions of dusk in the darkening atmosphere, and nightfall was early at hand.

"Wonder where he will bivouac, to-night?" the commandant suggested to the group of officers in the mess-hall before the great fireplace that half filled one side of the room, for they were all somewhat familiar with the topography of the region through which Raymond would have to pass and the names of the Cherokee towns.

It was a cheerful scene indeed. The aroma of a skilfully compounded punch pervaded it, and the great silver gilt bowl was genially disposed on the nearest end of the long table, within easy access of the group about the hearth. The fire roared joyously up the great cavernous chimney and was brilliantly reflected from the glimmering steel of the arms suspended on the walls,— trophies, curios, or merely decorations. The wide-spread wings of the white swan and the scarlet flamingo arranged above the wainscot in gorgeous alternations hardly now suggested a mere fiction of flight; they seemed to move, to flutter and flicker as the firelight fluctuated and the shadows danced. On a smaller table there was the steady, chaste white focus of candle-light, for the tapers were illumined in two tall candle-sticks, the cards were cut for Loo, and the expectant faces of the officers showed in the calm white gleam, with all the details of their red coats, their white belts, their powdered hair. Only one of the officers was smoking, an on-looker at the game, the quarter-master, but Captain Howard's snuff-box was repeatedly in his hands.

They all noted his signs of anxiety and agitation, but there was not an immediate response to his remark, for there could be no freedom of speculation with a superior officer upon the untoward probabilities of an enterprise which he had chosen to set on foot. The silence was the less embarrassing because of the absorptions of the matter immediately in hand, for the pool was being formed during the deal. But when the trump was turned, and the players had "declared," there was a momentary pause of expectation, each relying on some tactful comment of the other. Innis, the blond young ensign, looked demurely into the fire and said nothing. Lieutenant Jerrold, having already glanced through his hand and seeing "Pam" among the cards, thought it hard lines that the commandant should not betake himself to his own quarters and cease to interfere with the game. By way of promoting this consummation he suggested fatuously:—

"Raymond will pick a spot near good water."

"Water!" screamed Captain Howard. "Gad, sir. *Pick* a spot! Water! In this weather he has nothing to do but to hold his fool mouth open. *Water!*"

The lieutenant's unhappy precipitancy suggested the ambush of the highest card, and his eagerness to utilize it, to the mind of another player, Ensign Lawrence, who held the lead. He held also the ace of trumps.

At his sudden cry, "Be civil,—Pam, be civil," Captain Howard started from his preoccupation as if he had been shot, glancing from under his bushy eyebrows at the table on which the young officer was banging down the ace with great triumph.

The cabalistic phrase was of course only designed to secure the immunity of the ace from capture by "Pam," but somehow its singular aptness of rebuke and Captain Howard's attitude of sensitive expectation shook the poise of the board. Ensign Lawrence turned very red, and only clumsily made shift to gather in the trick he had taken, for "Pam," of course, could not be played, his civility having been bespoken, according to the rules of the game, and the holder following suit. The other officers made an effort to conceal their embarrassment. Bolt, the fort-adjutant, cleared his throat uneasily. The onlooking quarter-master with the pipe began a sentence, paused, forgetting its purport midway, and silence continued till Ensign Innis came hastily to the rescue with a suggestion which he thought a masterly diversion.

"I suppose it was an important matter which took Raymond to Choté in such weather, sir?"

Captain Howard withered him with a glance.

"You have been long enough in the service, sir, to know better than to ask questions," he replied sternly.

Then he rose and betook himself forth into the densely whirling snow, repenting of his irascibility, calling himself a condemned spoil-sport, and looking at the sky, which was all of a bleak blackness, as well as the buffeting flakes would permit. He noted the blur of orange light flaring out from barrack-windows and guard-house door, and guided his route to his own quarters by the situation of these oases in the surrounding desert of gloom.

His opening door gave him to view a great gush of firelight and gleam of candles; the room was perfumed with the sweet odors of the burning hickory and pine and cedar in the wide chimney and embellished by the presence of Arabella, whose grace made every place seem a parlor. Her golden-hued shawl hung in silken folds from the back of an arm-chair of the primitive frontier manufacture, and on the table lay her embroidery-frame, whereon roses seemed to bud at her magic touch and expand under the sunshine of her smiling hazel eyes. Her gown of canary sarcenet had a black velvet girdle and many black velvet rosettes for trimming, her golden hair gleamed in the rich glow of the fire, and in her hand was her lute, graced by long streamers of crimson ribbon.

Beside her was the captain-lieutenant, all bedight in the smartest of uniforms, his hair in a long queue of blond plaits, and with precise side-curls heavily powdered, a genteel fashion not always observed on the frontier.

She had been singing to him one of the songs that had become fashionable at Vauxhall during his long absence from London, and the air was still vibrant with the melody of voice and symphony.

And poor Raymond!—Captain Howard's inconsistent heart rebelled at the sight of their comfort and mirth and security,—out in the snow, and the black night, and the illimitable trackless wilderness on the march to Choté.

With the thought his anxiety and distrust of the subaltern's discretion were reasserted.

"He will reach Choté if he has a man left! I only hope he won't harry the town!" he exclaimed in the extravagance of his disaffection.

CHAPTER XVI

WHEN Ensign Raymond encountered the snow-storm he was already advanced some two days' march on his mission to Choté Great, the "beloved town," the city of refuge of the whole Cherokee nation. The tempest came first in a succession of capricious flurries; then the whole world seemed a maelstrom of dizzily whirling flakes. The young officer and his force pushed on with mettlesome disregard of its menace, although for days it persistently fell. Afterward it drifted with the wind into great mounds, it obscured the trail, hid the landmarks, set many a pitfall in the deep chasms and over the thin ice of unsuspected watercourses in narrow and steep ravines. Night brought hard freezes; the thaws of the rising temperature at noonday were resolved into ice at dusk, and the trees, ceasing to drip, were hung with icicles on every bough and twig. The great pearly moon, now and again showing above the mountains through gusty clouds, revealed strange endless forests glimmering with crystalline coruscations, despite the obscurity, as if endowed with some inherent source of light. The bivouac fires made scant impression on these chill primeval environments; the flare on the ruddy faces of the young soldiers, with their red coats and their snatches of song and their simple joy in the contents of their unslung haversacks, paled as it ventured out amidst the dense mysterious woods. The snowy vistas would presently grow dim, and shadows thronged adown the perspective. Before the ultimate obscurities were reached, the vanishing point, certain alien green glimmers were often furtively visible,—a signal for the swift replenishing of the fires and a renewed flaring of the flames high into the air, with great showers of sparks and a fierce crackling of boughs. For the number of wolves had hardly been diminished by the Cherokee War with the British, so recently at an end, although the easily affrighted deer and buffalo seemed for a time to have fled the country. The predatory animals had doubtless found their account in the slaughter of the battle-fields, and Raymond's chief anxiety at night was the maintenance of the vigilance of the fire-guard, whose duty it was to feed the protective flames with fuel. To drive off the beasts with musketry was esteemed a wanton waste of powder, so precious was ammunition always on the frontier. Moreover, the bellicose sound of British muskets was of invidious suggestion in the land of the sullen and smarting Cherokees, so reluctantly pacified, and recently re-embittered by the downfall of secret cherished schemes of the assistance of the French to enable them to regain their independence. Now the French were quitting the country. Canada was ceded; the southern forts were to be evacuated. The "great French father" had been overpowered and forced to leave them to their fate, and their treaties with the British, half-hearted, compulsory, flimsy of intention, were to be kept or broken at the peril of their national existence. They resisted this conviction,—so high had been their hopes. They had long believed that a confederation of the Indian tribes under French commanders would drive the British colonies of the south into the Atlantic Ocean and the Gulf of Mexico. They had grown heady with this expectation, and prophetically triumphant. They were now desperate with the sudden dissolving of this possibility forever,—vindictively inimical.

There was an incident of the march which might have seemed to an older man than Raymond far more menacing than the wolves that patrolled the camp. Nightly there came visitors to his fire, which was a little apart from the bivouac of the rank and file, as beseemed a commander's dignity. The soldiers were wont to gaze askance at the guests across the intervening spaces, as the fire threw their long shadows upon the snow. Feather-crested shadows they were, but never the same. Each night certain chiefs from the town nearest the end of the day's march appeared out of the darkness with protestations of welcome to the vicinity, and sat with the giddy young commander beside his fire and talked with faces of grave import, for the smattering of the Cherokee language that Raymond had picked up was such as might suffice for casual conversation. The soldiers wondered and doubted as they watched, for their lives hung on the discretion of this light-pated youth. They were brave men enough and versed in Indian warfare, but acquainted too with Indian treachery. The war was over, both with the French and the Indian tribes, but that gratuitous sacrifice of life, the death of the few occurring in the interval between the negotiation of a treaty and the slowly pervading news of the consummation of peace, has a peculiar horror for every soldier. They put their own heads together around the fire and questioned much what could these men, holding aloof all day, coming darkly, dubiously with the shadows, have in traffic with their "Babby" Ensign,— what subject of earnest persuasion. The lengthened discourse would be drawn out long after tattoo had sounded, and when the soldiers, constrained to keep to fixed hours, lay around the glowing coals like the spokes of a wheel, they still furtively watched the figure of the gay young commander, erect, alert, very wide awake in his dapper trim uniform, and his blanketed feather-tufted visitors, their eager faces shown by the fitful flicker and flare of the ensign's fire. An icy bough would wave above them, and so chill was the intervening atmosphere that the leaping flames wrought no change in its glittering pendants. A star would frostily glint high, seen through the snow-laden branches of the pine. Sometimes the clouds would part and the pearly moon would cast a strange supernal lustre on the scene,—the great solitary mountains on every side; the long vacant snowy valleys glimpsed through some clifty defile; the shadowy skulking figures of wolves, primeval denizens of the wilderness; the bivouac of the soldiers; and these incongruously colloguing figures beside the officer's fire.

The words of the visitors appeared destined to be in vain. For a head which seemed so easily turned Ensign Raymond's was curiously hard.

Not go to Choté? They thought it not worth the while?—he would always ask with a note of affected surprise, as if the subject had never before been broached.

For this was the gravamen of their arguments, their persuasion, their insistence—that he should not go to Choté.

Was there not Nequassee, on the hither side of the tumultuous Joree mountains? The head-men of the Cherokee nation would delight to meet him there and confer with him on whatever subject the splendid and brave Captain Howard might desire to open with them by the mouth of his chosen emissary, Ensign Raymond.

It was diplomacy, certainly, but it jumped with Raymond's adolescent relish of tantalizing, to give them no intimation of the fact that he, himself, had as yet no knowledge of the purpose of his embassy, his instructions being to open his sealed orders at Choté. Thus he turned, and evaded, and shifted ground, and betrayed naught, however craftily they sought to surprise him into some revelation of his intent.

Only to Choté he must go, he said.

Two Indians who sat with him particularly late one night, head-men from the neighboring town of Cowetchee, were peculiarly insistent,—first, that he and his command should accept the hospitality of their municipality, that he, himself, might lie in the comforts of their "stranger house," and then, since he could not so far depart from his orders as to break up his camp—if he must repair to one of the Overhill towns—how near was Talassee, just beyond a precipitous ridge of the mountains, or Ioco, or Chilhowee, or Citico,—but not to Choté, surely. So far,—nearly as far as Tellico Great! Not to Choté,—oh, no; never so far as to Choté!

"But to Choté," said Ensign Raymond, "to Choté must I go."

They never looked at each other, these crafty sages of Cowetchee. Only the suspicion bred of long experience could discern aught of premeditation in their conduct of the interview. One conserved a peculiarly simple expression. His countenance was broad, with high cheek bones and a long flat mouth. He had a twinkling eye and a disposition to gaze about the camp with a sort of repressed quizzical banter, as if he found the arrangement of the troops and their accoutrements, the dress and arms of the officer, the remnants of his supper, the methods of its service, the china and silver, all savoring strongly of the ludicrous and provocative of covert ridicule. He held his head canted backward as he looked from half-closed lids, across the shimmering heated air rising above the coals, into the young man's face, infinitely foreign to him. Youth is intensely averse to the slightest intimation of ridicule, and Raymond, with his personal pride, his impulsive temperament, his imperious exactingness, could not have brooked it for one moment had he not early observed that each demonstration was craftily designed to shake his equilibrium, and preceded some cogent question, some wily effort to elicit a betrayal of the purport of his mission to Choté, and only to the "beloved town." The other Indian was grave, suave, the typical chief, wearing his furs and his feathers with an air of distinction, showing no surprise at his surroundings, hardly a passing notice indeed. He was erect, dignified, and walked with an easy light tread, different in every particular from the jocose rolling gait affected by the Terrapin.

The giddy Raymond began to pique himself on his capacity to meet these emergencies which obviously Captain Howard had not anticipated. They invested the expedition with a subtler difficulty than either had dreamed he might encounter. He flushed with a sense of triumph, and his bright eyes were softly alight as he gazed on the glowing coals. He bethought himself with great relish how these adventures would garnish his account of his trip, and having naught to do with its official purpose might serve to regale the fireside group, where a golden-haired girl might be pleased again to call him "prodigiously clever." He was suddenly reminded of the string of pearls around her bare white throat which he had noticed at the commandant's table, with the depressing reflection that Captain Howard came of well-to-do people while he, himself, had little but his commission and his pay, and that Mervyn was rich,—rich in his own right,—and would eventually be a baronet. For here were pearls around the savage throat of the Terrapin,—pearls indeed of price. A single gem of his string were worth the whole of Arabella Howard's necklace. These were the fine fresh-water pearls from the *Unio margaritiferus* of the southern rivers, and they had a satin-like lustre and rarely perfect shape, which bespeak a high commercial value. The Terrapin wore strings of shell beads, which he appraised more dearly,—the wampum, or "roanoke" as the southern tribes called it,—and which fell in heavy fringes over his shirt of otter fur. He had a collar of more than two hundred elk teeth; his leggings were of buck-skin and solid masses of embroidery. As Ensign Raymond's well-bred observation, that sees all without seeming to notice aught, took in these details, he began to have an idea of utilizing the visit of the Indians in a method at variance with their weary marching and counter-marching upon the citadel of his secret,—the purport of his mission to Choté, Old Town.

He meditated gravely on this, as he sat in his camp chair by the smooth stump of a great tree, felled for fuel, on which had been laid his supper, serving as table, and now holding the case-bottle of brandy, the contents of which had been offered and sparingly accepted by the Indians, for the chiefs were by no means the victims of fire-water in the degree in which the tribesmen suffered.

"Tus-ka-sah," Raymond said suddenly, "tell me your real name. I know you are never the 'Terrapin.'" For an alias was reputed to be the invariable rule of Indian nomenclature. The Cherokees were said to believe that to divulge the veritable cognomen divested the possession of the owner, destroyed his identity, and conferred a mysterious power over him never to be shaken off. Thus they had also war names, official names, and trivial sobriquets sufficing for identification, and these only were communicated to the world at large, early travellers among the tribe recording that they often questioned in vain.

Tus-ka-sah's real face showed for one moment, serious, astute, suspicious, and a bit alarmed, so closely personal, so unexpected was the question. Then he canted his head backward and looked out from under heavy lowered lids.

"La-a!" he mocked. He had caught the phrase from English settlers or soldiers. "La-a!" he repeated derisively. Then he said in Cherokee, "If I should tell you my name how could I have it again?"

Raymond pondered a moment on this curious racial reasoning. "It would still be yours. Only I should know it," he argued.

"La-a!" bleated Tus-ka-sah derisively, vouchsafing no further reply, while the other Indian knitted his perplexed brow, wondering how from this digression he could bring back the conversation to the trail to Choté.

"I know what your name ought to be," declared Raymond.

Once more a sudden alarm, a look of reality flickered through the manufactured expressions of the Terrapin's face, as if the ensign might absolutely capture his intimate identity in his true name. Then realizing the futility of divination he said "La-a!" once more, and thrust out his tongue facetiously. Yet his eyes continued serious. Like the rest of the world, he was to himself an object of paramount interest, and he experienced a corrosive curiosity as to what this British officer—to him a creature of queer, egregious mental processes—thought his name ought to be.

"It ought to be something strange and wonderful," said Raymond, speciously. "It ought to be the 'Jewel King'—or," remembering the holophrastic methods of Indian nomenclature—"this would be better—'He-who-walks-bedizened.'"

The eyes of the Indian had no longer that predominant suffusion of ridicule. They were large, lustrous, and frankly delighted.

"*Agwa duhiyu! Agwa duhiyu!*" (I am very handsome), he exclaimed apparently involuntarily. He glanced down complacently over his raiment of aboriginal splendor, passing his hand over his collar of elk teeth and tinkling his many strings of shell beads, but it was only casually that he touched his necklace of pearls. The gesture gave Raymond an intimation as to the degree in which were valued the respective ornaments. It reinforced his hope that perhaps the pearls might be purchased for a sum within the scope of his slender purse. How they would grace the hair of the fair Arabella, her snowy neck or arm. To be sure, he could not presume to offer them were they bought in a jeweller's shop in London. But as a trophy from the wilderness, curiously pierced by the heated copper spindle, by means of which they were strung on the sinews of deer, the price a mere pittance as for a thing of trifling worth,—surely Captain Howard would perceive no presumption in such a gift, the young lady herself could take no offence. Nevertheless, the pearls were rarely worth giving in a sort he could not hope to compass otherwise, nor indeed she to own, for, but for the method of piercing, rated by European standards their size and lustre would have commanded a commensurate price.

"I should like to buy a jewel from the great chief, 'He-who-walks-bedizened,'" said Raymond, his cheek flushed, his ardent eyes afire. "There would be a peculiar interest to tell abroad that this was the necklace of the 'Jewel King.'"

The Fox flashed an aggrieved and upbraiding glance upon the Terrapin. Had they come hither to chaffer indeed of beads, when the trail to Choté lay open, and by the utmost arts the sages of all the towns could not thence divert this wayward soldier?

"How much?" demanded "He-who-walks-bedizened."

He pursed up his lips, canted his head backward, and set his eyes a-twinkle under their lowered lids.

Raymond's heart beat fast. He had all the sensitive pride of a poor man, highly placed socially. He would not for all the world have offered her the trifling personal ornament within his means,—such a compliment as Mervyn might well have paid. He tingled with jubilance at the thought of an actual munificence, which her father could not appropriately forbid her to accept because it was an aboriginal curio, costing so disproportionately to its beauty and value.

He laid a guinea on the table.

"La-a!" bleated the Terrapin, in the extremity of scorn.

Another guinea, and still another, and yet the Indian shook his head. The Fox, albeit his eyes gloated upon the gold, as if it appealed to an appetite independent of his individuality, growled out an undertone of remonstrance which the Terrapin heeded no more than if he had not heard.

Money slips fast through the fingers of a poor man of good station, but Raymond was schooled to a modicum of prudence by the urgency of his desire to possess the gems. Realizing that the demands of Tus-ka-sah would be limited only by his supposed capacity to pay and his willingness to part with his gold, he called a halt lest these, being over-estimated, frustrate the project that had become insistently, eagerly precious to him.

"Let the great chief name the price of his necklace," he suggested a trifle timorously, fearing a sum beyond the possibility of his wildest extravagance.

The eyes of both the Indians followed the gold pieces, as he swept them from the table and into his purse, with a glitter of greed akin to the look of a dog who gazes at a bone for which he is too well trained to beg. Then Tus-ka-sah, with a slow and circumspect motion, took the pearls from his neck and spoke with a deliberate dignity.

"When you return to your own country call all your people together,"— Raymond hardly smiled at this evidence of the Indian's idea of the population of England, so heartily were his own feelings enlisted in the acquisition,— "tell them this is the necklace of the 'Jewel King,' 'He-who-walks-bedizened.' Then name to them the pearls, for they have true names,—these, the smaller of the string, are the little fish that swim in the river, and these are the birds that fly in the clouds. These twelve large ones are the twelve months of the year,—this, the first, is the green corn moon; this is the moon of melons; this the harvest moon; this the moon of the hunter." As he told them off one by one, and as Raymond leaned forward listening like a three years' child, his cheek scarlet, his dark eyes aglow, the wind whisking the powder off his auburn hair despite his cocked hat, the Fox watched the two with indignant impatience.

If the Terrapin observed the officer's eagerness he made no sign,—he only said suddenly:—

"And *all* are yours—if—you go not to Choté."

The young officer recoiled abruptly—in disappointment, in mortification, in anger.

He could not speak for a moment, so sudden was the revulsion of sentiment. Then he said coldly, "You trifle with me, Tus-ka-sah!"

He checked more candid speech. For prudential reasons he could not give his anger rein. Harmony must be maintained. If cordial relations were not conserved it should not be the ambassador of a friendly mission to break the peace.

The Cherokees were as eager as he to let slip no chance. The Fox, understanding at last the trend of his colleague's diplomacy, uttered guttural soothing exclamations. But Tus-ka-sah, perceiving the reluctance of the officer's relinquishment of the opportunity, the eagerness of his desire, his angry disappointment, sought to whet his inclination and made a higher bid. He took from some pocket or fold of his fur garments a buck-skin bag and thence drew a single unpierced pearl, so luminous, so large, so satin-smooth, so perfect of contour, that Raymond, forgetting his indignation at the attempted bribery, exclaimed aloud in inarticulate delight, for this indeed was a gem which those who love such things might well fall down and worship.

It came from the Tennessee River. Tus-ka-sah made haste to recite its history to slacken the tension of the difference which had supervened.

The jewel king of the mussels, he said, had worn it on his breast; but when his shell, which was his house, was harried and his people scattered, and he torn ruthlessly out, this treasure fell as spoils to the victor. Only its custodian was Tus-ka-sah—this gem belonged to the Cherokee nation—one of the jewels of the crown, so to speak. And it too had a name, the "sleeping sun." The chief paused to point from the moony lustre of the great pearl, shown by the light of the fire, to the pearly lustre of the moon, now unclouded and splendid in the dark vault of the deep blue sky.

"The 'sleeping sun'!" Raymond exclaimed entranced, remembering Arabella Howard's joy in the fancy, and thinking how the unique splendor of this single pearl would befit her grace.

He had a prophetic intimation of the proffer even before it came.

"Since you scorn my necklace," Tus-ka-sah said in Cherokee, "this—this—the nation will give you if you go not to Choté, beloved town."

Raymond had never dreamed that his loyalty could be tempted by any treasure. He did not pique himself on his fidelity. It was too nearly the essence of his individuality, the breath of his life. An honest man cannot levy tribute for his integrity—he feels it a matter of course, impossible to be otherwise. Raymond was dismayed to find his distended eyes still fixed upon the gem,—they had a gloat of longing that did not escape the keen observation of the chiefs. For this was unique. This was a gift no other could bestow,—it was indeed fit for a princess.

He experienced a vague internal revolt against the authority of his superior officer. Why did the instructions specify Choté? Any mission to the headmen could be as effectively discharged at any of the seven great "mother-towns." As to the aversion of the chiefs to his appearance in the "beloved town," this was doubtless some vagary of their strange savage religion against the errors of which it was puerile and futile to contend. If they esteemed his presence at Choté a profanation of the "ever-sacred" soil, why persist in intruding logic upon their superstition—especially since compliance would be so richly rewarded? Moreover, there were practical considerations in their favor. Choté was yet distant half a hundred miles, perhaps,—a weary march in this frozen wilderness for the already exhausted detachment. Though seasoned to Indian warfare, they were new to the topography of this particular region. Hard at hand was the lesser town of Little Choté—thus even the casual talk of the troops could not betray him. Captain Howard need never know that he had not penetrated to Choté Great, "the beloved city." He could open here his sealed orders, accomplish every detail of his mission, he thought, and yet secure the rich guerdon of his compliance with so simple a request.

Raymond rose suddenly to his feet, trembling in every limb. Tempted—tempted thus by a bauble! Barter his honor for the lustres of the "sleeping sun"! His face was scarlet. His eyes flashed. His lip quivered.

"I am a poor man, Tus-ka-sah," he said, "and stop me, my heart grows very heavy for the sake of the 'sleeping sun.' I would give gold for it, to the extent of my power. Gad, I would willingly be poorer still for its sake. But you cannot bargain with me for my duty as a soldier. Go to Choté, says my superior, and to Choté I go."

He could hardly understand the deep disappointment expressed in the faces of the Indians who consciously were trembling on the verge of the accomplishment of their secret design. Tus-ka-sah first recovered himself with a fleer at the confession of poverty, so characteristically scorned by the Indians. "*Poor!* La-a! *Poor!*" He stuck his head askew with an affronting leer that made his grimace as insulting as a blow. "For no poor man!" he added, bundling up his great pearl into its buck-skin bag, with the air of indignantly terminating the interview, as if he had received the proffer of a sum beneath contempt for his valuable jewel.

Whether or not he would have devised some return to the negotiation, a sudden accident definitely terminated it. At last the great flare of the fire, the ascending column of heated air, began to affect the snow congealed upon the boughs of the pine above their heads. The thawing of a branch effected the dislodgment of a great drift that it had supported in a crotch. The snow fell into the fire with a hissing noise, and in one moment all was charred cinders and hot mounting steam where once were red-hot coals and the flash of flames. Raymond called out a warning to the fire-guard, who were presently kindling the protective blaze at a little distance, and as his servant, roused from sleep, began to shift his effects thither from the despoiled site of his camp, he sat on the edge of the stump, listening to the growling of the wolves which, encouraged by the obscurity, were now dangerously near. He had not marked when nor how the two Indians had disappeared, but they were gone in the confusion, and on the morrow he resumed his march.

CHAPTER XVII

IN the meantime the days dragged slowly by at Fort Prince George. The snow lay on the ground with that persistence which the weather-wise interpret as a waiting for another fall. All out-of-door diversions were interdicted. Sleighing was not to be essayed, for it was considered unsafe to venture beyond the range of the guns. There was no ice for curling. Save for the boisterous sport of the rank and file hurling snow-balls at each other about the parade, when the fall was fresh and the novelty an appeal to idleness, the storm had brought none of its characteristic pastimes.

There was a rumor heard in Keowee Town of a blockade higher up in the mountains, where the fall had been of unprecedented depth. It became bruited abroad somehow,—not that aught had been disclosed of the fact,—perhaps by subtle intuition, perhaps only because the circumstances warranted the surmise, that Captain Howard was extremely uneasy as to the progress and fate of Ensign Raymond and his soldiers. Now and again an Indian straggling from some party out on "the winter hunt" came in at Fort Prince George with a story of having met the detachment in the wilderness. He would be eagerly welcomed by Captain Howard, regaled with French brandy and roast beef to loosen his tongue, the fraud discovered only when too late, the man's description of the personnel of the force, elicited under keen inquisition, failing to tally with the facts in a single particular. It was impossible for Captain Howard to set his mind at ease in the assurance that all were well and progressing finely, when the commander was described as a beautiful old man in buck-skin with a long white beard, or a squat fat man with a big stomach, and a red face, and a splendid bag-wig. The fumes of the brandy and the beef penetrated far beyond the gates of Fort Prince George, for rumor diffused and extended the aroma, and Indian idlers made their racial craft and tact serve the simple purpose of refreshing their inner man at the government's expense by the simple expedient of professing to have seen Ensign Raymond in the mountains commanding Captain Howard's soldiers. So anxious for news did he become that he seemed to have lost his normal suspicion, and on each occasion he returned to his hope of trustworthy information with an eager precipitancy that made him an easy prey.

Mervyn watched with cynical secret amusement this exhibition of vacillating character, as he deemed it. Why had Captain Howard despatched the detachment if he straightway wanted it back again, he demanded of himself. He was fond of observing from an outside standpoint the perplexity and the floundering mistakes of other men, especially his superiors in military rank, with the inner conviction how much more efficiently he could have discharged his obligations and disposed of the matter were he in their position. It was perhaps because of mental exercitations of this nature that he did not respond with the genial endorsement of the commandant's course which Captain Howard obviously expected and coveted, when he said one evening as they sat in the parlor before the fire, after dinner, entirely apropos of nothing:—

"This snow-storm, now—I couldn't possibly have foreseen this."

He lifted his eyes, his bushy brows bent, and fixed them on Mervyn's face interrogatively, yet with a certain challenge of denial.

"Well, sir," Mervyn hesitated, primly, judicially, "*I have never thought the backbone of the winter broken as yet.*"

"Gad, sir—why didn't you say so?" snapped Captain Howard. "If you are such a weather-prophet as to have foreseen a fall of twenty-six inches,—a thing never heard of before in this region,—why didn't you give me the benefit of your wisdom?"

"Oh, sir," said Mervyn, and there was rebuke even in his temperate voice, and his expression was calmly disclaiming, "I did not foresee the depth of the fall, of course. And it would ill become me to offer advice to an officer of your experience. I only thought the winter not fairly ended."

Despite the chill in the outer air, the flowers seemed blooming in royal profusion in Arabella's tambour-frame. She was constantly busy with the particolored skeins in these dark days, scarcely ever lifting her eyes as she listened. Now she sat close to the table for the sake of the light from the candles in the two tall candle-sticks. She had paused to thread her needle, and glanced up.

"The snow, papa, is out of all reasonable expectation—both as to season and depth. You must know that. You couldn't doubt it, except for your over-anxious sense of responsibility for the safety of the expedition. Lord, sir, nobody ever heard, as you say, of such a snow."

"That's no comfort to me," said Captain Howard, visibly comforted, nevertheless.

Mervyn, roused from the soft conceits of superiority, sought to follow her lead.

"I think, since you permit me to express my opinion, sir, that the detachment is in far less danger from the inclemency of the weather than from Ensign Raymond's inexperience. A judicious officer would have faced about at once and returned to the fort before he could be blockaded, with the drifts filling the mountain defiles. I should, I am sure."

"And a very damn fool you would have been!" exclaimed Captain Howard, testily.

"Dear Brother! In *Arabella's presence!*" Mrs. Annandale admonished him, as she sat in her big arm-chair, busy with her knotting, which she dextrously accomplished without other illumination than the light of the fire, which was reflected from the jewels on her slender twinkling fingers and flashed back from the glittering beads of her gorgeous knotting-bag. She deprecated this caustic discourtesy to Captain-Lieutenant Mervyn.

"I am not afraid Arabella will learn to swear, and I don't see any other harm that anything I say can do to her," retorted Captain Howard. He was even less pleased with the suggestion that the man to whom he had entrusted the lives of twenty of his soldiers was an unwise selection, than that, if he had had more prudential forethought, he might have divined the coming of the obstructive tempest.

Mervyn was rather more stiffly erect than usual, and his long pale face had flushed to the roots of his powdered hair. It was most obvious, despite his calm, contained manner that he considered himself needlessly affronted. "But like father, like daughter," Mrs. Annandale reflected, when Arabella, without the scantiest notice of his aspect, once more joined in the discussion.

"Now that is just how I think you show your knowledge of men and opportunities, papa," she remarked. "A more experienced officer than Mr. Raymond—Mr. Mervyn, for instance—would have turned back and lost your opportunity, who knows for how long, and the men would have been so demoralized by relinquishing the march for a snow-storm that they might not have made their way back even to Fort Prince George—remember how sudden it was, and how soon those nearest defiles were full of drifts. A man can be snowed under in twenty miles of forest as easily as in a hundred. But a young, ardent, dreadnaught like Mr. Raymond will push the men through by the sheer impetus of his own character. His buoyant spirit will make the march a lark for the whole command."

Mervyn's eyes widened as he listened in stultified surprise. He was amazed at his lady-love's temerity, to thus suggest Raymond's superiority to him in aught. He sought to meet her eye with a gaze of dignified reproof. But she was evidently not thinking of him. In truth, Arabella's heart was soft with sympathy for the commandant, yearning after his twenty odd hardened, harum-scarum young soldiers, as if they were the babes in the wood. He was afraid he had unduly exposed them to danger, and in the thought no woman could have been more troubled and tender,—in fact, for such a cause his sister could never have been so softened, so hysterically anxious.

"You are right, Arabella; Raymond has something better than caution or judgment. He is pertinacious and insistent, carries things before him, won't take no for an answer—he is a very good fighting man, too."

"But his lack of experience, sir," Mervyn interpolated with lifted eye-brows, "the very rank and file comment on it. They call him 'the hinfant,' and 'the babby ensign'!"

Captain Howard flushed scarlet.

"They are mighty careful that it doesn't reach his ears," he said, sternly. "Ensign Raymond knows how to maintain his dignity as well as any man twice his age I ever saw."

"Oh, papa, he does!" cried Arabella, eagerly corroborative. "I often notice when he is serious how noble and thoughtful he looks."

Mrs. Annandale was not near enough to give her niece a warning pinch; from such admonitions against girlish candor Miss Howard's delicate arm sometimes showed blue tokens. Like Mervyn, but with a different intent, the schemer tried to catch the young lady's eye. Now she felt she could no longer contain her displeasure, and her anxiety lest the matter go further than prudence might warrant impaired her judgment.

"Dear me, Arabella," she said, with an icy inflection, "one would think you are in love with the man."

The obvious response for any girl was, in her opinion, a confused denial, and this necessity would warn Arabella how far in the heat of argument she was going.

To Mrs. Annandale's astonishment Arabella softly laid the tambour-frame on her knee as if better to contemplate the suggestion. She held the needle motionless for an instant, her eyes on the fire, and suddenly she said as if to herself:—

"Sometimes I, too, think I am in love with him."

Mervyn shot a furious glance at her, but she had hardly looked at him all the evening, and she now continued blandly unaware. If Captain Howard marked what she had said it must have seemed a jest, for he went on, magnifying Raymond's capacity to take care of himself and to bring his detachment safely home.

Despite these arguments Captain Howard continued ill at ease, watchful of the weather, anticipating a renewal of snow or hopeful of tokens of thaw; eager to confer with any stray Indian, who Mervyn believed often came from no greater distance than the town of Keowee across the river; comparing reminiscences of distances and the situation of sundry notable Indian towns with veterans of the two campaigns during the previous years in the Cherokee country. In addition to the information of some of the garrison on this point, he was able to glean items from the very intimate knowledge of all that region possessed by the Reverend Mr. Morton, now contentedly installed at Fort Prince George, and holding forth at close intervals for the soul's health of the soldiery. But even he had a thrust for the tender sensibilities of Captain Howard's military conscience.

"Ensign Raymond," he said, apropos of the mooted safe return of the expeditionary force, "is of a very impetuous and imperious nature. God grant that he be not hurried into any untoward and reckless course. We can but pray for him, sir."

"Gad! I ought to have prayed beforehand," exclaimed the commandant.

"And that is very true," said the missionary.

But Captain Howard had not intended to be entrapped into confession, and he found Mr. Morton cheerless company in these days of suspense. For it was his faithful belief that a proper disposition of forces and munitions of war is calculated to induce Providence to fight on one's side and an omission of these rules and precautions is wilful neglect of means of grace. He saw little of the minister in these days, but Mrs. Annandale professed herself vastly edified by the good man's discourse, and kept him in conversation on one side of the fireplace while the two young people were ranged upon the other. Even the old man, inattentive to such matters, fell under the impression that the young lady and her cavalier seemed not a little disposed to bicker, and one evening when their voices were raised in spirited retort and counter-retort, Mrs. Annandale took occasion to say to him behind the waving feathers of her fan, that they were betrothed, and that their lovers' quarrels wearied her out of all patience.

He inclined his head with its straggling wig, which Rolloweh, with courteous compliments, had punctiliously sent down from Little Tamotlee; in its shabby similitude to the furnishings of humanity it had the look of being of low spirits and maltreated, and as if in its natural estate it might have been the hair of some poor relation. Mr. Morton observed that he hoped the young people were fully aware of the transitory nature of earthly bliss.

"Oh, they know that fast enough—their snappings and snarlings are a proof of its transitory nature, if they had no other," said Mrs. Annandale, sourly.

For Mervyn was not disposed to pass by, without an explanation, Arabella's statement that she sometimes thought she was in love with Raymond.

"He is a presuming puppy!" declared Mervyn, angrily, breathlessly, looking at her with indignant eyes.

"I can't see in what respect he presumes," she stipulated. "He has never said a word of love to me."

"But you said—"

"Only that I sometimes thought I was in love with him."

"You want to tantalize me—to make me miserable. For my life I can't see why."

He fared better when he appealed only to her generosity, for she realized that in his way he loved her. She had begun to realize that she did not, that she had never loved him, and was prone to remind him that she had always stipulated that he must consider nothing settled.

"She only wants to feel her power," Mrs. Annandale had reassured him.

"They tell me these Indians are cannibals on occasion," she said to herself, for there had come to be no one in whom she could really confide. "I wish they would eat Raymond—he would doubtless prove a spicy morsel—and I really don't see any other means to dispose of him out of harm's way."

Mervyn found a melancholy satisfaction in the enforced silence, when he could not upbraid nor Arabella retort, as they sat side by side on the dreary snowy Sundays in the mess-hall, where the garrison attended divine service. A drum mounted upon the table reached the proper height of a prayer desk, and all the benches and settees in the barracks, guard-house, and officers' quarters were laid under requisition to furnish forth sittings for the force. Captain Howard was duly wakeful during the long and labored homily, although he felt in his secret soul that the most acceptable portion of the service was concluded when Arabella's voice, soaring high above the soldiers' chorus, had ceased to resound, sweet and indescribably clear, and sunk into silence. Mervyn found the psalms for the day for her, and they read and sang from the same book. She wore, in deference to the character of the occasion, her formal church attire, and he was reduced to further abysses of subjection by the sight of her lovely face and head, unfamiliar, and yet the same, in such a bonnet as should have graced her attendance at the parish church at home. A white beaver of the poke or coal-scuttle form framed her golden hair, and accented the flush in her cheeks and the warm whiteness of brow and chin. Her ermine muff and tippet were inconceivably reminiscent of home and church-going. Her long black velvet pelisse gave her an air of rich attire which enhanced her beauty and elegance with the idea of rank and wealth which it was to be his good fortune to bestow on her. Never had she been so beautiful as with that look of staid decorum, of solemnity and reverence. Captain Howard might well have enjoyed his regular Sabbatical nap—her attention was so sedulous it might have sufficed for all the family. But he was noting the manners of the garrison, and as they were conscious of the commandant's eye naught could have been more seemly. Jerrold, and Innis, and Lawrence, themselves, were not more reverential than Robin Dorn, who raised the tune of psalm and hymn to the correct pitch with a tuning fork, then piped away with a high tenor, now and again essaying with good measure of success a clear falsetto. The non-professional tenors held to the normal register, the basses boomed after their kind, and above all, it might seem an echo from heaven, the clear soprano voice. The big fire flashed, hardly so red as the mass of red coats in the restricted limits of one room, ample though its size, and its decorations of red and white feathers, of grotesque paintings on buffalo hides, of flashing steel arms and gaudy bows and quivers, all glimmered, and gleamed, and flickered, and faded as the flames rose and fell.

And the homily—it was not likely that the congregation knew much about the significance of the Pentateuchal types and analogies, but if the idea of such crass ignorance could have occurred to Mr. Morton, he would have said it was time they were finding out somewhat. Perhaps as he drew near his sixthly division and began to illustrate a similarity of the religious customs of the Jews and Indians, they may have pricked up their ears, and still more when he deduced an analogy between the cruelty of the temper of the ancient Hebrews toward their enemies and the torture practised by the modern Indian. He cautioned his hearers on the danger of prying into the religious ceremonies of the Cherokees as if his audience shared the pious fervor which consumed him, but said he did not despair of using these similarities as an introduction of the Christian religion, of which they were a forerunner and type. Then he talked of the legends of the lost tribes, till Captain Howard felt that it would be a piety to fall on his own sword like the military heroes of Scripture, world-weary. At last he ended with:—

"'Woe—woe is me if I preach not the Gospel!'"

"And—woe—woe, surely, is thy hearer!" Mrs. Annandale mimicked below her breath, as hanging on her brother's arm she walked decorously across the snowy parade to the commandant's quarters. Mervyn and Arabella followed in silence, the young man's thoughts on the ivy-clad church of Chesley Parish, and the walk thence through the lush greenth of the park to Mervyn Hall, with this same fair hand laid lightly on his arm.

CHAPTER XVIII

ENSIGN RAYMOND was no polemic nor versed in the Hebraic analogies rife at that day among those who ascribed a Semitic origin to the American Indian and sought to recognize in them the "lost tribes of Israel." When at last he set foot on the "ever-sacred" soil of the city of refuge and opened his sealed orders, it was less a resemblance to ancient Jewish customs that appealed to him than an appreciation of the prudence of his commander in choosing this site for the delivery of his mission. For he had that to say to the head-men of the Cherokee nation which elsewhere might cost him his life. Here, however, at the horns of the altar, had he, himself, been the shedder of blood, he was safe. Here his blood could not be shed. He was under the shadow of the "wings of peace." The "infinitely holy" environment protected him and his.

When he drew up his command and addressed the soldiers, ordering them on no account to venture beyond the limits of the "beloved town," the amazement and flouting ridicule on their florid Irish and Cockney faces marked the difficulty which the ordinary mind experiences in seeking to assimilate the theories of eld. With the heady severity characteristic of a very young officer, he replied to the nettling surprise and negation in their facial expression.

"It may sound like a fool notion to you, but you must remember that you are only a pack of zanies, and don't know a condemned thing but the goose-step. They had this same sort of immunity 'way back in the Bible times,"—he was himself a trifle vague,—"cities of refuge, where, in the case of involuntary manslaughter, the slayer might find protection, and in this 'old peaceable town' of Choté no hurt may be done even to a wilful man-slayer, no blood may be shed here,—now, do you understand?"

The heads were all erect; the position was the regulation "attention" with "eyes front," but so round were these eyes with amazement that "the greasy red-sticks" had aught similar to customs "'way back in the Bible times," that the caustic young commander was moved to add: "You are a set of heathen, too, or you would have learned all that long ago,—about holding to the horns of the altar, as an effective defensive measure. Anyhow," he summed up, "if you choose to go off the 'sacred soil' and get yourselves slaughtered, you cannot say that you have not been fairly warned. You will disobey orders, you will be put under full stoppage of pay, and—*your* bones will not be buried."

The parade was dismissed and they marched away, much marvelling at his strange discourse.

The allusion to their bones remained rankling in his mind. For there was a fence of human bones at Choté, very grievous for a British soldier to look upon,—a trophy, a triumphal relic, of the massacre of the British garrison of Fort Loudon after its capitulation. It had been difficult for Raymond to control the righteous wrath of his soldiers in the presence of this ghastly mockery,—notwithstanding their scanty number and the realization that any demonstration would be but the sacrifice of their own lives the moment they should quit the soil of immunity. The assurance of their commander that he would report the indignity to the government, when doubtless some action would be taken, was necessary to avert disastrous consequences.

Raymond, himself, had great ado to contend with the storm of anger a-surge within his own breast when the Cherokees ceremoniously received him, beating the drums of the late Captain Demeré, who had marched out of Fort Loudon with the full honors of war, with flags and music and their assurance of safeguard.

"This is not well," Raymond could not refrain from saying, as he stood in the centre of the "beloved square" in the midst of the town, with the headmen, splendidly arrayed in their barbaric fashion, gathered to greet him. "The articles of capitulation reserved to Captain Demeré the colors, drums, and arms of the garrison—he had the solemn assurance of the Cherokee nation,—and—" Raymond was very young; his face turned scarlet, the tears stood in his eyes, he caught his breath with something very like a sob, "the remains of that honorable soldier are entitled to Christian burial."

He was sorry a moment later that he had said aught. The Indians' obvious relish of his distress was so keen. They replied diplomatically, however, that all this had happened long ago, nearly three years, in fact, and that if they had done aught amiss, the British government had amply avenged the misdeed in the distressful wars it had waged against the Cherokee nation, that had indeed been reduced to the extremity of humiliation.

Raymond, breathing a sigh of solace, was accepting this logic with the docile rudimentary reasoning of youth, when one of the chiefs, with a countenance at once singularly fierce and acute, the great Oconostota, added blandly that he, himself, had known Captain Demeré with something of intimacy and desired to withhold naught of advantage from him. If Ensign Raymond was sufficiently acquainted with his bones to select them from out the fence, he would be privileged to remove them. But this applied to none of the other bones, for the consent of other warriors controlled the remainder of the structure.

When he paused a ripple of mirth, like a sudden flash of lightning on a dull cloud, appeared on the feather-crested faces and disappeared in an instant. They all stolidly eyed Raymond, standing with his hand on his sword, his heart swelling as he realized the fleer with the ludicrous ghastliness of the dilemma it presented. Then it was that Raymond showed the soldier. The cub, despite its immaturity, has all the inherent mettle of the lion. His eyes still flashed, his cheek glowed, his voice shook, but he replied with a suavity, which was itself a menace, that being only a subaltern he did not feel authorized to take the initiative in so serious a matter, but that he would report the offer to Captain Howard, commanding at Fort Prince George, with whom Oconostota was also acquainted, and with, he believed, some degree of intimacy.

That the Indians were adepts in every art of propitiation was amply manifest in the urbanities that Raymond enjoyed after this apt suggestion, and if aught could have obliterated its provocation from his mind, this would have been compassed by the courtesies and attentions showered upon him and his men during the days that intervened between his arrival and the time when etiquette permitted the business of his mission to be opened.

Raymond seemed to have brought the spring to Choté, that lovely vernal expectation which holds a charm hardly to be surpassed by the richness of fulfilment. Soft languors were in the air, infinitely luxurious. A large leisure seemed to pervade the world. The trees budded slowly, slowly. At a distance the forests had similitudes of leaflets, but as yet the buds did not expand. It was evident that the grass was freshly springing, for deer were visible all a-graze on the opposite banks of the Tennessee River. Far away the booming note of buffalo came to the ear, and again was only a soft silence. A silver haze hung in the ravines and chasms of the mountains, austere, dark, leafless, close at hand but in the distance wearing a delicate azure that might have befitted a summer-tide scene.

After the long, toilsome, wintry march Raymond found a sort of luxury in this interval of rest, despite the unaccustomed barbaric manners of his hosts. He sought to make due allowance for the differing standards of civilization, but there was much that was irksome notwithstanding the utmost endeavors of his entertainers to win his favor. From morning to night he was attended by an obsequious young warrior called "Wolf-with-two-feet" with half a dozen braves who tried to anticipate his every wish, and when he was relegated to his repose at night in the "stranger house," a guard was placed before the door to protect the guest from intrusion or harm. Raymond thought this cordon of braves was also effective in preventing on his part any reconnoitring expedition thence, when Choté, old town, lay asleep and at the mercy of the curiosity of the inquisitive British officer. This suspicion, however, seemed contradicted by the disposition of his cicerone during the day. He was dragged hither and thither over every inch of the "sacred soil" as it appeared, and every object of interest that the town possessed was paraded before him to titillate his interest. The Indians of Choté, an ancient and conservative municipality, yet retained a certain pride in their national methods despite the repeated demonstration of the superiority of the Europeans both in war and manufactures. Had Raymond possessed a theoretical interest in such matters, or were he skilled in anthropological deductions, he might have derived from them some information concerning the forgotten history of the people. But it was only with the superficial attention of the desperately idle that he watched the great weaving-frame on which they made their cloth, of porous quality—few yards indeed now being produced since the Indian trade had brought English textile fabrics to the Tennessee River. He had never seen a better saddle than the one a leisurely wight was finishing—lying down in the sun at intervals and sleeping an hour or so to reward some unusual speed of exertion. Raymond committed the solecism of laughing aloud when told that a year's time was necessary to complete a saddle to the satisfaction of the expert. He took more interest in their pottery—a wonderfully symmetrical pattern, in deep indentations in checks or plaids, baffled his conjecture as to how it was applied in the decoration of jars and bowls of the quaintest shape imaginable. His guide, philosopher, and friend challenged him to a dozen guesses, breaking out in guttural glee and ridicule at every untoward suggestion, till at last Raymond was shown the baskets, deftly woven of splints or straw or withes, which were lined with clay, and set to bake in the oven, the plastic material taking not only the shape of the mould but the pattern of the braiding.

Raymond thought it was his interest in this primitive art that had defied his conjectures which influenced his attention toward another plastic impression different from aught he had seen in the Cherokee country. Still accompanied by Wolf-with-two-feet he had left the main portion of the town, and the two were idly strolling along the river-bank. Raymond was thinking that Wolf-with-two-feet was not a poor specimen of a host considering his limitations, his strange, antiquated, savage standards, and his incapacity for civilization in a modern sort. He had kept the shuttle-cock of conversation tossing back and forth for two days. He had gotten up a horse-race and a feather-dance to entertain the guest. He had fed him on his choice of an imitation of British fare and appetizing Indian dainties, and of the latter Raymond partook with distinct relish. He had shown the town and descanted on the value of its methods of government and its manufactures, and save that now and again he turned his sharp, high-featured face, with its polled head and feather crest, toward him with a fiery eye, his upper lip suddenly baring all his narrow white teeth set in a curiously narrow arch, the officer could see naught of the wolf in him.

The sky was beginning to redden; the air was bland and filled with the scent of the spring-tide herbs; some early growth of mint was crushed under their feet and sent up a pungent aroma; the ground was moist and warm, as it had been for several days; Raymond noticed on the shelving shore the mark, still distinct, of the prow of the canoe in which he had landed at Choté,—for during the last stages of the march the Indians of the various riverside towns of the vicinity had come forth and proffered their boats for the remainder of the journey. He now spoke of the circumstance and identified the spot and the canoe, for there was the print of his London-made boot distinct amongst the tracks of a dozen Indian moccasins. His men had followed in a pettiaugre, formerly belonging to Fort Loudon, and had landed a little below the town.

Perhaps it was this idle interest that kept him still looking at the ground,— for, as they skirted a point and came again on a marshy level beneath a row of cliffs, he suddenly paused and pointed out a different impression on the earth.

"But what is that?" he said, thinking first of some queer fish or amphibious animal, for the natural history of America was of vast interest to Europeans, and there were many fables current of strange creatures peculiar to the new world.

The Wolf-with-two-feet turned and looked down at the spot at which Raymond was staring.

"Where?" he asked in Cherokee, for the British officer spoke the language with enough facility to enable them in casual conversation to dispense with an interpreter.

The impression was of a deep indentation in the centre, surrounded at the distance of some inches by a ring, plainly marked but less deep, and this had an outer circular imprint very symmetrical but still more shallow. Raymond saw that for one moment the eyes of the Indian rested upon it, but still saying, "Where?" he stepped about, looking now in every direction but the one indicated; all at once, as if inadvertently, he pressed his foot deeply into the marshy soil, and the water rushing up obliterated forever the impression of the deep indentation and the two concentric circles.

Raymond called out to him pettishly that he had spoiled the opportunity of discovering the cause of so strange a mark.

"'Twas the track of a snake, perhaps, or a tortoise," the Wolf suggested.

When he was assured that this was something circular and symmetrical, he said he did not know what it could have been, but some things had big hoofs. Perhaps it might have been Mr. Morton's Big Devil, whom he was so fond of preaching about!

"In Choté?" asked Raymond.

"Oh no—not in Choté," the Wolf made haste to say—"Mr. Morton could not preach in Choté. Cunigacatgoah has a sacred stone, an amulet, that belongs to the Cherokee people, and it would not suffer a word about Mr. Morton's very wicked Big Devil in the city of refuge."

"An amulet against evil," said Raymond sarcastically—"and yet the Devil walks along the river-bank of the 'ever-sacred' soil and leaves his big footprint in defiance!"

"True,—true,"—said the Wolf, doubling like his own prey, "then it couldn't have been the Devil. It must have been a buffalo,—just a big bull buffalo."

"A big bull buffalo with one foot," sneered Raymond, logically, "there is no other track near it,—except," he continued looking narrowly at the earth, "the imprint of a number of moccasins of several sizes." He was merely irritated at the balking of his natural curiosity, but he noticed with surprise that Wolf-with-two-feet was very eager to quit the subject, and digressed with some skill and by an imperceptible gradation from the character of this spongy soil, so plastic to impressions, to the alluvial richness of the whole belt along the watercourses and thence to the large yield of the public fields that lay to the southwest of Choté, and which were even now, early as it was, in process of being planted. And then, as if suddenly bethinking himself, he changed the direction of their stroll to give Raymond an exhibition of the primitive methods of agriculture practised with such signal success at Choté Great. At this hour the laborers had quitted the fields, leaving, however, ample token of their industry. For in the whole stretch of the cultivated land the fresh, rich, black loam had been turned, but with never a plough, and daily large numbers of women and girls repaired thither under the guidance of the "second men" of the town to drop the corn. Though the world was so full of provender elsewhere, the birds took great account of this proceeding, and thronged the air twittering and chattering together as if discussing the crop prospects. Now and again a bluejay flew across the wide expanse of the fields, clanging a wild woodsy cry with a peculiarly saucy intonation, as though to say, "I'll have my share! I'll have my share!"

But birds were builders in these days, and he could hardly see a beak that was not laden with a straw. Oh, joyous architects, how benign that no foreknowledge of the storm that was to wreck these frail tenements, so craftily constructed, or of the marauder that was to rifle them, hushed the song or weighted the wing! Human beings have a hard bargain in their vaunted reason.

There was none of the delight in the spring; none of the bliss of sheer existence in days so redundant of soft sheen, of sweet sound, of fragrant winds, of the stirring pulse of universal revivification; none of that trust in the future which is itself the logic of gratitude for the boons of the past, expressed in the hard-bitten faces of the head-men and in the serious eyes of the young officer when they sat in a circle around the fire in the centre of the council-house at Choté. They were all anxious, troubled, each determined to mould the days to come after the fashion of his individual will, only mindful enough of the will of others to have a sense of doubt, of poignant hope, and a strenuous realization of conflict. Thus the young officer was wary, and the Indian chiefs were even wilier than their wont as he opened the subject of his mission.

The interpreter of each faction stood behind his principal, for a long time silent as the official pipe was smoked. The council-house of the usual type, a great rotunda built on a high mound near the "beloved square," and plastered within and without with red clay, was dark, save for the glimmer of the dull fire and the high, narrow door, through which could be seen the town of similar architecture but of smaller edifices, with here and there a log cabin of the fashion which the pioneers imitated in their earlier dwellings, familiar to this day, and the open shed-like buildings at each side of the "beloved square." The river was in full view, a burnished steely gray, and the further mountains delicately blue, but more than once, as Raymond glanced toward them, his eyes were filled with a blinding red glare, sudden, translucent, transitory.

Only the nerve of a strong man, young, hearty, well-fed, enabled him to be still and make no sign. The first thought in his mind was that this was a premonition of illness, and hence it behooved him to address himself swiftly to the business in hand that no interest of the government might suffer. As he pressed his palm to his brow for a moment, it occurred to him that the strange feather-crested faces were watching him curiously, inimically,—but perhaps that was merely because they doubted the intent of his mission.

And so in Choté, in the unbroken peace of its traditional sanctity, he began with open hostility.

"You signed a treaty, Cunigacatgoah," he addressed the ancient chief, "and you Oconostota, and other head-men for the whole Cherokee nation,—in many things you have broken it."

Several chiefs held out their hands to receive "sticks," that they might reply categorically to this point when he had finished. But he shook his head. He did not intend to conform to Indian etiquette further than in sitting on a buffalo rug on the floor, with his legs in their white breeches and leggings folded up before him like the blades of a clasp knife. He gesticulated much with his hands, around which his best lace frills dangled, and he wore a dress sword as a mark of ceremony; his hair was powdered, too, and he carried his cocked hat in his left hand. He did not intend to be rude, but he was determined to lose no time in useless observances, because of that strange affection, that curious red glare which had seemed to suffuse his eyes, portending some disturbance of the brain perchance.

"No," he said firmly, declining to receive or to give the notched sticks, "I am not going to enter into the various details. There is only one thing out of kilter about that treaty which I am going to settle. It relates to the cannon which you brought here after the capitulation of Fort Loudon. They were to be delivered up to the British government according to the last treaty. Eight of these guns were taken down to Fort Prince George, one was burst by an overcharge at Fort Loudon, but others you have not relinquished. You have evaded compliance."

A long silence ensued, while the chiefs gazed inscrutably into the fire. Their pride, their dignity suffered from this cavalier address. All their rancor was aroused against this man,—even his callowness was displeasing to them. They revolted at his incapacity for ceremonial observance, save, indeed, such as appertained to his military drill, which they esteemed hideous and of no value to the British in the supreme test of battle. They resented his persistence in having ensconced himself here under the protection of the sanctities of Choté until after his offensive mission should be disclosed and answered. He had evidently neither the will nor the art to disguise it with euphemistic phraseology that might render it more acceptable to a feint of consideration. It was not now, however, at the moment of the French withdrawal, that the Cherokees could resist by force an English demand. Diplomacy must needs therefore fill the breach. In some way Captain Howard had evidently learned that the three missing cannon were not sunk in the river by the garrison of Fort Loudon as the Cherokees had declared. With this thought in his mind, Cunigacatgoah said suddenly, "Only three cannon failed to be relinquished,—they had been in the river, and they were all sick,—they could not speak."

"Sick,—are they? I have a sovereign remedy for a sick cannon," declared Raymond. "They shall speak and—" Once more as he glanced mechanically through the open door toward the brilliant outer world, with the gleam of the river below the clifty mountains and a flight of swans above, that curious translucent red light flashed through his eye-balls.

This time he was quicker,—or perhaps accident favored him, for as, half-blinded, his glance returned, he saw the red light disappearing into the ample sleeve of one of the Indians who sat on the opposite side of the fire.

Raymond's first feeling was an infinite relief. No illness menaced him, no obscure affection of the nerves or brain. Some art of conjuring,—some mechanical contrivance, was it?—they were employing to distract his attention. In their folly and fatuity did they dream that they might thus undermine his purpose, or weaken his intellect, or destroy his sight, or work a spell upon him? He marked how they watched his every motion.

He looked vaguely, uncertainly, about the shadowy place, with its red wall. The decorated buffalo hides suspended on it showed dully against its rich uniform tint. The circle of the seated Indian chiefs in the shifting shadow and the flickering light, with their puerile ornaments of paint and feathers and strings of worthless beads about the barbaric garb of skin and fur, was itself vague, unreal, like a curious poly-tinted daub, some extravagant depiction of aboriginal art. Each face, however, was expressive in a different degree of power, of perspicacity, of subtlety, and many devious mental processes, and he marvelled, as many wiser men have marvelled since, that these endowments of value should fail to compass the essentials of civilization, theorizing dimly that the Indians were a remnant of a different order of being, the conclusion of a period of human development, the final expression of an alien mind, radically of an age and species not to be repeated.

There was absolutely no basis of mutual comprehension, and Raymond was definitely aware of this when he said, "I can cure a disabled cannon,—show me the guns,"—and a sudden silence ensued, the demand evidently being wholly unexpected.

"Tell me," he urged, his patience growing scant, "where are the guns now?" Then catching the shifty expression of the chief, Cunigacatgoah, he was moved to add, disregarding the interpreter, "*Gahusti tsuskadi nigesuna.*" (You never tell a lie.)

Now and again his knowledge of the Cherokee language had enabled him to detect the linguister for the British force softening his downright candid soldierly phrases. The interpreter was seeking to mitigate the evident displeasure excited by the commander's address, which he thought might rebound upon himself, as the medium of such unpleasant communication. There was something so sarcastic in this feigned compliment that it might well have seemed positively unsafe, even more perilous than overt insult, but as Raymond, with a wave of his cocked hat in his left hand and a smiling bow of his heavily powdered and becurled head, demanded, "*Haga tsunu iyuta datsi waktuhi?*" (Tell me where they are now?) a vague smile played over the features of Cunigacatgoah, and he who was wont to believe so little, found it easy to imagine himself implicitly believed, the model of candor.

He instantly assumed an engaging appearance of extreme frankness, and abruptly said, "Now, I, myself, will tell you the whole truth."

Raymond looked at him eagerly, breathlessly, full of instant expectation.

"The cannon are not here,—they have all three sickened and died."

The soldier sat dumbfounded for a moment, realizing that this was no figurative speech, that he was expected to entirely believe this,—so low they rated the intelligence of the English! He experienced the revolt of reason that seizes on the mind amidst the grotesqueries of a dream. He had no words to combat the follies of the proposition. Only with a sarcastic, fleering laugh he cried aloud, "*Gahusti tsuskadi nigesuna!*" (You never tell a lie.)

The next moment he felt choking. He was balked, helpless, hopeless, at the end. He knew that Captain Howard had anticipated no strategy. The savages could not by force hold the guns in the teeth of the British demand, and the commandant of Fort Prince George had fancied that they would be yielded, however reluctantly, on official summons. They were necessary to Captain Howard, to complete his account of the munitions of war intrusted to his charge, upon being transferred from Fort Prince George. And this was the result of Raymond's mission,—to return empty-handed, outwitted, to fail egregiously in the conduct of an expedition in which he had been graced with an independent command,—Raymond was hot and cold by turns when he thought of it! Yet the guns had disappeared, the Indians craftily held their secret, the impossible checks even martial ardor. Raymond, however, was of the type of stubborn campaigner that dies in the last ditch. The imminence of defeat had quickened all his faculties.

"*Ha-nagwa dugihyali?*" (I'll make a search), he blustered.

But the threat was met with sarcastic smiles, and Cunigacatgoah said again with urgent candor,—"*Agiyahusa cannon.*" (My cannon are dead.)

As Raymond hesitated, half distraught with anxiety and eagerness, the red light suddenly flashed once more through his eye-balls from its invisible source. He was inherently and by profession a soldier, and it was not of his nature nor his trade to receive a thrust without an effort to return a counter-thrust.

"Hidden!" he cried suddenly, with eyes distended. "Hidden!" he paused, gasping for effect. "I know the spot," he screamed wildly, springing to his feet; for he had just remembered the peculiar track he had noticed on soft ground near the river, and he now bethought himself that only the trunnion of a dismounted gun could have made an imprint such as this. It suggested a recent removal and a buoyant hope. "The cannon are in the ravine by the river. I know it! I know it!"

In the confusion attendant upon this sudden outburst they all rose turning hither and thither, awaiting they hardly knew what in this untoward mystery of divination or revelation. Making a bull-like rush amongst them, actually through the fire, Raymond fairly charged upon the conjurer, felling him to the ground, and ran at full speed out into the air and down the steep mound.

"Fall in! Fall in!" he cried out to his "zanies" as he went, hearing in a moment the welcome sound of his own drum beating "the assembly."

He led the way to the locality where he had seen the track, followed by all his score of men at a brisk double-quick. In a ravine by the river a close search resulted in the discovery of the guns ambushed in a sort of grotto, all now mounted on their carriages. Not so sick were they but that they could speak aloud, and they shouted lustily when the charges of blank cartridges issued from their smoking throats. For the giddy young officer had them dragged up to the bluffs and trained them upon the "beloved town" of peace itself, and by reason of the Indians' terror of artillery hardly five minutes elapsed before Choté was deserted by every inhabitant.

Raymond found his best capacity enlisted to maintain his authority and prevent his twenty men flushed with victory, triumphant and riotous with joy, from pillaging the city of refuge, thus left helpless at their mercy. But the behests of so high-handed and impetuous a commander were not to be trifled with, and the troops were soon embarked in the large pettiaugre belonging to the British government, which chanced to be lying abandoned at the shore. In this they transported the three guns, which they fired repeatedly as they rowed up the Tennessee River, with the echoes bellowing after all along the clifty banks and far through the dense woods,—effectually discouraging pursuit.

CHAPTER XIX

WHY the recoil of the pieces did not sink the old pettiaugre with all on board, to their imminent danger of drowning in the tumultuous depths of the spring floods, Captain Howard could never understand, except on the principle that "Naught is never in danger," as he said bluffly, now that his anxiety was satisfied. The heavy rainfall and the melting of the snows had swollen the watercourses of the region to such a degree that they had risen out of their deep, rock-bound channels, and this enabled Raymond to secure water-carriage for the guns the greater part of the return journey. He had some hardships to relate of a long portage across country when the pack animals which had carried his supplies and ammunition had been utilized as artillery horses, and had drawn the guns along such devious ways as the buffalo paths from one salt spring to another might furnish. Then they had embarked on the Keowee, and had come down with a rushing current, firing a salute to Fort Prince George as they approached, eliciting much responsive cheering from the garrison, and creating more commotion than they were worth, the commandant gruffly opined.

He hearkened with a doubtful mien to the ensign's report of the vicissitudes of the expedition, and was obviously of the opinion that the whole mission could have been as well accomplished in a less melodramatic and turbulent manner.

"I knew," he said, "that the official demand for the guns would anger the chiefs, for they have long craved the possession of a few pieces of artillery, and nothing in their hands could be so dangerous to the security of the colonies. But I was sure that being in Choté, you were safe, and that if you should find it necessary to seize the guns they would protect you against all odds on your march back to Fort Prince George. I did not imagine the chiefs would venture so far as to conceal the cannon, and of course that gave you a point of great difficulty. But the feint of firing on the town was altogether unnecessary. There was no occasion for incivility."

"Stop me, sir, if it had not been for their lies and conjuring tricks I should have been as polite as pie."

Captain Howard listened with an impartial reservation of opinion to the detail of the magic red light, but his face changed as Raymond took from his pocket a gem-like stone, large, translucent, darkly red, and caught upon it an intense reflection from the dull fire in the commandant's office.

"This must be their famous 'conjuring-stone,'" he said gravely.

"The fellow dropped it when I knocked him down," Raymond explained, graphically. "I lost my balance, and we rolled on the ground together, and as I pulled loose I found this in my hand."

Early travellers in this region describe this "conjuring-stone" of the Cherokees as the size of a hen's egg, red and of a crystalline effect, like a ruby, but with a beautiful dark shade in the centre, and capable of an intense reflection of light.

The next day Captain Howard received from the Indians the strange complaint that the British ensign had their "religion," with a demand that he be required to return it. They stated that they had searched all their country for the sacred amulet, and they were convinced that he had possessed himself of it. They were robbed of their "religion."

"This is idolatry," exclaimed the old missionary, rancorously, vehement objection eloquent on his face.

"They tried to put my eyes out with their 'religion,'" declared Raymond. "They shall not have the amulet back again. They are better off without such 'religion.'"

"That is not for *you* to judge," said Arabella, staidly.

They were all strolling along the rampart within the stockade after retreat. The parade was visible on one side with sundry incidents of garrison life. The posting of sentinels was in progress; a corporal was going out with the relief, and the echo of their brisk tramp came marching back from the rocks of the river-bank; the guard, a glitter of scarlet and steel, was paraded before the main gate. From the long, dark, barrack building rose now and again the snatch of a soldier's song, and presently a chorus of laughter as some barrack wit regaled the leisure of his comrades. The sunset light was reflected from the glazed windows of the officers' quarters; several of the mess had already assembled in their hall to pass the evening with such kill-time ingenuities as were possible in the wilderness. Now and again an absentee crossed the parade with some token of how the day had been passed;—a string of mountain trout justified the rod and reel of an angler, coming in muddy and wet, and the envy of another soldier meeting him; at the further end, toward the stables, a subaltern was training a wild young horse for a hurdle race, and kept up the leaping back and forth till he "came a cropper," and his sore bones admonished him that he had had enough for one day.

The air was soft and sweet; the Keowee River, flush to its brim with the spring floods, sang a veritable roundelay and vied with the birds. Sunset seemed to have had scant homing monitions, for wings were yet continually astir in the blue sky. All the lovely wooded eminences close about the fort, and the Oconee mountain, and the nearer of the great Joree ranges, were delicately, ethereally green against the clear amethystine tone of the mountain background.

And as if to fairly abash and surpass the spring, this dark-eyed, fair-haired girl herself wore green, of a dainty shadowy tint, and carried over one arm, swinging by a brown ribbon, a wide-brimmed hat, held basket-wise, and full of violets, while the wind stirred her tresses to a deeper, richer glitter in the sunset after-glow. For these violets Raymond had rifled the woods for fifty miles as he came, and she turned now and again to them with evident pleasure, sometimes to handle a tuft especially perfect.

Despite his hopelessness, in view of the impression he had received as to Mervyn's place in her good graces, Raymond set a special value on aught that seemed to commend him. He had greatly enjoyed the pose of a successful soldier, who had returned from the accomplishment of a difficult and diplomatic mission. He cared not a *sou marqué* for the criticism of several of the other officers of the post who opined that it was a new interpretation of the idea of diplomacy to train cannon on commissioners in session and bring off the subject of negotiation amidst the thunders of artillery. He had felt that it was enough that he was here again, all in one piece, and so were the cannon,—and he had brought off, too, it seemed, the "religion" of the Cherokees. He experienced a sudden reaction from this satisfaction when Arabella turned from the violets, and pronounced him unfit to judge of the Indian's religion.

"Why not? I am as good a Christian as anybody," he averred.

Mervyn at this moment had a certain keenness of aspect, as if he relished the prospect of a difference. This eagerness might have suggested to Raymond, but for his own theory on the subject, that the placid understanding which seemed to him to subsist between Arabella and the captain-lieutenant was not as perfect as he thought.

The Reverend Mr. Morton paused, with his snuff-box in his hand, to cast an admonitory glance upon the young ensign.

"There is none good,—no, not one," he said rebukingly.

He solemnly refreshed his nose with the snuff, although that feature seemed hardly receptive of any sentiment of satisfaction, so long and thin it was, so melancholy of aspect, giving the emphasis of asceticism to his pallid, narrow face, and his near-sighted, absent-minded blue eyes.

"I mean, of course, by ordinary standards, sir. I'm as good a Christian as Mervyn, or Lawrence, here, or Innis, or—or—the captain," Raymond concluded, with a glance of arch audacity at the commandant.

"Hoh!" said Captain Howard, hardly knowing how to take this. He did not pretend to be a pious man, but it savored of insubordination for a subaltern to claim spiritual equality with the ranking officer.

"When we are most satisfied with our spiritual condition we have greatest cause for dissatisfaction," declared the parson.

With his lean legs encased in thread-bare black breeches and darned hose,— he had been irreverently dubbed "Shanks" during the earlier days of his stay at Fort Prince George,—his semi-ludicrous aspect of cadaverous asceticism and sanctity, so incongruous with the haphazard conditions of the frontier, it would have been difficult for a casual observer to discern the reason of the sentiment of respect which he seemed to command in the minds of these gallant and bluff soldiers. Their arduous experience of the hard facts of life and the continual defiance of death had left them but scant appreciation of the fine-spun sacerdotal theories and subtle divergencies of doctrine in which Mr. Morton delighted. Seldom did he open his oracular lips save to exploit some lengthy prelection of rigid dogma or to deliver the prompt rebuke to profanity or levity, which in the deep gravity of his nature seemed to him of synonymous signification. He might hardly have noticed the subject of conversation of the party as he walked by the commandant's side along the rampart, but for the word "religion." He seemed to be endowed with a separate sense for the apprehension of aught appertaining to the theme that to him made up all the interest of this world and the world to come. Therefore he spoke without fear or favor. His asceticism was not of a pleasing relish, and his rebukes served in no wise to commend him. It was his fearlessness in a different sense that had made his name venerated. The rank and file could not have done with rehearsing, with a gloating eye of mingled pride, and derision, and pity, how he had driven the gospel home on the Cherokees, in season and out, they being at his mercy, for by the rigid etiquette of the Indians they were forbidden to interrupt or break in upon any discourse, however lengthy or unpalatable. And how he had persisted, albeit his life was not safe; and how the head-men had finally notified Captain Howard; and how Captain Howard had remonstrated in vain; and how at last Ensign Raymond had had the old parson literally brought off in the arms of two of their own command. It is to be feared that it was neither learning nor saintliness that so commended the old missionary to the garrison of Fort Prince George.

Now it seemed that the Cherokees had lost their own religion, if this amulet represented it, for by their curious racial logic Raymond possessed its symbol and therefore they no longer had the fact.

"It is a heathen notion that I have got their religion," protested Raymond. "They never had any religion."

"It is religion to them," said Arabella. "Religion is faith. Religion is a conviction of the soul."

"True religion is a revelation to the mind direct from God," said Mr. Morton, didactically. "The name doth not befit the hideous pagan follies of the Indians."

She did not feel qualified to argue; she only said vaguely with a certain primness, in contrast with her method of addressing the young men:—

"Faith always seems to me the function of the soul, as reason is of the mind. You can believe an error, but mistakes are not founded on reason."

Then she asked him suddenly if the stress that the Cherokees laid on this amulet did not remind him of the attributes of the ark of the Hebrews and their despair because of its capture.

"The ark was a type,—a type," he declared, looking off with unseeing eyes into the blue and roseate sky and launching out into a dissertation on the image and the reality, the prophecy and its fulfilment, with many a digression to a cognate theme, while Captain Howard affected to listen and went over in his mind his quarter-master's accounts, the state of the armament of the fort, and the equipment of the men, all having relation to the settling of his affairs in quitting his command. The younger people chatted in low voices under cover of the monologue, it not being directly addressed to them.

They had slowly strolled along the rampart as they talked, the two elderly men in the rear, the girl in the centre, with her charming fair-haired beauty, more ethereal because of that pervasive, tempered, pearly light which just precedes the dusk, while the young officers, in the foppery of their red coats, their white breeches, their cocked hats, and powdered hair, kept on either side. The party made their way out from the dead salient of the angle, only to be defended by the musketry of soldiers standing on the banquettes, and ascended the rising ground to the terre-pleine, where cannon were mounted *en barbette* to fire above the parapet.

As Arabella noticed the great guns, standing a-tilt, she said they reminded her of grim hounds holding their muzzles up to send forth fierce howls of defiance.

"They can send forth something fiercer than howls," said Raymond, applausively. He was a very young soldier, and thought mighty well of the little cannon. Captain Howard, who had seen war on a fine scale and was used to forts of commensurate armament, could not repress a twinkle of the eye, although for no consideration would he have said aught to put the subaltern out of conceit with his little guns.

The other cannon were pointed through embrasures beneath the parapet. One of them had been run back on its chassis. She paused beside it, and stood looking through the large aperture, languid, and silent, and vaguely wistful, at the scene from a new point of view.

As she lingered thus, all fair-haired in her faint green dress, with her hat on her arm full of violets, one hand on the silent cannon, she seemed herself a type of spring, of some benison of peace, of some grave and tender mediatrix.

The foam was aflash on the rapids of the Keowee River; the sound of its rush was distinct in the stillness. Now and again the lowing of cattle came from some distant ranch of pioneer settlers. The Indian town of Keowee on the opposite side of the river was distinct to view, with its conical roofs and its great rotunda on a high mound, all recognizable, despite the reduction of size to the proportions of the landscape of the distance. No wing was now astir in the pallid, colorless sky. One might hardly say whence the light emanated, for the sun was down, the twilight sped, and yet the darkness had not fallen. A sort of gentle clarity possessed the atmosphere. She noted the line of the parapet of the covered way, heretofore invisible because of the high stockade, and beyond still the slope of the glacis, and there—

"What *is* that?" she said, starting forward, peering through the embrasure into the gathering gloom. A dark object was visible just beyond the crest of the glacis. It was without form, vague, opaque, motionless, and of a consistency impossible to divine.

"Why,—the Indian priests or conjurers," Mervyn explained. "They have been there all day."

"They are called the *cheerataghe*,—men possessed of divine fire," Raymond volunteered.

The captain-lieutenant somewhat resented the amendment of his explanation. "They are the only people in the world who believe that Raymond has any religion of any sort." He laughed with relish and banteringly.

"Don't you think that is funny, Mr. Mervyn?" she demanded, her tone a trifle enigmatical. She did not look at him as she still leaned with one hand on the cannon, her hat full of violets depending from her arm.

"Vastly amusing, sure," declared Mervyn,—and Ensign Innis laughed, too, in the full persuasion of pleasing.

"I can't see their feathers or bonnets," she said.

"No," explained Raymond, "they have their heads covered with the cloth they weave, and they heap ashes on the cloth."

"Oh-h-h!" cried out Arabella.

"Watch them,—watch them now," Raymond said quickly. "They are heaping the ashes on their heads again."

There was a strange, undulatory motion among the row of heavily draped figures, each bending to the right, their hands seeming to wildly wave as they caught up the invisible ashes before them and strewed them over their heads, while a low wail broke forth. "And you think this is funny?" demanded Arabella of the young men, looking at them severally.

"I can't say I think it is *un*funny," said Innis, with a rollicking laugh.

"I think it is very foolish," said Lawrence.

"I don't believe they have lost a religion because I've got it in my pocket," said Raymond.

"And they are old men—are they?" she asked.

"Old?"—said Mervyn. "Old as Noah."

"And they have had a long journey?"

"Pounded down here all the way from Choté on their ten old toes."

"And how long will they stay there, fasting, and praying, and wailing, and waiting, in sackcloth and ashes?"

"Perhaps till they work some sort of spell on me," suggested Raymond. She laughed at this in ridicule.

"Till the fort is evacuated, I suppose," said Mervyn.

"So long as that!" she exclaimed, growing serious. All at once she caught her breath with a gasp, staring at the Indians in the gathering gloom, as with a sudden inspiration.

"I would speak with them!—Oh, la!—what a thing to tell in England! Take me down there,—quick. Tillie vallie!—there is no water in the fosse. What a brag to make in Kent! There can be no danger under the guns of the fort. Lord, papa,—*let me go!*"

Captain Howard hesitated, but made no demur. The war was over, and there was indeed no risk; and Arabella's pilgrimage into primeval realms would be infinitely embellished by this freak. All of the young officers accompanied her, the interpreter, hastily summoned, following; the commandant and the parson watched from the rampart.

She went through the gray dusk like some translucent apparition, the figment of lines of light. The moon, now in the sky, hardly annulled the tints of her faint green gown; her hair glittered in the sheen; her face was ethereally white.

The wailing ceased as her advance was observed. The swaying figures were still. A vague fear seized her as she came near to those mysterious veiled creatures, literally abased to the ground. She wavered for a moment,—then she paused on the crest of the glacis in silence and evident doubt.

There was an interval of suspense. The odors of violets and dust and ashes were blended on the air. Dew was falling; the river sang; and the moon shone brighter as the darkness gathered.

"Good people," she said, with a sort of agitated, hysteric break in her clear voice, for she was realizing that she knew not how to address magnates and priests of a strange alien nation.

The croak of the interpreter came with a harsh promptitude on each clause.

"Good people, I hear a voice,"—she paused again, and corrected her phrase,—"I feel a monition—to tell you that your prayers are answered. Your 'religion' I have the power to restore. To-morrow, at the fort, at high noon, it shall be returned to you. If you help the helpless, and feed the hungry, and cherish the aged, and show mercy to captives, it will be a better religion than ever heretofore. I promise,—I pledge my word."

She wavered anew and shrank back so suddenly that Raymond thought she might fall. But no! She fled like a deer, her green draperies all fluttering in the wind, the moonlight on her golden hair and in her shining eyes. The officers followed, half bewildered by her freak, Raymond first of all. He overtook her as she was climbing through the fraise of the steep exterior slope of the rampart, clutching at the sharp stakes to help her ascent.

"Stop! stop!" he said, catching at her sleeve and pausing to look up gravely into her eyes as she, laughing, gasping, half-hysterical, looked down at him standing on the berme below. "Are you in earnest?" he demanded.

"Yes,—yes,—I shall give back the amulet."

She seemed hardly to realize that it was his; that he had captured it in a mêlée; that it was now in his possession; that he had a word in the matter, a will to be consulted.

"I don't understand—" he hesitated.

"Oh,—la,—*you*! You make no difference. *I* have worked a spell on *you*,—as you know!"

She laughed again, caught her breath with a gasp, and began once more to ascend swiftly through the fraise. But he was beside her in a moment. He caught her little hand trembling and cold in his.

"Arabella," he cried, in agitated delight, "you know I worship you,—you know that you have indeed all my heart,—but only a subaltern,—I hardly dared to hope—"

"La! you needn't bestir yourself to hope now! Sure, I didn't say *you* had worked any spell on *me*."

Not another word was possible to him, for the others had overtaken them, and it was in a twitter of laughter that she climbed through the embrasure, and in a flutter of delighted achievement that she breathlessly detailed the adventure to her father and the parson. Then hanging on the commandant's arm she demurely paced to and fro along the moonlit rampart, now and again meeting Raymond's gaze with a coquettish air of bravado which seemed to say:—

"Talk love to me *now*,—if you dare!"

The embassy of Indians had disappeared like magic. The party from the fort declared that upon glancing back at the glacis the row of veiled, humiliated figures had vanished in the inappreciable interval of time like a wreath of mist or a puff of dust.

One could hardly say that they returned the next day,—so unlike, so far alien to the aspect of the humble mourners, who had wept and gnashed their teeth and wailed in sackcloth and ashes on the glacis of the fort in the dim dusk, was the splendidly armed and arrayed delegation that high noon ushered into the main gate. Their coronets of white swan's feathers, standing fifteen inches high, with long pendants trailing at the back, rose out of a soft band of swan's-down close on the forehead. They wore wide collars or capes of the same material, and the intense whiteness heightened the brilliancy of the blotches of decorative paint with which their faces were mottled. Each had a feather-wrought mantle of iridescent plumage, the objects of textile beauty so often described by travellers of that date. They bore the arms of eld, in lieu of the more effective musket, wearing them as ornaments and to emphasize the fact that they were needed neither for defence nor aggression. The bows and arrows were tipped with quartz wrought to a fine polish, and the quivers were covered with gorgeous embroidery of beads and quills. Their hunting shirts and leggings were similarly decorated and fringed with tinkling shells. They were shod with the white buskins cabalistically marked with red to indicate their calling and rank as "beloved men." Their number was the mystic seven. They were all old, one obviously so infirm that the pace of the others was retarded to permit him to keep in company. They advanced with much stateliness, and it was evidently an occasion of great moment in their estimation.

Captain Howard, adopting the policy of the government to fall in with the Indian ceremonial rather than to seek to force the tribes to other methods, met them in person, and with some pomp and circumstance conducted them to the mess-hall in one of the block-houses, as the most pretentious apartment of the fort. He was an indulgent man when off duty. He was rather glad, since to his surprise Ensign Raymond had suddenly declared that he was willing to return the amulet, that the Indians should have the bauble on which they set so much value, and he was altogether unmoved by Mr. Morton's remonstrance that it was a bargaining with Satan, a recognition of a pagan worship, and a promotion of witchcraft and conjure work to connive at the restoration of the red stone to its purpose of delusion.

Inclination fosters an ingenuity of logic. "I am disposed to think the stone is a symbol—a type of something I do not understand," Captain Howard replied; evidently he had absorbed something of Mr. Morton's prelections by the sheer force of propinquity, for certainly he had never intentionally hearkened to them. "You, yourself, have often said the Cherokees are in no sense idolaters."

The officers of the post had no scruples. They were all present, grouped about the walls, welcoming aught that served to break the monotony. Mrs. Annandale, cynical, inquisitive, scornful, and deeply interested, was seated in one of the great chairs so placed that she could not fail to see all of what she contemptuously designated as "the antics." Norah stood behind her, wide-eyed and half-frightened, gazing in breathless amazement at the proceedings. The room was lighted only by the loop-holes for musketry, looking to the outer sides of the bastion, and the broadly flaring door, for there was no fire this warm, spring day. The great chimney-place was filled with masses of pine boughs and glossy magnolia leaves, to hide its sooty aperture, and on the wide hearth, near this improvised bower, stood Arabella, looking on, a pleased spectator, as Raymond advanced to the table in the centre of the floor, and laid upon it the great red stone, which shone in the shadowy place with a translucent lustre that might well justify its supernatural repute. The interpreter repeated the courteous phrases in which Ensign Raymond stated that he took pleasure in returning this object of beauty and value which had by accident fallen into his possession.

His words were received in dead silence. The Indians absolutely ignored him. They looked through him, beyond him, never at him. He had been the cause of much anguish of soul, and the impulse of forgiveness is foreign to such generosity of spirit as is predicable of the savage.

A moment of suspense ensued. Then the tallest, the stateliest of the Indians reached forth his hand, took the amulet, passed it to a colleague, who in his turn passed it to another, and in the continual transfer its trail was lost and the keenest observer could not say at length who was the custodian of the treasure.

Another moment of blank expectancy. There were always these barren intervals in the leisurely progress of Indian diplomacy. The interview seemed at an end. The next incident might be the silent filing out of the embassy and their swift, noiseless departure.

Suddenly the leader took from one of the others a small bowl of their curious pottery. It was full of fragrant green herbs which had been drenched in clear water, for as he held them up the crystal drops fell from them. There was a hush of amazed expectancy as he advanced toward the young lady. With an inspired mien and a sonorous voice he cried, casting up his eyes, "*Higayuli Tsunega!*"

"Oh, supreme white Fire!" echoed the interpreter.

"*Sakani udunuhi nigesuna usinuliyu! Yu!*"

"Grant that she may never become unhappy! Yu!"

Then lifting the fresh leafage aloft, the cheerataghe, with a solemn gesture, sprinkled the water into her astounded face.

"Safe! Safe!" the interpreter continued to translate his words. "Safe forever! She and hers can never know harm in the land of the Cherokee. Not even a spirit of the air may molest her; no ghost of the departed may haunt her sleep; not the shadow of a bird can fall upon her; no vagrant witch can touch her with malign influence."

"*Ha-usinuli nagwa ditsakuni denatlu hisaniga uy-igawasti dudanti!*" declared the cheerataghe.

"We have keenly aimed our arrows against the accursed wanderers of darkness!" chanted the interpreter.

"*Nigagi! Nigagi!*"

"Amen! Amen!"

A breathless silence ensued. No word. No stir. The amazement depicted on the faces of the staring officers, the dubitation intimated in Captain Howard's corrugated, bushy eye-brows, the perplexity in Mrs. Annandale's eagerly observant, meagre little countenance, were as definite a comment as if voiced in words. This was all caviare indeed to their habits of mind, accustomed as they were to the consideration of material interests and the antagonisms of flesh and blood. But the pale ascetic face of the old missionary was kindled with a responsive glow that was like the shining of a flame through an alabaster vase, so pure, so exalted, so vivid an illumination it expressed, so perfect a comprehension this spark of symbolism had ignited.

As a type of covenant the suggestions afforded by this incident occupied several learned pages of Mr. Morton's recondite work on "Baptism in its Various Forms in Antient and Modern Times," published some years afterward, a subject which gratefully repays amplification and is susceptible of infinite speculation. The peculiar interest which the occasion developed for him served to annul the qualms of conscience which he had suffered, despite which, however, instigated by the old Adam of curiosity, he had permitted himself to be present at the restoration of the conjuring-stone to its mission of delusion.

A mention of the amulet as a "lost religion" was the next moment on the lips of the interpreter, echoing the rhetorical periods of Yachtino, the chief of Chilhowee, who had stepped forward and was speaking with a forceful dignity of gesture and the highly aspirated, greatly diversified intonations of the Cherokee language, illustrating its vaunted capacity for eloquent expressiveness, and affording the group a signal opportunity of judging of the grace of oratory for which these Indians were then famous.

The gratitude of the Indians, the spokesman declared, was not to be measured by gifts. Not in recognition of her beneficence, not in return for her kindness,—for kindness cannot be bought or repaid, and they were her debtors forever,—but as a matter of barter the Cherokee nation bestowed upon her their pearl, the "sleeping sun," in exchange for the amulet which she had caused to be returned by the ruthless soldier.

Forthwith the chief of Chilhowee laid upon the table the beautiful freshwater pearl which Raymond had seen at Cowetchee.

Heedless of all the subtler significance of the ceremony, and, under the British flag, caring naught for the vaunted puissance of Cherokee protection against the seen and the unseen, the astonished and delighted young beauty gazed speechless after the embassy, for their grotesquely splendid figures had disappeared as silently as the images of a dream, feeling that the reward was altogether out of proportion with the simplicity of the kindly impulse that had actuated her girlish heart. Because they were very old and savage, and, as she thought, very poor, and were agonized for a boon which in their ignorance they craved as dear and sacred, she had exerted the influence she knew she possessed to restore to them this trifle, this bauble,—and here in her hand the tear of compassion, as it were, was metamorphosed into a gem such as she had never before beheld.

Mounted by a London jeweller between prongs set with diamonds it was famous in her circle for its size and beauty, and regarded as a curio it could out-vie all Kent. She long remembered the Cherokee words which described it, and she entertained a sort of regretful reminiscence of Fort Prince George, soon dismantled and fallen into decay, where the spring had come so laden with beauty and charm, and with incidents of such strange interest.

Mrs. Annandale also remembered it regretfully, and with a bitter, oft-reiterated wish that Arabella had never seen the little stronghold or the officers of its garrison. She used her utmost endeavors against Raymond's suit, but threats, persuasion, appeals, were vain with Arabella. She had made her choice, and she would not depart from it. Her heart was fixed, and not even the reproach to which her generous temper rendered her most susceptible,—that she had caused pain and unhappiness to Mervyn, encouraging him to cherish unfounded hopes,—moved her in the least. She reminded them both that she had warned him he must not presume on her qualified assent as a finality; she had always feared she did not love him, and now she knew it was impossible.

"I can't imagine how Ensign Raymond had the opportunity to interfere," Mrs. Annandale said wofully to her brother in one of their many conferences on the unexpected turn of the romance the match-maker had fostered. "I am sure I never gave him the opportunity to make love to her; it was dishonorable in him to introduce the subject of love when he knew of her engagement."

"He did not introduce the subject of love," said Arabella, remembering the scene in the fraise above the scarp, and laughing shyly. "I, myself, spoke first of love."

Then awed by her aunt's expression of horror and offended propriety, she added demurely:—

"It must have been the influence of that amulet. He had it then. They say it bestows on its possessor his own best good."

Captain Howard also remembered Fort Prince George regretfully, and also with a vague wish that she had never seen the little stronghold. He was not exactly discontented with Raymond as a son-in-law, but this was not his preference, for he had advocated her acceptance of Mervyn's suit. His own limited patrimony lay adjoining the Mervyn estate, and he thought the propinquity a mutual advantage to the prospects of the two young people, and that it materially enhanced Arabella's position as a suitable match for the Mervyn heir. The succeeding baronet was a steady conventional fellow, and had been very well thought of in the regiment before he sold out upon coming into his title and fortune. Raymond would be obliged to stick to the army, having but small means, and he would doubtless do well if he could be kept within bounds.

"But," Captain Howard qualified, describing the absent soldier to an intimate friend and country neighbor in Kent, over the post-prandial wine and walnuts,—"but he is such a frisky dare-devil! If he could be scared half to death by somebody it would tame him, and be the making of him."

In a few years it might have seemed that this had been compassed, for it was said that Raymond was afraid of his lovely wife. He was obviously so solicitous of her approval, he considered her judgment of such peculiar worth, and he thought her so "monstrous clever," that when impervious to all other admonitions, he could be reached, advised, warned, through her influence.

When he became a personage of note, for in those days of many wars he soon rose to eminence, and it was desired to flatter, or court, or conciliate him, a difficult feat, for he was absolutely without vanity for his own sake, it was understood that there was one secure road to his favorable consideration,—he was never insensible to admiration of his wife's linguistic accomplishments, which included among more useful tongues, the unique acquisition of something of the Cherokee language. Then, too, he was always attentive and softened by any comment, in some intimate coterie, upon the jewel, now called a pendant, which, hanging by a slender chain, rose and fell on a bosom as delicately white as the gem itself. The great pearl was associated with the most cherished sentiments of his life, his love and his pride in his professional career,—with the inauguration of his dear and lasting romance, and his first independent command. With a tender reminiscent smile on his war-worn face, he would ask her to repeat the word for the moon in the several dialects, and would listen with an unwearied ear as she rehearsed her spirited story of the "sleeping sun," and the method of its barter for the amulet.